Attachment *in* Therapeutic Practice

Sara Miller McCune founded SAGE Publishing in 1965 to support the dissemination of usable knowledge and educate a global community. SAGE publishes more than 1000 journals and over 800 new books each year, spanning a wide range of subject areas. Our growing selection of library products includes archives, data, case studies and video. SAGE remains majority owned by our founder and after her lifetime will become owned by a charitable trust that secures the company's continued independence.

Los Angeles | London | New Delhi | Singapore | Washington DC | Melbourne

Attachment *in* Therapeutic Practice

Jeremy Holmes
Arietta Slade

Los Angeles | London | New Delhi
Singapore | Washington DC | Melbourne

Los Angeles | London | New Delhi
Singapore | Washington DC | Melbourne

SAGE Publications Ltd
1 Oliver's Yard
55 City Road
London EC1Y 1SP

SAGE Publications Inc.
2455 Teller Road
Thousand Oaks, California 91320

SAGE Publications India Pvt Ltd
B 1/I 1 Mohan Cooperative Industrial Area
Mathura Road
New Delhi 110 044

SAGE Publications Asia-Pacific Pte Ltd
3 Church Street
#10-04 Samsung Hub
Singapore 049483

Editor: Susannah Trefgarne
Editorial assistant:Talulah Hall
Production editor: Katherine Haw
Copyeditor: Sarah Bury
Indexer: Elizabeth Ball
Marketing manager: Camille Richmond
Cover design: Sheila Tong
Typeset by: C&M Digitals (P) Ltd, Chennai, India
Printed in the UK

Library of Congress Control Number: 2017939971

British Library Cataloguing in Publication data

A catalogue record for this book is available from
the British Library

ISBN 978-1-4739-5328-4
ISBN 978-1-4739-5329-1 (pbk)

At SAGE we take sustainability seriously. Most of our products are printed in the UK using FSC papers and boards.
When we print overseas we ensure sustainable papers are used as measured by the PREPS grading system.
We undertake an annual audit to monitor our sustainability.

For Alkisti, Carol, Edgar, and in memory of Shao Kun
J.H.

For Sam,
and for my mother, so missed
A.S.

Contents

About the Authors

Jeremy Holmes, MD was for 35 years NHS Consultant Psychiatrist/Medical Psychotherapist at University College London and then in North Devon, UK. He was Chair of the Psychotherapy Faculty of the Royal College of Psychiatrists 1998–2002. He is visiting Professor at the University of Exeter, and lectures nationally and internationally. In addition to 200+ papers and chapters in the field of psychoanalysis and attachment theory, his books include *John Bowlby and Attachment Theory*, *The Oxford Textbook of Psychotherapy* (co-editors Glen Gabbard and Judy Beck), *Exploring In Security: Towards an Attachment-informed Psychoanalytic Psychotherapy*, and *The Therapeutic Imagination: Using Literature to Deepen Psychodynamic Understanding and Enhance Empathy*. Like Arietta, he was recipient of a New York Attachment Consortium Bowlby-Ainsworth Founders Award. Gardening, Green politics and grand-parenting are gradually eclipsing his lifetime devotion to psychoanalytic psychotherapy and attachment.

Arietta Slade, PhD, is Clinical Professor at the Yale Child Study Center, and was for 31 years Professor of Clinical Psychology at the City College and City University of New York. A theoretician, clinician, teacher, and researcher, she has written widely about the development of parental reflective functioning, the development of symbolisation, and the implications of attachment and mentalisation for child and adult psychoanalytic psychotherapy, and regularly presents her work nationally and internationally. She is one of the founders and co-directors of *Minding the Baby*®, an interdisciplinary reflective home visiting programme for high-risk mothers, infants, and their families, at the Yale Child Study Center and School of Nursing. Dr Slade is editor, with Jeremy Holmes, of the six-volume set, *Major Work on Attachment* (SAGE Publications, 2013), with Elliot Jurist and Sharone Bergner, of *Mind to Mind: Infant Research, Neuroscience, and Psychoanalysis* (Other Press, 2008), and with Dennie Wolf, of *Children at Play* (Oxford University Press, 1994). She has also been in private practice for over thirty-five years, working with individuals of all ages.

Acknowledgements

AS

It was my particular good fortune to meet and work with Mary Ainsworth and Mary Main just as I was ready to explore the world beyond the secure base of psychoanalysis. And to then some years later hear Peter Fonagy sketch out the fundamentals of what was to become mentalisation theory. It is hard to put into words just how much these experiences changed everything. I am deeply grateful to my patients for their trust and courage, my students for their enthusiasm and passion, and the dear friends and colleagues who have so sustained and encouraged me over the years: Larry Aber, Betsy Brett, Jude Cassidy, Nancy Crown, Daphne de Marneffe, Wendy Haft, Alicia Lieberman, Patty and Tom Rosbrow, Alan and June Sroufe, Mary Target, and Steve Tuber. And to my wonderful colleagues at *Minding the Baby*®, especially Lois Sadler, you are the ultimate secret base. And to my family, including Esther (canine oxytocin machine), your love and support mean more than you can imagine.

JH

Many people and organisations have contributed to the secure matrix from which this book has emerged. Thanks: first to my patients for their forbearance, loyalty, and unbidden teaching; to the Department of Psychology, University of Exeter for hosting me, and especially to colleagues Richard Mizen, Nic Sarra, Janet Reibstein and Eugene Mullan, and to my students and supervisees there; third, since science knows no borders, to friends and colleagues in the wider world: Evrinomy Avdi, Peter Fonagy, Suzanne Hicks, Sebastian Kraemer, Howard Steele, Miriam Steele, Alessandro Talia, Mary Target, Saman Tavakoli, and Kristin White. As ever, my family, past, present and future are the *sine qua non*.

Jeremy and Arietta Acknowledgements

We are hugely indebted to Ros Holmes and Madeleine Terry for their help in the last stages of putting this 'baby' to bed, and of course to the many people at SAGE who encouraged us, prodded us, and kept us on course, including Katherine Haw, Charlotte Meredith, and Sarah Bury for the copyediting. And a special thank you to Susannah Trefargne, who never wavered in believing that we had a book to write and that we would, in fact, write it.

1

Introduction

Attachment matters: its role, development, maintenance, and disruption are major themes in the social and biological sciences. Rooted in the work of Darwin and Freud, attachment theory came into being in the 1940s when John Bowlby, a psychiatrist and psychoanalyst, noted that the majority of the delinquent boys in his practice had experienced early separations and loss. He theorised that human infants are born with a fundamental, biological, and human need for connection and attachment, and that the quality and stability of these early relationships shape a range of developmental, relational, and clinical outcomes. His trilogy, *Attachment* (1969), *Separation* (1973), and *Loss* (1980) set the stage for what is now one of the dominant paradigms in psychology, psychiatry, and neuroscience. His collaborator Mary Ainsworth was crucial to this evolution, and she is recognised as the co-creator of attachment theory and research. Her most important contribution was the development of the Strange Situation Procedure (SSP) (Ainsworth & Wittig, 1965), an experimental method that has been used for the last 50 years to assess the quality of attachment in parent–infant pairs.

Beginning in 2012, we undertook a project aimed at selecting and collecting – 'curating' – the most significant papers in the field of attachment study into six volumes. The result was *Attachment Theory* (Slade & Holmes, 2014). Our goal was to celebrate Bowlby's and Ainsworth's work in creating the attachment paradigm, benchmark its history, highlight its later achievements, and justify its current status as a prime theme in psychological science.

We are both practising psychotherapists. Our early exposure to attachment theory strongly shaped our approach to clinical practice (e.g., Holmes, 1996, 2001, 2010; Slade, 1999, 2000, 2014). However, despite the centrality of attachment in developmental and other forms of academic psychology, we found the literature on the clinical implications of attachment theory and research[1] relatively limited. As Bowlby himself noted in 1988:

> It is a little unexpected that, whereas attachment theory was formulated by a clinician for use in the diagnosis and treatment of emotionally disturbed patients and families, its usage hitherto has been mainly to

promote research in developmental psychology. Whilst I welcome the findings of this research as … of the greatest clinical relevance, it has none the less been disappointing that clinicians have been so slow to test the theory's uses. (1988: ix–x)

Clinicians undoubtedly recognise the importance of attachment: a Google search of attachment and psychotherapy yields over 4 million hits (July, 2016). The question is: how can attachment ideas and research be brought to bear on clinical practice? In both the clinical literature and popular writing on parenting and relationships, the term is often used to describe any close relationship to a significant other. Though not incorrect, this definition strips attachment of the *motivational* and *dynamic* aspects that lie at the heart of Bowlby's theory. This 'motherhood-and-apple-pie' tendency means there has been little systematic and focused examination of how attachment principles might shape, influence, underpin, inform, and improve psychotherapeutic practice. That – based on our own experience and ways of working – is what we have set out to do here. Our rationale is the belief that attachment, possibly uniquely, leads to a therapeutic practice that is intimately linked with its scientific foundations.

Who is This Book for?

Despite an exuberance of theory, once in the consulting room, psychotherapy is a practice in search of a theory. Attachment research provides therapists with an account of the psychobiology of healthy relationships, and how these can be harnessed to understand and alleviate suffering. We hold that absorbing the attachment message can enhance the work of all psychotherapy practitioners, of whatever stripe, and hope that this book will be helpful and relevant for clinicians from beginners to the more experienced – from novitiates through to master-craftsmen and women.

Who Are We?

Both of us were exposed to attachment theory at the start of our careers. In his psychiatric training JH was drawn to Bowlby's project of aligning science and psychoanalysis, and sought out Bowlby as a mentor (Holmes, 2014a). Like most clinical psychology students of her generation, AS had little exposure to attachment in her psychoanalytically oriented training, but was introduced to the Strange Situation while a postdoctoral fellow. Shortly thereafter, she met Mary Ainsworth, whose approach to anxiety seemed to make far more sense than prevailing psychoanalytic models.

These pivotal moments early in our careers have defined us as psychotherapists, and shaped our work in large and small ways. We try to bring this thinking and experience alive in this volume. Our collaboration began 25 years ago, when AS beat her way – in a brave 'exploratory' move from rural

Connecticut, past NYC and London, to equally rural Devon – to meet JH. Since then, despite being, in Churchill's words, 'separated by everything except a common language', we have regularly discussed the ramifications of attachment: in person, and via Skype and email. We have used one another as port of first call for draft papers and chapters, and shared our professional doubts, delights, and dilemmas. With due hubris, we like to think of our collaboration as mirroring the collaborative spirit of Bowlby and Ainsworth.

Outline

The shape of the book follows a well-established schema in the field of integrative psychotherapy (Castonguay & Hill, 2012; Holmes & Bateman, 2002). Effective therapies are generally agreed to entail three key components: a therapeutic relationship (Chapters 5–8), an explanatory framework (Chapters 9 and 10), and a means of producing change (Chapters 11–14).

Chapters 2, 3, and 4 are introductory. We begin, in Chapter 2, with a brief history of the principals and principles of attachment theory and research. Chapter 3 encapsulates our credo, outlining our particular approach to attachment and its relevance to psychotherapy and summarises – we hope in a fresh way – the history and main attachment characters and principles. In Chapter 4 we describe the role of affect regulation in attachment relationships and psychotherapy.

Chapters 5 and 6 address how research findings about secure and insecure care-seeker/caregiver relationships can be applied to the processes of psychotherapy. In Chapter 5, Ainsworth's concept of parental sensitivity, mirroring, and playfulness are discussed, while Chapter 6 addresses the neurobiology of parental and – speculatively – therapeutic sensitivity.

As a continuation of this caregiver–care-seeker/therapist–patient parallel, Chapter 7 is devoted to a single, but crucial, attachment-informed therapeutic concept: mentalising.

Chapter 8 addresses both the relational foundations of attachment and their clinical applications, and introduces the concept of earned security, so relevant to attachment-informed therapy. These are discussed in relation to resilience, a current hot topic in mental health.

Although the non-conscious, paralinguistic, bodily, and contextual aspects of the therapeutic relationship play a vital role in helping to bring about attachment security, ultimately psychotherapy is a verbal interchange. The starting point for Chapters 9 and 10 is the importance of discourse style as a marker of psychological health or disease. Chapter 9 focuses on organised forms of attachment insecurity, while Chapter 10 applies these ideas to severe and complex disorders in which disorganised attachment prevails. These chapters illustrate how, through therapy, clients' discourse becomes more elaborated, complex, and nuanced as it begins to encompass previously excluded or unformulated aspects of psychic life.

Chapters 11 and 12 move to the change-catalysing aspects of attachment-informed psychotherapy. Chapter 11 looks at how secure attachments are promoted in the therapeutic setting, while Chapter 12 proposes a neuroscience-informed model of psychotherapeutic change based on Bayesian probability. We suggest that psychotherapy is not so much, in Freud's phrase, an 'impossible' profession, as an 'improbable' one.

The concluding chapters move on from the hitherto predominant emphasis on individual therapy with adults. Chapter 13 focuses on attachment approaches to child psychotherapy, while Chapter 14 looks at how attachment ideas can be applied to couple and family work.

Chapter 15, our concluding chapter, moves to the wider context. It looks at secure and insecure attachments at a societal level, and the implications for resilient organisations and societies.

We hope, by the end, that readers will feel familiar with attachment as a framework with which to inform and enhance their daily psychotherapeutic work. Ultimately, we aspire to communicate our journey towards understanding the lineaments of attachment security, both in ourselves and our patients.[2]

Notes

1. The bibliography includes a list of monographs on the clinical applications of attachment theory and research.

2. Note on nomenclature, gender and confidentiality: we use the terms 'patient' and 'client' interchangeably throughout; we have tried to be even-handed as to gender of both clients and therapists. We have observed strict confidentiality, except where explicit permission has been granted. Case-vignettes are 'fictionalised' but, we hope, still ring true.

2

Attachment's Principals and Principles

When reading books with a large cast, a list of principal characters and their roles can be very helpful. We subscribe to Whitehead's (1916) aperçu that: 'science that fails to forget its founders is doomed', but believe that going back to the originators of a new paradigm helps us see ideas in their historical context, as well as highlighting the difficulties with which they were wrestling. What follows is a summary of some of the main attachment characters, themes, and concepts that inform this book.

John Bowlby

Like many cultural and scientific advances, attachment theory arose from juxtapositions: conceptually between ethology and psychoanalysis; professionally between John Bowlby and Mary Ainsworth. Nevertheless, the founding father was undoubtedly Bowlby, who claimed that: 'in 1956 when this work was begun I had no conception of what I was undertaking' (Bowlby, 1969: xi). This 'undertaking' turned out to be no less than a new paradigm, with implications for child development and childrearing, psychology, psychiatry, parent–infant research – and psychotherapy.

New scientific theories arise out of 'paradigm shifts', typically preceded by discomfort with existing theories' failure to fit the facts (Kuhn, 1977). Bowlby's preoccupation was the parent–infant bond, which he saw as fundamental to all subsequent relationships. He was dissatisfied with the prevailing psychoanalytic model, which saw relationships as arising out of feeding and/or infantile sexuality. Like Ainsworth, he was equally unimpressed with the behavioural view that mother love boiled down to associative propinquity. Both approaches, he felt, failed to account for *the primacy of relationships*.

For Bowlby the drive to relate – holding, clinging, playing, exploring, providing safety – was a dynamic in its own right, needing new theories and research.

Bowlby's initial aims were relatively modest. In 'The influence of early environment in the development of neurosis and neurotic character' (Bowlby, 1940), he presented his experiences of working in UK Child Guidance Clinics to his fellow-psychoanalysts, hoping, with a typical homespun trope, to persuade them that it was 'as important for analysts to study the early environment as it is for a nurseryman to make a scientific study of the soil' (1940: 155).

Even at this early stage he realised how vital the subtleties of the emotional atmosphere in the home were for children's well-being. More palpable trauma is addressed in his paper 'Forty-four juvenile thieves: Their characters and home-life' (Bowlby, 1944), earning him the nick-name 'Ali Bowlby and his 44 thieves'. This case-series suggested a link between delinquency in adolescence and early loss of mother. The separation theme was then developed in his joint paper with Robertson (Bowlby & Robertson, 1952) studying children in hospital with tuberculosis and so separated for long periods from their parents. In it they outline the now familiar phases of emotional response to unredeemed loss: denial, protest, and despair.

The three classic *International Journal of Psychoanalysis* articles (Bowlby, 1958, 1960, 1961) form the core of Bowlby's contribution, each of which was expanded into a volume of the 'trilogy' (Bowlby, 1969, 1973, 1980). In *Attachment*, he proposed the attachment bond as a primary motivational force, whose 'set goal' is physical proximity to a 'secure base' when a child is threatened, stressed, or ill. *Separation* set out a novel understanding of anxiety disorders in children and adults as responses to trauma and/or the failure of parents to provide safety. It also conceptualises anger and violence to self and others (see too, Bowlby, 1984) as pathological manifestations of healthy protest, part of the normal response to separation. In *Loss*, Bowlby described loss as an irreversible separation, proposing the then heterodox claim that children experience grief and mourning no less intensely than adults, and developing an attachment model of pathological mourning and depression applicable throughout the life-cycle.

Bowlby's trilogy remains the secure foundation for half a century of post-paradigmatic 'normal science'. Throughout, he remained true to his original objectives: opening psychoanalysis to cross-fertilisation with other disciplines such as ethology and cybernetics; acknowledging that real trauma and deprivation were as important in psychopathology as phantasy; helping build secure scientific foundations for the art of psychotherapy.

Bowlby's intellectual giants[1] were Darwin (Bowlby, 1991) and Freud. His own development and experiences as a teacher of disturbed children provided the seedbed for his later theories (van Dijken et al., 1998). As a psychoanalytic candidate in the British Psychoanalytic Society in the 1930s and 1940s, he was affected by Melanie Klein and her followers, if only to try to convert them to more environmentally sensitive and scientific points of view.

His open-mindedness made him a ready enthusiast for the ethological theories of Konrad Lorenz, which he encountered in a pre-publication draft of *King Solomon's Ring* (1961), given him by the evolutionary biologist Julian Huxley (Bretherton, 1992). Another major ethological influence was Harry Harlow (1958), who famously showed that infant monkeys sought out security and 'holding' from a cloth mother-substitute in preference to feeding from a milk-providing but comfortless 'wire mother'. This provided experimental support for attachment theory's fundamental postulate of the primacy of 'contact comfort' over feeding/oral drive-reduction as the basis for early relationships. Harlow's mantle has been carried forward by Steven Suomi, who in five decades of primate research has established beyond doubt the significance of early rearing on gene expression, stress regulation, neuro-endocrine functioning, and socioemotional development (Suomi, 2016). Suomi's oeuvre, perhaps more than any other, provides empirical support for Bowlby's fundamental premise that early attachments matter and have long-range developmental implications. The ornithologist and later primatologist Robert Hinde (Van der Horst, Van der Veer, & van IJzendoorn, 2007) was another important colleague and mentor; he and Bowlby developed the Darwinian idea of the 'environment of evolutionary adaptedness', in which protection from predation through attachment conferred selective advantage for vulnerable human infants.

The most seminal of these collegial relationships was with Mary Ainsworth. Attachment theory can truly be said to be their joint creation, and could not have become the force it is today without their complementary skills and backgrounds.

Mary Ainsworth and the Strange Situation

Life is full of fortunate accidents. An American-born, Canadian-raised clinical psychologist and researcher, Ainsworth had a background in clinical diagnosis and psychotherapy, having collaborated with Bruno Klopfer on what was to become a classic textbook on the Rorschach (Klopfer et al., 1954). In 1950 she answered an advertisement in the London *Times Education Supplement* placed by John Bowlby, and was immediately hired to help with his studies of maternal separation at the Tavistock Clinic.

Ainsworth's autobiographical essay (1983) describes this eye-opening trans-ition in her intellectual journey. At first sceptical about Bowlby's objections to drive theory and his insistence on the primacy of the mother–infant attach-ment relationship, Ainsworth was eventually fully persuaded. Like all good scientists, the decisive factor was data. She moved to Uganda in 1954, where she studied Ganda mothers and infants in everyday settings (Ainsworth, 1967). This groundbreaking work described in detail the evolution of the attachment system, culminating in fully developed attachment to the mother around the first birthday. Her observations also underscored the crucial role of *maternal sensitivity* in shaping a child's sense of security and interest in the world around him.

In 1961 Ainsworth returned to the USA, joining the faculty at Johns Hopkins University in Baltimore, Maryland. Building on her Ganda observations, but in this very different environment, she followed 26 infants and their mothers from birth to one year. This gave rise to her greatest contribution, the Strange Situation Procedure (SSP), a tool for the assessment of the quality of infant–mother attachment (Ainsworth, Blehar, Waters, & Wall, 1978).

Ainsworth began by observing infants and their mothers in the home. Meticulous analysis confirmed the presence, from birth, of an increasingly complex behavioural system with which the infant signals his needs for comfort and safety to the caregiver. She identified systematic individual differences in the *quality* of the caregiving environment, particularly in mothers' sensitivity to, and acceptance of, babies' needs for contact and comfort. Ainsworth then devised a mildly stressful laboratory procedure, in which one-year-old children are separated from their mothers for three minutes and left, first with a stranger, and then by themselves (Ainsworth & Wittig, 1965). The SSP, an 'in vitro' separation paradigm, was designed to mimic everyday separations in which infants might be left with strangers or momentarily on their own.

The SSP laid the foundations for the now familiar attachment classification, dividing infants into one of three main groups. The securely attached had been recipients of sensitive and responsive care throughout the first year of life; their mothers provided them with a 'secure base' from which to explore; upon reunion they turned to their mothers – usually with appropriate but readily assuaged distress and protest – for comfort and safety. Children with somewhat rejecting parents tended on reunion to damp down their emotional responses, failing to protest, hovering inhibitedly near their caregiver, just out of arms' reach. These Ainsworth called 'avoidant' (also referred to here as 'deactivating'). The third group, 'anxious/resistant' ('hyperactivating'), had caregivers who were inconsistent in their responses; the children would cling to their caregiver but without being easily pacified, also failing to return to exploratory play upon reunion. Reunion behaviour in the SSP thus yielded vital information about the mother–child relationship and its history (Ainsworth et al., 1978).

This simple, elegant paradigm and the identification of the three patterns of attachment in her Baltimore sample have served as the foundation for four decades of attachment research. Ainsworth is responsible for two other key principles of attachment theory: (a) the notion that the caregiver provides the child with a '*secure base from which to explore*'; and (b) the '*attachment–exploration balance*', in which children find a path between the need for safety with the wish to strike out into the larger world.

Long-term Studies

Mary Ainsworth's development of the SSP, her discovery of the three primary patterns of infant–mother attachment, and her establishment of the links between early caregiving and individual differences in attachment organisation set the stage for attachment research as we know it today. The next steps came from Alan Sroufe at the University of Minnesota's Institute of Child Development. He learned about attachment theory from his graduate student, Everett Waters, who had joined him after undergraduate studies with Ainsworth at Johns Hopkins. Their collaboration (Sroufe, 1979; Sroufe & Waters, 1977) challenged the prevailing behaviourism in psychology, emphasising the 'coherence' of an individual life-history arising out of the interplay of developmental processes and the environmental context.

Waters (1978) and his colleagues established the validity and reliability of the SSP, based on their 20-year 'follow-along' study of a low-risk sample. They found links between infant security on the SSP and persistence, enthusiasm, cooperation, and positive affect in play during the toddler period (Matas, Arend, & Sroufe, 1978; Sroufe, 2005; Waters, Wippman, & Sroufe, 1978), providing the first evidence that attachment classification had long-range effects on adaptations and competencies well beyond infancy. Brian Vaughn, another Sroufe graduate student, replicated Waters' 1978 study with a high-risk sample (Vaughn et al., 1979). With his colleagues he found that the more unstable the caregiving environment, the more likely were children to be insecurely attached and to shift from secure to insecure in the face of environmental upheaval. This research was critical in identifying the risks to children living in high stress, disadvantaged environments. Sroufe and Byron Egeland went on to follow 200 of these families for over 30 years (Sroufe et al., 2005).

These and a wealth of other studies (see Grossmann, Grossman, & Waters, 2005) have established the predictive validity of the child's attachment classification. Taken together, they confirm the role of attachment in the organisation and stability of personality, and provide scientific underpinning for psychoanalytic emphasis on the importance of early relationships as a template for later development, healthy and otherwise. They provided strong support for Bowlby's emphasis on the role of the environment in promoting or compromising the children's psychological development and its likely long-term impact on mental health.

Mary Main and the Adult Attachment Interview

The early evolution of attachment theory and research can be thought of as a series of quantum leaps. Bowlby established the foundational theory, while Ainsworth developed observational and empirical methods critical to attachment's evidence base. Mary Main, originally Ainsworth's graduate student, took the field in two crucial new directions. First, she extended Ainsworth's research on mother–infant attachment to the study of attachment in adults. Rather than adult behaviour, she studied adult attachment *narratives*, moving attachment study to 'the level of representation' (Main, Kaplan, & Cassidy, 1985). Second, she delineated a fourth category of attachment – '*insecure disorganised*' (D). Both discoveries radically altered the landscape of attachment, with major implications – to be explored in this book – for clinical theory and practice.

Main followed a cohort of mothers and infants longitudinally, having first assessed the infants' attachment classifications at one year. As the study proceeded, she became curious about the attachment patterns of the *parents* of the children she was following. Together with graduate students Carol George and Nancy Kaplan, she developed the Adult Attachment Interview (AAI) (George, Kaplan, & Main, 1996), which was administered to mothers and fathers when the study children were six years old. Like the SSP, the AAI was intended to *activate* the subject's attachment system – as opposed to merely describing the past – by asking the parents to re-live in their minds their early experiences with caregivers. From a therapist's point of view, the AAI is thus comparable to a psychotherapy assessment interview in which significant childhood experiences, including early losses and traumata, are described, affectively evoked and explored.

Main identified systematic attachment-related patterns in these adult narrative accounts of early childhood experiences that were comparable to Ainsworth's patterns of infant behaviours. Adults judged 'secure' in relation to attachment represented their early attachment experiences in coherent and affectively balanced ways, childhood trauma and difficulty nothwithstanding. Adults judged 'insecure', by contrast, revealed a range of defences against expressing childhood longings and disappointments; their narratives were contradictory, vague, incoherent, or dysfluent. Main identified two distinct insecure 'states of mind in relation to attachment': 'dismissing', in which the impact of early experiences is disavowed and minimised, leading to clipped, contradictory, and affectively barren narratives; and 'preoccupied', in which the affects and effects of early experiences are heightened, autonomy downplayed, reflected in chaotic, emotionally uncontained, and incoherent narratives.

This delineation of adult categories of attachment allowed Main and her colleagues to examine the relationship between child and parent attachment classifications. They found high rates of correspondence: infants judged secure at one year were more likely to have mothers secure in relation to attachment; those judged avoidant were more likely to have mothers who dismissed the impact of early attachment experiences; the resistant or anxiously attached were more likely to have mothers with preoccupied states of mind.

Internal Working Models

Main saw patterns in adult attachment narratives as reflecting distinct '*internal working models*' (IWMs) of attachment. This was Bowlby's term for the representation of the self-in-relation-to-others that shapes a person's emotional life. In Main's view, the linguistic patterns noted on the AAI revealed representational models arising out of accumulated and recurrent real-life experiences of self–other (especially care-seeker/caregiver) interactions. IWMs are distinct, in important ways, from the 'internalised object representations' of object relations theory, representations shaped more by the child's unconscious fantasies than actual relationships and experience. Bowlby had been influenced in his thinking about IWMs by the psychologist Kenneth Craik's (1943) seminal notion of 'mental maps', which are needed by animals in order to navigate and negotiate their physical and social environment. IWMs are 'descriptively' unconscious (i.e., out of awareness but not due to repression) but nevertheless determine both how a person interacts with others, and the underlying assumptions that shape those interactions. IWMs can be formulated in terms of self-to-self statements (e.g., *is this person trustworthy? Will they attend to me when I'm in distress?*), etc.

Patricia Crittenden, another student of Ainsworth, makes an important psychotherapy-relevant point about IWMs:

> Internal representational models are postulated to assist individuals in two ways. First, such models can help an individual to interpret the meaning of others' behaviour and to make predictions regarding others' future behaviour. 'Open' models are open to new interpretations and predictions. 'Closed' models interpret all behaviour in terms of the existing model. Second, such models can facilitate the organization of a response. 'Working' models allow cognitive manipulation of possible responses. 'Nonworking' models do not allow cognitive exploration of behavioural alternatives. The responsiveness of the model to new information and the ability of individuals to use the model to organize their responses are relevant to the adaptiveness of the model. (1990: 265)

IWMs are thus the basis of the transferences which psychotherapists are adept at 'reading', and aim to bring into therapeutic discourse. Psychotherapy helps prise open these 'closed models', and jump-start those that are 'non-working', so that people begin to learn from experience and reach towards new ways of understanding themselves, others, and the world.

Disorganised Attachment

Main's second great contribution, made with the help of her graduate student Judith Solomon[2] (Main & Solomon, 1990), was the identification of a third insecure attachment type, 'insecure/disorganised' (D). This discovery arose from observing that a small proportion of children in their community sample could not be reliably classified in the SSP system. On separation and reunion in the SSP, this group showed some or all of the following behaviours: odd postures or behaviours (such as physical 'collapse'), apprehension, stereotypies, contradictory behaviours, trance-like expressions, freezing, disorientation, and/or repetitive hand and head movements.

Main and her colleagues noted that this group of infants alternated between proximity-seeking and avoidance in a way that suggested that they were *afraid of their caregivers*. Main and Hesse (1990) then hypothesised that the caregivers of disorganised infants are – as a result of their *own* unresolved loss or trauma – either frightened *by*, or frightening *to* their infants. Such infants then face an insoluble paradox, in which the caregiver is both a 'source of and the solution to its alarm' (1990: 163). Follow-up studies have linked D classification, found to be the prevalent pattern in high-risk groups, with 'controlling/punitive' or 'controlling/caretaking' behaviours at age 6 (Main & Cassidy, 1988), and psychopathology in childhood, adolescence, and early adulthood (Carlson, 1998; Lyons-Ruth & Jacobvitz, 2016; van IJzendoorn & Bakermans-Kranenburg, 2009). Schuengel, Bakermans-Kranenburg, and van IJzendoorn (1999) provided meta-analytic support for the links between frightening maternal behaviour and disorganised attachment; Lyons-Ruth and her colleagues later expanded this to a range of atypical maternal caregiving behaviours (including, but not limited to, frightened/frightening behaviour) that predicted infant disorganisation, expanding the potential pathways for the emergence of disorganised attachment (Lyons-Ruth, Bronfman, & Parsons, 1999). These themes will be discussed in Chapter 10.

The observation that *fear of the caregiver* played a pivotal role in infant disorganisation led Hesse and Main (2000) to return to the AAI, and to add a fourth category, 'unresolved' (U), in which the effects of parental trauma or loss are manifest as lapses in narrative fluency and meta-cognitive monitoring (i.e., the capacity to reflect on one's own thought processes), as well as disorientation in time and space. Lyons-Ruth later linked a variety of disruptions in narrative fluency and voice to 'pervasively unintegrated mental states', manifest in the AAI as Hostile/Helpless (H/H) states of mind and even more predictive of infant attachment disorganisation (Lyons-Ruth et al., 2005) than U status. Clinically, manifestations in narrative of both U and H/H are highly significant.

Crittenden's Dynamic Maturational Model (Crittenden, 2006) reframes Ainsworth's and Main's attachment categories as self-protective strategies learned in interaction with caregivers, in the context of maturational and individual biological differences. Like Main, she noted that there were some infants who could not be classified using the organised insecure classification system. Rather than D, she proposed a fourth category: *combined* avoidant/resistant. Crittenden's circumplex model generates a range of attachment subtypes, attempting to capture individual differences – which is of course where psychotherapists' main interest lies.

Mentalising

As the twenty-first century dawned, a new attachment concept came to the fore: mentalising. Emerging from the groundbreaking work of Peter Fonagy,

Miriam and Howard Steele, and Mary Target, mentalising marks, in two distinct ways, yet another leap forward. First, it illuminates some of the *mechanisms* underlying the intergenerational transmission of attachment. Second, it provides a clinical slant on attachment theory, which was useful in understanding both the early roots of severe psychopathology and in guiding treatment (cf. Allen, 2012a).

Fonagy, Steele, and Steele (1991) initially set out to examine the link between prenatal parental attachment classification and infants' later attachment. They noticed that adults who were secure on the AAI were able to appreciate and reflect upon mental states (thoughts, feelings, and intentions) relating to their early childhood experiences and relationships. This contrasted with their insecure peers, who had difficulty imagining their own or their parents' minds. Their ideas extended Main's work on metacognition, and led to an AAI code of 'reflective self-function', later shortened to 'reflective functioning' (RF) (Fonagy et al., 1998). This then mutated into the more general concept of 'mentalising'.

Mentalising refers to the process whereby we *make meaning* of the interpersonal world; RF is mentalising in action. Fonagy and his colleagues found that the *meta-representational* process, whereby pregnant parents reflect upon their own or another's psychic experience, was predictive of their subsequent infants' attachment classification (Fonagy et al., 1995). Importantly, they also found that even highly stressed, developmentally deprived parents, *in the presence of high RF*, had securely attached children at one year, as compared with similarly traumatised low-RF parents (Fonagy et al., 1995). Other studies found that adults with good reflective capacities were less likely to develop borderline personality disorder following childhood trauma than their less reflective peers. Secure attachment in childhood provides the context for a reflective self and a theory of mind (Fonagy & Target, 1996, 1997), which in turn contributes to later resilience, in part because mentalising capacities are intimately linked with self-agency, a crucial component of psychological well-being (see Chapter 8). The finding of the protective effects of RF immediately suggests psychotherapy's role in enhancing mentalising skills.

Fonagy et al. (2002) pinpoint the role of impaired mentalising in child maltreatment. The child is exposed to the 'double whammy' of a maltreating caregiver, by definition unable or unwilling to mentalise the impact of the neglect and/or abuse they inflict, and unable to foster the very mentalising capacity that would help the child actively make sense of and circumvent the impact of their maltreatment.

Explicit in Fonagy and his colleagues' work was the notion that a parent's capacity to make sense of the *child's* mind is a crucial aspect of maternal sensitivity and suggests a mechanism for the *intergenerational transmission of attachment*. This led researchers to study how parents 'hold their children in mind' by examining the ways they speak with (Meins et al., 2001), or about, their child (Grienenberger, Kelly, & Slade, 2005; Oppenheim & Koren-Karie, 2013; Slade, 2005; Slade, Grienenberger, et al., 2005). Parents differ widely in their capacity to see infants as sentient beings, with projects, desires, and affects of their own, and how good they are at factoring in their *own* states of mind when talking about their relationship with their child. Such differences significantly impact on infant attachment security and their subsequent attachment histories.

Ainsworth's formulations had from the start differentiated between mothers' capacity to respond to their infants' signals and the 'appropriateness' of that response, although that distinction got somewhat lost by later researchers. 'Appropriateness' assumes that a caregiver needs two skills: first, the capacity to 'read' her infant – i.e., to mentalise; second, to gauge and pitch her own responses in the light of those 'readings'. This goes beyond Main's (1995) notion of a 'fluid-autonomous' parental discourse style to a more interactive model of sensitive parenting in which the child's and the caregiver's actions and reactions are mutually cued. This is clearly relevant to psychotherapy, where the 'appropriateness' of therapists' interventions – the 'how' of their interventions as much as the specific contents and theoretical basis – may be crucial in determining outcome.

Fonagy and his collaborators have recently argued that the psychosocial 'purpose' of secure attachment is to create in the child a state of 'epistemic trust' (Fonagy & Allison, 2014). The caregiver creates an ambiance in which an infant feels accurately known and can rely on the relationship to be based on truthfulness and benign support, rather than exploitation. On this basis, children absorb the cognitive and emotional skills needed to flourish in the social context in which they find themselves, especially to learn from their own and others' experience. Epistemic *mis*-trust, arising out of insecure, especially disorganised, attachments, compromises this process, leading either to inefficient lone-wolf 'reinventing the wheel' strategies, or slavish and compliant imitation of bad models (cf. Laland, 2017). Psychotherapeutic 'techniques', however 'evidence-based', will be ineffective unless and until epistemic trust, via secure attachment, is first reinstated.

Conclusion

As a pointer to what is to come, we end this chapter with Bowlby's much-quoted invocation of how therapy should provide:

> ...the patient with a secure base from which he can explore the various unhappy and painful aspects of his life, past and present, many of which he finds it difficult or perhaps impossible to think about and reconsider without a trusted companion to provide support, encouragement, sympathy, and, on occasion, guidance. (1988: 138)

Note Bowlby's characteristically cautious use of the negative, describing what is 'difficult' and 'impossible' 'without' a trusted companion, rather than what will happen '*with*' one. Our aim in this book, with the hoped-for collaboration and blessing of our readers, is to transform that negative into a positive.

Summary

- John Bowlby laid the observational and theoretical foundations of attachment theory. His *magnum opus* is his 'trilogy' – *Attachment, Separation* and *Loss*.

- Mary Ainsworth is the co-founder of attachment theory and research. Her Strange Situation Procedure (SSP) continues to be used to classify infants' attachments as secure, organised insecure (deactivating and hyperactivating), and disorganised. She also proposed parental sensitivity and appropriateness of response as key determinants of secure attachment, and observed the relationship between secure attachment and confident exploration from a secure base.

- Long-term studies of children's attachments were initiated by Alan Sroufe and Everett Waters.

- Mary Main moved the study of attachment to the 'level of representation' by developing the Adult Attachment Interview (AAI). Analysis of parents' narrative patterns when describing their own childhood leads to a classification of their attachment status as secure-autonomous, dismissing, or preoccupied. She identified a third type of insecure attachment in infants: disorganised ('D'), whose AAI analogue is unresolved ('U').

- Main saw 'D' as an 'approach–avoidance dilemma' in which children turn to a caregiver who is the very source of the threat that stimulates the attachment dynamic. Lyons-Ruth extended this to the idea of 'hostile-helpless' ('H/H') caregivers who are either frightened by their children's distress or frightening to them.

- Peter Fonagy, Howard and Miriam Steele, and Mary Target developed the concepts of 'reflexive function' ('RF') and then 'mentalising', which are typical of secure-making parents who are able to see their children as sentient beings with motives, projects, and experiences of their own. Despite adversity, mentalising mothers can still transmit security to their offspring. Important functions of psychotherapy include establishing a secure relationship, instilling epistemic trust, and enhancing mentalising skills.

Notes

1. Newton: 'If I have seen further it is by standing on the shoulders of giants.'
2. Note the 'intergenerational transmission of attachment' from Bowlby and Ainsworth to her students (Bretherton, Cassidy, Crittenden, Kobak, Lieberman, Main, Waters), and on to *their* colleagues and students as well.

3

Attachment-informed Psychotherapy

Definition and Overview

What is Attachment?

We begin with a working definition of human attachment. At its most basic level, attachment refers to the observation that from the start of life, in common with other mammals, we develop inextricable connections with those who care for and protect us. These connections are motivated by infants' drive to survive, and are maintained and elaborated by parents' no less instinctual imperative to ensure their offspring's survival. 'Survival' here refers to physical survival, but also to survival as feeling, thinking, connected, fully *human* beings.

Without attachments the child would be at best, lost; at worst, cease to exist. The emphasis on survival as a primary motivator, and the analysis of how threat and concomitant anxiety are managed (i.e., 'defences'), is central to attachment theory, and to its relevance to psychotherapy.

For infants and young children, the most dangerous threats are those that directly imperil their caregiver bonds; maintaining these ties is of overriding importance. As a result, children develop strategies that minimise disruptions to these primary relationships. They do so by *adapting* or accommodating to the nurturing ecology in order to ensure proximity (literal or figurative) to their caregivers,[1] even if this means minimising or amplifying their emotions to suit the caregiver's needs (Cassidy, 1994). In his classic paper 'On knowing what you are not supposed to know and feeling what you are not supposed to feel', Bowlby (1979) described how children unconsciously suppress feelings and actions they have learned diminish their parents' emotional and physical availability. Staying attached under adverse circumstances comes at a price.

These adaptations to the caregiving environment – their flexibility, rigidity, or vulnerability – determine the openness and freedom with which children explore the world around them. 'Exploration' here encompasses learning based on imitation, mirroring, and modelling as well as innovation, imagination, and creativity. An irony of the attachment dynamic is that the more secure and connected people feel, the more able they are to venture *away* from their caregivers. The nature and quality of peoples' attachments encompass their stance towards 'being with' and 'being away from' intimate others.

As originally conceptualised by Bowlby and Ainsworth, attachment is a dynamic system, activated by threats (real or imagined) to safety (and hence survival). When infants are startled by a loud noise, the attachment system is activated, and they seek proximity to their caregiver. Once safe, the attachment system is deactivated and they can return to exploratory play. This dynamic system is not phased out at school age or adolescence. Attachment operates throughout life, with threats to safety – literal or figurative – taking precedence over other motivational systems, such as hunger or sex. These security searches can be overt and behavioural, as when survivors of a terrorist attack hug complete unknowns, or covert and internal, with soothing others brought to mind. Our evolutionary heritage ensures that when threatened we turn to a real or imagined 'secure base'.

Bowlby saw the attachment dynamic as a control/feedback system in which child and caregiver adjust their mutual proximity as well as their excursions away from one another in exquisite synchrony (see Solomon & George, 1996). In the attachment 'Circle of Security' model, Powell et al. (2013) depict how parents and children continuously monitor the balance between security-scaffolded exploration and the need for re-connection when threatened. Parents' pre-existing attachment systems come into play as they pull their children close or push them away – hence the 'intergenerational transmission' of attachment dispositions via parents from grandparent to grandchild.

These dynamic properties, which include both members of the dyad (seeker and sought), slowly become internalised as internal working models of attachment (IWMs) (Bowlby, 1980). The attachment dynamic is transposed into the growing child's, and later adult's, mental representations, or '*internal* secure base' (Holmes, 2010). A well-functioning attachment system ensures safety and security in intimate relationships as well as in autonomous exploration. In contrast to classical object relations theories, Bowlby emphasised the importance of 'mature dependence' and the lifelong role of internalised *and* external others as the basis for independence and autonomy.

Secure people survive as infants, thrive as children, and flourish as adults. Insecure attachment can compromise intellectual and social childhood development, and in severe forms is a long-term risk factor for physical and mental ill health in adult life.[2] As we shall describe in the pages that follow, psychotherapy aims to reverse or mitigate the impact of these adversities, and help move clients towards more secure forms of thinking and relating.

Attachment-informed Psychotherapy

We now come to the question of attachment-informed psychotherapy. In the section below, we will briefly outline what we see as the theoretical and scientific assumptions, guiding principles, and therapeutic competencies of attachment-informed psychotherapy. These form both the core of our approach and establish the structure of this book.

Theoretical and scientific assumptions

Based on the history of attachment theory and research described in Chapter 2, and expanded upon throughout this book, we assume that most of the patients who come to us are struggling with *insecure* ways of being in the world that cause them (and those close to them) pain and suffering.

We further assume that these ways of being – whether they are conscious or unconscious, and whether suffering is overt or covert – have arisen legitimately out of the patient's life experience. Attachment sees character and its discontents largely in terms of efforts to survive (emotionally and sometimes literally) in the immediate and wider environment in which people grow up, and given the biology with which they were born.

When we speak of 'ways of being', we are referring to defences against thoughts and feelings that are perceived as threats to survival. These can be conceptualised in terms of 'attachment organisations' (the attachment approach), 'patterns of defence' (the more psychodynamic position), or biologically based systems for stress and distress regulation (the position of affective neuroscience). All refer to modes of thinking, feeling, and regulating relational closeness and distance whose primary function is to achieve a modicum of emotional safety.

Because individuals' primary relationships and biology tend to be relatively stable (even if, as in disorganised attachment, 'stably unstable'), the 'states of mind in relation to attachment' that bring clients to our consulting rooms are likewise fairly stable, and reflect efforts to cope and stay emotionally (or, in dire circumstances, physically) alive within the perceived – and to an extent self-created – parameters of their interpersonal world. But equally, attachment-based research strongly suggests that change is possible, thanks to the power of certain types of new relationships to alter even the most entrenched relational patterns.

Guiding principles

The theoretical and scientific assumptions we have outlined inform the basic principles of attachment-informed psychotherapy. These can be listed as follows.

1. Attachment defences or organisations will be observed in patients' everyday relationships, as well as in the therapeutic relationship.

2. An essential psychotherapeutic skill is awareness of and sensitivity to patients' attachment-based ways of being – in relationship to themselves and others.

3. Therapists aim to *soften* rigid and non-productive states of mind, *enhance* flexibility and open-ness, and *promote* genuine safe closeness and rich exploration and autonomy. Clinical work typically involves understanding and modifying adaptations/defences.

4. These processes arise out of therapeutic relationships that – as we will describe – have many components of secure attachment. This forms the foundation for moving from insecure to more secure ways of being.

5. Transformative patient–therapist relationships depend on the therapist's capacity to maintain a stance that is:

   - Regulating
   - Non-threatening
   - Sensitive
   - Synchronous
   - Mentalising
   - Radically accepting

6. The capacity to respond in regulating, sensitive, and accepting ways is crucial to diminishing the threat patients feel both in addressing their pain and suffering, and allowing themselves to get close to, and gradually, often with many false starts, to trust their therapist (Slade, 2014; Slade et al., 2017).

7. In order to truly provide a secure base for patients, therapists need to be aware of and reflect upon their own attachment states of mind (see Dozier, Cue, & Barnett, 1994), 'core sensitivities', and vulnerabilities (Powell, et al., 2013). As we shall see, their intrusion can threaten the therapeutic process and its protagonists in a variety of ways.

Key Therapeutic Competencies

Based on these principles, we can delineate the key competencies of attachment-informed psychotherapists, as manifest – consciously and/or procedurally – in their working practice. These include the capacity to:

1. Establish a *relationship*:

- form and sustain secure trusting relationships.
- sensitively regulate affects – in oneself and one's client.

- mentalise in its three facets: self-reflection (i.e. reflect upon and regulate one's own attachment states of mind in the countertransference), reflections on clients' inner world, and reflection on the interactions (countertransferential and transferential) between them.

- validate the client's intrinsic autonomy and agency.

- adopt a position of 'radical acceptance' of clients' adaptations and their necessity for survival.[3] This is especially important when working with very disturbed people.

2. *Make meaning*

- imagine and describe the early emotional environment underlying clients' attachment dispositions.

- identify and work with attachment-shaped defences as they manifest themselves dynamically in the therapeutic relationship.

- conceptualise for the patient the adaptive role and survival function of such defences as strategies for managing threats to attachment security.

- foster narrative competence, and through it an enlarged, affectively coherent sense of self.

3. *Promote change*

- help patients generalise from secure therapeutic relationships to their everyday lives.

- facilitate learning from experience.

- encourage an epistemology of truthfulness in two senses: being 'true to one's self' (i.e. authenticity); and in developing a methodology which, through reflection, leads to more comprehensive and nuanced self-narratives.

- help clients to feel safe enough to be open to surprise and 'improbability', and thus prepared to revise outmoded attachment patterns and assumptions.

The Three Paradoxes of Psychotherapy

It might be argued that this list is hardly attachment-specific and could be applied to any competent therapist. Our response to this is wholehearted agreement! But, as we hope to show, we are convinced that the science and art of attachment have much to contribute to improved psychotherapeutic understanding, practice, and outcome. Before embarking on our exposition we turn briefly to some fundamental paradoxes of psychotherapy, each of which, we believe, can and must be turned to advantage.

With a few diagnostic exceptions,[4] the overwhelming bulk of evidence favours as the prime mover of therapeutic change 'common factors', and especially *the therapeutic relationship*. The latter encompasses the quality of the alliance; therapist empathy; and interpersonal skills (Safran, Muran, & Proskurov, 2009; Wampold, 2015). As the American Psychological Association Task Force on Empirically Supported Treatments puts it:

> the therapy relationship makes substantial and consistent contributions to psychotherapy outcome *independent of specific type of treatment.* (Ackerman et al., 2001, our italics)

Thus, despite minor differences, the efficacy of most valid and structured psychotherapies is roughly comparable (Shedler, 2010; Wampold, 2015): 60–65% of patients will improve (n.b. 10% deteriorate), irrespective of the modality of therapy. Luborsky's inspired invocation of the 'Dodo-bird's verdict' (Luborsky et al., 2002), in which that now extinct avian calls a halt to the Caucus race in *Alice in Wonderland* by announcing that 'everyone has won and all shall have prizes', has stood the test of time.

The importance of the therapeutic relationship in promoting change does not obviate the need for specific modality training, however. The vast majority of practitioners start their professional life by absorbing and identifying with a *specific* psychotherapeutic modality – Rogerian, systemic, CBT, psychoanalytic, psychodynamic, group analytic, etc. Implicitly, and sometimes unashamedly, therapists tend to believe their own brand of therapy is better – more effective (CBT), more deep-reaching (psychodynamic), more socially sensitive (systemic) – than its rivals. Grounding oneself in a core set of concepts is unavoidable and necessary. Language acquisition starts from one's mother-tongue; multilingualism comes later; later still, perhaps, an appreciation of the 'deep grammar' that underlies all languages. But here's the paradox: the majority of psychotherapy practitioners and clinical psychologists ultimately describe themselves as 'integrative' (Holmes & Bateman, 2002), as they move from exclusivity to therapeutic multilingualism.

Regardless of modality, we argue that attachment provides the *scientific and practical basis for effective deployment of the relationship in psychotherapy*. If the key to therapeutic success is the client–therapist relationship, then an attachment perspective is indispensable, since it taps into the fundamentals of secure relationships and how they form the springboard for development and change.

But here our project is up against another paradox. While attachment provides a theoretical, research-based, and clinically relevant set of principles that inform and permeate psychotherapeutic work in all its forms and modalities, it is not a psychotherapeutic modality in its own right:

> Understanding the nature and dynamics of attachment and mentalization *informs* rather than *defines* intervention and clinical thinking ... without needing to jettison other, equally important and valid kinds of clinical understanding. (Slade, 2008a: 763)

The last thing the field needs is yet another brand-named therapy.[5] Practitioners must learn their trade as though their chosen modality were the best and only effective one. But if it is accepted that the interactive *process* rather than the theoretical persuasion of the therapist ultimately determines psychotherapy outcome, attachment's evidence-based understanding of intimate relationships has a special contribution to make. We hope to guide therapists towards the attachment principles that will enhance their particular therapeutic practice, whatever it may be.

This brings us to a third paradox. Bowlby's last published work was his biography of Darwin (Bowlby, 1991). Darwin's qualitative and observational studies provided powerful evidence for his (and Wallace's) theory of the origin of species through natural selection. But Darwin – pre-Mendel, pre-Watson and Crick – was entirely ignorant of of the cellular and biochemical *mechanisms* underpinning evolutionary change. Contemporary psychotherapy finds itself in a comparable situation. There is no doubt that psychotherapy *works*, but how exactly does it bring about change? What are its 'active ingredients', and how do they impact on the troubled psyche? We aim to show how attachment – as a theory, a body of research, and a *practice* – provides a window into these fundamental mechanisms.

Summary

- The fundamental assumptions of attachment theory guide attachment-informed practice.

- Attachment-informed psychotherapy places special importance on the therapeutic relationship to reduce threat, soften defences, and support autonomy and exploration.

- Attachment provides an explanatory framework for both therapist and patient with which to make meaning of the patient's suffering.

- The key competencies of an attachment-informed psychotherapist include the capacity to provide a secure base for the patient, be sensitive to attachment processes, and to make use of the self in illuminating these processes.

- 'Attachment-informed psychotherapy' is a scientifically based conceptual and pragmatic framework for thinking about helping relationships rather than a new species of psychotherapy.

Notes

1. In line with contemporary attachment theory, we use the term 'caregiver'; the person caring for a child is usually, but not invariably, the mother.
2. Evidence for these rather bald assertions will emerge in the course of this book.
3. 'Radical acceptance' here differs from Linehan's (1993) use of the term. She refers to the *patient's* capacity for 'radical acceptance' of things the way they are. Here we describe the *therapist's* stance.
4. Exceptions to the 'common factors' rule include the unsuitability of psychoanalysis in schizophrenia (Fonagy, 2003) and the comparative effectiveness of CBT in OCD (Veale, 2007).
5. Currently over 500 and counting! (Lilienfeld & Arkowitz, 2012).

4

Affect Regulation in Attachment and Psychotherapy

As we noted in the previous chapter, the therapeutic relationship is what makes transformation possible. We described the key competencies of attachment-informed pyschotherapists as regulating and non-threatening. In this chapter we will approach the question of affect regulation more systematically, looking at its role in a variety of attachment relationships: caregiver and infant, romantic/spousal partners – and therapist and patient. We will also suggest – contrary to 'classical' attachment theory – that a range of intense, intimate relationships, including that with the therapist, can be considered *attachment relationships*.

Affect and Affect Regulation in Attachment Theory

Bowlby (1969: 158) maintained that

> only if an animal, human or sub-human, is reasonably accurate at assessing the mood of another is he able to participate in social life.

Implicit in this is the view that the very fabric of social life is based on affective exchange. Humans love, hate, procreate, nurture, destroy, and die under the aegis of reciprocally expressed emotions. Stripped of emotion we are unable to effectively appraise, bond, collaborate, quarrel, and repair our relationships with others.

The affect system is evolution's way of guiding individuals through the maze of feelings that the intensely social nature of our species' existence engenders.

Panskepp's (2010) list of primary emotions – seeking, panic, fear, rage, lust, care, and play – are deeply embedded in our palaeo-cortex, and are to be found in all mammals. But, as Bowlby recognised, in humans and higher primates they *are harnessed, given meaning, and shaped within the interpersonal field*. The affect system is an interpersonal system: joy, happiness, excitement, love – alongside hate, fear, rage, envy, and disgust – only make sense in a relational context (Stern, 1985). Emotions are relational experiences.

Attachment theory is, in many ways, a theory of affect and affect regulation. As Bowlby saw it, safety-seeking is *motivated by an internal, affective* state, primarily the sense of being threatened. He saw threat as coming primarily from the outside world, prompting fear and consequent proximity-seeking in the child. But, given his psychoanalytic background, he also recognised that threat could come from within. Feelings – especially negative ones – can themselves threaten the relationship with the caregiver, hence the need for adaptation and accommodation. Ainsworth added a positive dimension, expanding it to include 'felt security'. Here the child is motivated not just to banish fear and threat, but also to bask in an internal feeling state of safety and security. These 'good' feelings are surely part of what is ordinarily meant by 'love'; indeed, near the end of his life Bowlby referred to attachment theory as a theory of love (R. Bowlby, personal communication, AS, 2011).

The Developmental Framework of Affect Regulation

Crucial features of human development are its slow pace, and the primacy of instruction and learning over instinct (Laland, 2017). Infants need help if they are to use their emotions to negotiate the complexity of the interpersonal environment. In the early stages of life the long (albeit in milliseconds) journey from *sensation* (sense organs' environment-stimulated impulses travelling towards the central nervous system (CNS) from the periphery) to *perception* (meaning-infused emotion, with its behavioural consequences, e.g., approach or avoidance) needs the help of the 'borrowed brain' of the caretaker. The attachment relationship is the primary locus for this 'sensitive period' of affect co-regulation, collaboratively first 'holding' a feeling – then understanding, naming, and acting upon it.

> A child wakes up in the night from a bad dream, and finds himself surrounded by darkness, alone, beset by nameless threats. The contours of trusted reality are blurred or invisible; in the terror of incipient chaos the child cries out for his mother. It is she who has the power to banish the chaos and to restore the benign shape of the world. (Berger, 1970: 54)

Berger is describing here how the caregiver 'regulates' the child's emotion, in the sense of understanding its meaning, but always in the context of a mentalising perspective in which regulatory hypotheses are *provisional*, modified by the child's *feedback*, and subject to continuous *revision*. In Berger's example, the child is presumed to have had a bad dream, but mother will also be considering other possibilities: is my baby hungry, too hot, too cold, needing a nappy change, bored and wanting stimulus, etc.? Her motherly 'intuition' is a result of the current context, her prior experience both of this particular child and others, and of comparable caregiving situations, including her own in relation to *her* mother. Her Bayesian brain (see Chapter 12) will be assigning probabilities to the various options, and acting accordingly.

As the child grows, this affect-regulatory process gradually becomes internalised. Children begin to move from co-regulation to self-regulation, acquiring the skills to 'read' their own emotions: '*Mum, I'm hungry*', '*I'm tired*', '*I'm upset*', etc. This emerging capacity for coping with, and being guided by feelings, creates affective 'envelopes' in which raw emotion is *contained* by the modulatory processes of verbalising and counter-balance (e.g., '*I'm hungry, but it's not that bad; I can wait till Mum's ready to give me a feed; most of the time she's there when I need her*').

With development, this co-regulation becomes internalised as children gradually learn to cope with their own emotions, while retaining the life-long capacity to elicit co-regulation with an intimate other if feelings threaten to overwhelm.

The school entry child will cope 'bravely' with a minor injury or bullying in the playground, but once collected by a parent from school and in the privacy of home or car, may burst into tears and need comfort. Adolescents cultivate a furious independence, but will regularly return to home base for warmth, food, and sometimes even advice! Adults continue to need secure base figures who help co-regulate extremes of emotion, positive and negative.

The 'good enough' parent meets the child's affects and his need for regulation with acceptance and holding, facilitating complex emotional expression and organisation. The attachment figure has a reciprocal emotional resonance to the child's search for connection, and draws on and expresses her own affects in response; she does so in gesture and physical posture, tone and timbre of voice, and, of course, words. The parent's own affects help her to make meaning of the child's affective experiences and reflect them back in a 'digestible' way. She attunes to and modulates his emotional state, and helps him – in whatever way is appropriate – make meaning of his experience. The child's feelings are retuned, recalibrated, contextualised, soothed, amplified, and verbalised.

But of course, just as safety is social, so too is danger. The proximity inherent in attachment makes us vulnerable to exploitation, neglect, harm, and loss. For many parents, their children's emotions are triggering and potentially dysregulating. One way of dealing with this is to transform the child's affect into something they *can* bear, by denying, suppressing, distracting, distancing, or even exaggerating it. Here the child's affect is, to a greater or lesser degree, subsumed or obliterated by the parent's affect, necessitating, in Winnicott's terms (1965), 'compliance'. The child quickly learns which affects can be tolerated and which must be modified in order to mollify the caregiver and maintain whatever safety is possible. The 'false self' is born. We are reminded again of Bowlby's classic paper (1979) 'On knowing what you are not supposed to know and feeling what you are not supposed to feel'. The child's survival depends upon his regulating his affects – which in many cases means suppressing them – so as to preserve his essential relationships. In extreme cases it may also mean holding the parent's projections and distortions, identifying with them, at whatever cost to the child's own integrity. An open, secure relationship is one that can hold the breadth of the child's feelings; closed, insecure ones invariably place constrictions on what can be borne – by either party.

Thus, children's affective experience and inner world are profoundly coloured by the way they are understood, responded to, and regulated by key figures in their life (Beebe & Lachmann, 2013; Schore & Schore, 2008; Tronick, 2007). For example, a child will be implicitly aware of the maternal affect accompanying his own: e.g., '*When I get angry in my attempts to alert Mum to my need and distress, she pulls away.*' Feeling 'A' is thus dynamically and relationally linked to feeling 'B' (in the example, anger → abandonment).

In Main's formulation (Main et al., 1985), these 'actions and outcomes' are the basis for IWMs. They can also lead to self-alienating identifications with the parent, as in Anna Freud's (1936) classic concept of 'identification with the aggressor'. The attachment–affect dynamic is internalised, so that the parental *response* to the child's affect becomes as much a part of the child's state of mind with respect to attachment as are their own feelings (Lyons-Ruth et al., 2005; Sroufe & Fleeson, 1986).

For psychotherapists, the key point of the above account is that the affect regulatory process is re-awakened in the therapeutic relationship, but in ways that can be subject to examination and so modification.

Attachment Patterns and Affect Regulation

Secure and insecure attachment reflect varying 'strategies' for affect regulation (Cassidy, 1994; Kobak & Sceery, 1988) learned in the crucible of the child's primary relationships. The distressed (fearful, threatened, unwell) child seeks out a secure base with the capacity to soothe (i.e., regulate) 'bad' feelings and evoke 'good' ones (feeling safe, held, warm, happy, cheerful, amused, interested, excited). The parent of a secure child allows for the full expression of emotions, both positive and negative. The child learns that all affects – good, bad or indifferent – are tolerable and regulable. Snuggling up, the secure child can say 'I *hate* you Mum when you go away', confident that she will not be rejected.

Parents of insecure children do well enough when the going is good, but find it hard to cope with their children's negative affects, which may persist in raw form or be suppressed. In response to their parent's recoil at intense affect, avoidant children dampen down misery and rage for the sake of proximity to a rejecting or aggressive caregiver; hoping not to activate maternal aversion – fearing to bite the hand that feeds – resentful or hostile feelings are suppressed or diverted, but cannot be entirely eradicated. Their suffering is manifest in elevated heart rate, raised cortisol levels, and reduced interpersonal sensitivity and pleasure (Dozier et al., 2008; Sroufe et al., 2005; Sroufe & Waters, 1977). At the other pole of insecure attachment, resistant/anxious infants amplify emotion and helplessness, hopeful of activating the distracted or inconsistent caregiver's attention, but run the risk of becoming suffused with negative affect, inconsolable and unable to resume exploratory play. The toll taken by this strategy is inhibited exploration and diminished sense of agency; the child fails to move along the pathway from co- to self-regulation. In disorganised attachment, the parent's frightening or frightened responses leave the child alone and desperate with bad feelings, resorting to various forms of ineffective or even harmful self-soothing.

This continuum of insecure attachment patterns can be seen as differential responses to the threat of losing a vital connection to the parent (Slade, 2014). From earliest infancy, infants are sensitive to potential threats to whatever security is possible in their relationships. Secure children can express an array of feelings and needs without compromising the connection to the caregiver; when parents are unavailable or non-responsive (which even the best parents are, regularly!), the stress is still tolerable. The insecure organised patterns result when parents fail to 'meet' (Winnicott, 1965) the child's thoughts and feelings; the child learns that these must be diverted and defended against in order to protect the relationship. These avoidant and resistant/anxious responses to threat are manifestations of the 'flight' and 'fight' responses described in the stress regulation literature (Porges, 2011). Avoidant individuals flee from negative affects, while the resistant/anxious find it hard to extricate themselves from them, in both cases because to do so would be to threaten the child's most vital relationships.

The most serious danger to children's emotional integrity and even physical survival arises when the parent or parents themselves are the source of threat, and thus – quite directly – to their survival. This leads to the range of 'freezing' responses that life-threats trigger: dissociation, numbing, confusion, disorientation, and disintegration.

In sum the basis for the widely accepted psychoanalytic concept of 'defences', is the threats to children's key attachments, and the need to find some way, however diminishing or self-defeating, to negotiate a route between safety and danger.

As Main's work has made clear, given that the need for attachment is life-long, rather than outgrown, these affect-regulatory principles apply as much to adults and their relationships as they do to children. Mikulincer and Shaver (2016) have shown in a series of ingenious studies how attachment status colours the ways in which individuals handle feelings, their own and others. To illustrate, in one study (Mikulincer & Shaver, 2005), subjects were asked to describe an episode of conflict with a partner in the previous week and how, if at all, it was resolved. The securely attached were able readily to supply such instances. By contrast, dismissive people tended to find it hard to recall conflict at all, while the hyperactivating groups were short on convincing narratives of repair. In both groups, therefore, the collaborative affect regulation we describe was compromised. Intriguingly, subliminal or supraliminal messages of love and security (words like 'mother' or 'home', but not neutral words like 'chair', flashed on a screen with or without the subject's awareness) helped insecure people's narratives move in a more affect-containing and reparative direction.

Extending the Definition of Attachment

From Bowlby's perspective (cf. Cassidy, 2016), only the parent–child relationship qualified as an attachment relationship. Thus Bowlby avoided using the term 'attachment' to describe the parental side of the attachment system because for him attachment implied safety *seeking* and not safety *providing*. Likewise, he avoided describing romantic relationships as attachments because of the involvement of sexual and reproductive systems.

For us, attachment as a term has face validity as a description of deep, intimate, regulating emotional connections, and this we believe applies to a range of important relationships in a person's life. For that reason, we propose extending the definition to include any intimate relationships in which affect regulation or co-regulation – of both negative and positive affect – are at its core. Thus, *alongside security provision, an attachment relationship is defined here as one that is person-specific, intimate, and affect-regulating*. This allows us to extend the idea of attachment beyond that between parent and child to spouses/partners, siblings, close friendships, some sporting or military 'buddies' – and the psychotherapeutic relationship. This expansion retains the motivational aspect of Bowlby's original formulation in that the imperative of emotional survival (his 'set goal') depends on affect co-regulation with the help of a secure base. When suffused with feelings – negative or positive – we feel an overwhelming need for another with whom to share our sorrows and joy.

While mutual regulation (see too Beebe & Lachmann, 2013; Tronick, 2007) is a feature of all attachment relationships, the developmental context and ecology of the relationship determines who takes the lead in this co-regulation. In the case of infants and caregivers, this is predominantly unidirectional, or 'lopsided' (Barratt, 2016); it is the carers' job to regulate their infants' feelings. The same is largely true for therapists *vis-à-vis* their clients. Danger threatens when the care-seeker/caregiver relationship, whether parent–child or therapist–patient, is role-reversed. Here, the child or patient assumes responsibility for regulating and containing the other's feelings, often, if in an entrenched pattern, with disastrous consequences. In adult romantic attachments, co-regulation is two-way and mutual, although at any given moment it is often unidirectional, as one member's attachment dynamic is activated by stress or threat, and the other's reciprocal caregiving dynamic comes into play. The pattern turns and turns about, depending on circumstances. When both members of the dyad's attachment needs are aroused, for example through the illness or even death of a child, and neither is therefore able to offer care, relationship difficulties and mal-'adaptation' and sometimes irretrievable separation can result.

With this possibly heretical proposition explicitly stated, we turn to the question of affect regulation and attachment in the therapeutic relationship.

Affect Regulation and Psychotherapy

Affect regulation is central to what psychotherapists do. Attuned therapists mirror, resonate with, and help verbalise clients' feelings; these are all aspects of 'regulation' in the sense of modulating feelings so they became available for mentalising – soothing, stimulating, dampening, as needed. Examining the discrepancy between these efforts, and the ways in which pre-existing attachment representations manifest themselves in transference, becomes a lever for psychic change (see Chapter 11).

Faced with patients' entrenched and rigid defences, seemingly seeking to repeat or maintain destructive relationships, therapists must constantly remind themselves of the *unregulated affects* that lie at the heart of these *adaptations*, and try to picture and give voice to the affective environment that brought them about. They strive to create a contrasting environment within the consulting room, where the emotions and expectations that have hitherto triggered defences can, often for the first time, be available for co-regulation. They do so by providing a secure base, identifying and then working with the attachment dynamic, and always aiming for co-regulation of the affects, typically but not exclusively negative, that this engenders.

Providing a regulating secure base

Another sometimes overlooked therapeutic paradox is that alongside the psychological troubles that bring people for help, seeking help in itself will activate the attachment dynamic. For many clients, the invitation to share their thoughts and feelings, and thus implicitly or explicitly open themselves to the therapist, is itself potentially threatening. Where intimate relationships have been shaped by disappointment, betrayal, absence, or violence, the invitation to enter into this new relationship brings its own fear. Daring to give up entrenched survival patterns, however threadbare, spells danger, evoking the attachment dynamic that established them in the first place.

As we shall reiterate throughout this book (see especially Chapters 5 and 6), part of our work is to help clients find ways to regulate these threats, just as secure caregivers regulate threats for their children. Especially in the early stages of therapy, and often at the beginning and end of sessions, patients will be seeking comfort and security rather than exploration. Therapists will at these moments sense a caregiving pressure towards reassurance and soothing. Under the sway of the attachment dynamic, the free-associative aspect of psychotherapy will be in abeyance, and attempts to instigate it often ineffective or counter-productive. As one new patient exasperatedly replied when asked by the analyst, faithful to his Freudian roots, to say whatever came into his head, however irrelevant or embarrassing, 'If I could do that I wouldn't need to be here in the first place.'

For these reasons, it can be important for the therapist to feel free to provide a degree of comfort to the patient. Reassuring comments may be needed, often in a soothing tone of voice: '*Maybe it feels pretty scary having to come in here and lay bare your soul*', or '*Sometimes getting going in a session can be difficult.*' Similarly, at the end of sessions, therapists frequently make conventional, yet actually significant valedictory remarks such as: '*See you tomorrow/ next week.*' They may make eye-contact and smile. These reinforce a secure base representation that helps tide the sufferer over until the next encounter. While this active security-provision on the part of therapists is often needed, once the attachment dynamic is in abeyance it is important to find ways to reflect upon – i.e., mentalise – it. For example:

Th: I've noticed you seem to feel pretty tense when you first come in, shall we think about that a bit...?

P: Yeah, well I'm sure you think I'm making a big fuss about nothing, and just need to get on with things...

Th: It sounds as though you imagine I'm about to judge you and find you wanting...?

P: Well I never was the brilliant, popular, successful and articulate chap my Mum wanted me to be...

Identifying the attachment dynamic

The raw materials of psychotherapy are the full panoply of negative emotions – conflict, anger, rage, envy, grief, sadness. A fundamental therapeutic skill is the capacity to identify and encourage the expression of negative feelings, especially when denied or repressed. And yet the invitation to give voice to these emotions in therapy will activate defences, developed in order to survive in the context of one's original, vital attachments.

An early and urgent task for therapists is to explore clients' specific attachment *dynamics*. What were the nature, function, and meaning of their unique and necessary adaptations to the developmental circumstances in which they found themselves? The key question is not whether they are secure or insecure, for the majority are insecure (van IJzendoorn & Bakermans-Kranenburg, 2009). Rather, we are concerned with dynamic efforts to regulate fear and anxiety; that is, *it is these efforts rather than the categories themselves that deserve our clinical attention.* The varieties of insecure attachment, despite providing a useful rubric, take us only so far. They are broad-brush categories mainly useful for research. As clinicians, we are concerned with the specificity and uniqueness of individual lives.[1] Also, within the psychotherapeutic context defences shift and change, so that avoidance may give way to rumination, and then to anxiety and extreme neediness at different points in the treatment. The hope is that these will eventually give way to a more secure organisation. Because attachment is a dynamic rather than static system, and is activated by the relational processes of psychotherapy, both recapitulation and transformation become possible. This is the *how* of attachment – the living, breathing, fast-moving, ever-changing, here-and-nowness of affective communication, whether between parents and children, lovers and spouses, and patients and their therapists.

Clinicians will be asking themselves the following kinds of questions. How does this person try to *stay safe*? How do they *regulate* closeness? How robust is the sense of their *agency*? Are they inhibited and paralysed by doubt or do they rush blindly into risk without apparent thought? Do they minimise their needs for intimacy and proximity, or exaggerate them? What has led them to defend against either closeness or exploration? What were the unique qualities of their early relationships, and how did these inform their sense of themselves and their capacities for self-regulation? What attachment or relational triggers spark off self-defeating or dysfunctional thoughts, feelings, and behaviours? What is the downside of the specific strategies they have chosen for staying safe and regulating emotion? And how are these processes being reactivated in the therapeutic relationship?

As we shall see, recognising and understanding patients' attachment dynamics is helped by the research literature on infant–mother attachment and its sequelae, and by advances in affective neuroscience. But the relevance of attachment's empirical basis to clinical practice goes beyond scientific validation, important though that is. Attachment research provides a framework and language for understanding how people adapt – even if in seemingly dysfunctional ways – to the environment in which they grow up.[2] This sensitises therapists to the primal need for security, and to the perils achieving it can bring. The attachment perspective alerts therapists to listen, respond to, and use the language of safety, security, and its obverse – loneliness, fear, anger, and yearning – and so help patients to feel heard and understood.

Working with the attachment dynamic

How do we respond to the specific attachment orientations our clients bring? Just as secure-making parents bring different patterns of love and attention to their children's different needs, stages and personalities, so flexibility is an essential feature of good therapists. While research suggests that encouraging the expression of negative emotions is helpful to clients with avoidant attachment styles, it can be less so with resistant/enmeshed/hyperactivating clients. Here, 'dwelling in the negative' is a habitual stance; this may be reinforced by a relentless emphasis on rage/anger/envy, etc., fostering yet more misery-perpetuating rumination rather than transcendence. From an attachment perspective, a capacity to notice and encourage a 'Dutchman's trousers' smidgeon of blue in an otherwise overcast emotional sky, is an equally important therapeutic skill (Slade, 2016).

If therapy is to be successful, therapists must first validate the patient's emotional stance before gently challenging the assumptions that underlie it. In the early stages of the therapeutic alliance, clinicians are likely to respond 'in style' to patient defences: for example, not pushing too hard for an avoidant person to open up, and gently tolerating hyperactivating emotional overchargedness. This mirroring helps patients feel understood and validated. As therapy progresses, however, and the relationship becomes more secure, therapists move towards responding in ways that are 'out of style': dismissing patients are pushed to express intolerable emotions and become more engaged, while preoccupied patients are helped to contain powerful emotions, function more autonomously, and deintensify transference manifestations and expectations. Dismissing clients' rigid, emotionless accounts need 'breaking'; with the preoccupied/enmeshed, the need is for 'making' coherent stories out of overwhelming, unbounded, and chaotic emotion (Holmes, 2001). Gentle challenges to the patient's attachment organisation have the effect of softening rather than provoking characteristic defensive styles, thereby enhancing flexibility and change (see Daniel, 2014; Daly & Mallinckrodt, 2009).

Easier said than done. Weiss and Sampson (1986) conceptualise therapy in terms of a 'test' set by clients for therapists. Will prior expectations (i.e., transferential projections) of inadequate care be confirmed or disconfirmed? An attachment approach suggests that the appropriate response to this 'test' will depend on the client's attachment style. Let us say the client is talking about a loss, perhaps the death of a parent in childhood, or the ending of a recent relationship. An avoidant client might recount the events surrounding the loss but fail to communicate or describe her own feelings about it. A validating response from the therapist here might be:

> 'It sounds as though your feelings of sadness and fear when your mother died were so overwhelming they had to be put to one side – almost had to be *not* felt.'

This type of response would help build trust, as it acknowledges both the patient's defence and the reasons for it. However valid, it would be premature to move to a more challenging transference-based comment:

'You have told me everything about the loss except for your own emotional reactions to it. It's as though you put your feelings about the loss into cold storage, and this plays out now in the way you reacted to your girlfriend leaving you, and indeed to my holiday breaks, when you told me – I'm not sure I quite believed you – that it was "fine, OK – everyone deserves a holiday – and, boy! You therapists need them more than most".'

A more enmeshed/preoccupied client might dissolve in tears while telling the story of the loss. Here the therapist might gently say:

'It sounds as if all this is still very real for you today – almost unbearably painful.'

This would help contain the raw emotion. Again, an 'interpretation'/challenge would need to wait until deeper trust had been established:

'I wonder if these overwhelming feelings mean that it doesn't feel safe to you to let go of your dead mother – as though if you were to move on, all you would be left with would be a hollow emptiness; maybe even a horrible feeling that you were in some way responsible for her death...'

With disorganised/unresolved clients there might be sudden switches of topic or incoherence in the client's discourse surrounding the death. Here the therapist might notice her own feeling of emotional pain, or find herself silently tearful. This exemplifies the 'borrowed brain' at its most resonant, picking up split-off feelings, which, if sufficiently co-regulated, could now perhaps be faced:

'Listening to you I felt a great wave of sadness come over me; it's so hard – and doesn't really feel safe – to put that sort of pain or trauma into words, does it?'

Ironically, therapists 'fail' the test when they respond in ways consistent with the patient's expectations. Avoidant patients will anticipate rebuff, thereby suppressing feelings before expecting they are brushed aside ('getting their retaliation in first'!). Preoccupied people might expect the therapist to join them in their pool of negativity, and to be equally unable to extricate themselves from it, hence the caution about reinforcing depressive ruminations. The disorganised patient is hair-triggered for neglect and betrayal: momentary insensitivity, distractedness, misunderstanding, or clumsy interjection on the part of the therapist will be taken as a sign that the client is beyond help and on her own. Often at first fruitlessly, therapists aim to tailor their responses to soften, not reinforce, these defences.

To conclude the message of this chapter, a key feature of therapeutic affect co-regulation entails the identification and 'softening' of defences. In so far as it is itself a 'soft' concept, our use of this self-representing (cf. Hobson, 2013) word tries to capture yet another paradox of therapy: that therapeutic change entails becoming 'more' rather than less oneself. 'Softening' means putting one's history and difficulties overcome to good use, rather than aspiring to an illusory 'new self', a precursor to further disappointment and despair. We shall discuss these themes further in Chapters 9 and 10, especially in relation to the language and verbal interactions of therapeutic discourse.

Summary

- Attachment theory is an interpersonal theory of affects and their co-regulation.

- Children rely on their parent(s) to regulate the affects that are part of everyday experience.

- The success or failure of these efforts at regulation play a big part in the development of secure or insecure attachments. In the latter, when negative affects threaten the relationship, they tend either to be suppressed or exaggerated.

- The definition of an attachment relationship can be extended to describe any close, intimate, mutually affect-regulating or co-regulating relationships.

- Affect regulation is at the heart of attachment-informed psychotherapy.

Notes

1. This remains true even when attachment categories are expanded into a number of sub-categories, as in Crittenden's (2006) 'circumplex model'.
2. Just as it is useful to pyschoanalytic candidates to conduct infant observations, so it is useful for attachment-informed psychotherapists to be exposed to attachment's observational research methods.

5

Sensitivity, Mirroring, and Play

Foundations of Attachment Security in Caregivers and Therapists

As described in Chapters 3 and 4, a key therapeutic skill is to create – in the face of insecure attachment dispositions – a secure therapist–patient relationship. Attachment provides the scientific basis for the exploratory curiosity, emotional empathy and responsiveness, validation, appropriate verbal interplay and developmental narrative constructions that are the hallmarks of good clinical practice. The responsibility for the formation and maintenance of the therapeutic relationship rests squarely on the shoulders of the therapist, whose patients' insecurity will inevitably mean that they struggle to form a solid alliance and working relationship. Therapists who are able to provide a secure and safe base for their patients, to remain emotionally present and compassionate, while managing complex and potentially intense affects, are likely to be those best able to facilitate their patients' development.

The minutiae of parent–child attachments – secure and insecure – have much to teach us about successful and ultimately secure therapeutic relationships. In this chapter, we home in first on Ainsworth's central concept, parental *sensitivity*, and compare her formulations with aspects of the therapist–patient relationship. We then turn to two other key aspects of the parent–child relationship – mirroring and play – and discuss their relevance to the clinical situation.

Ainsworth's Sensitivity Scales and their Therapeutic Parallels

Ainsworth's view of attachment security is as relevant and fresh today as it was nearly 50 years ago. From Uganda to Baltimore and beyond, she never wavered in her view that maternal *sensitivity* is the crucial characteristic of securely attached mother–infant dyads, as compared with their insecure counterparts. Ainsworth developed a series of scales to measure maternal sensitivity; scores on these scales were used as the basis for overall attachment classification (Ainsworth et al., 1978). They are organised around four aspects of early care: (a) *receptiveness to infant signals*, (b) *cooperation vs. interference*, (c) psychological and physical *availability*, and (d) *acceptance vs. rejection* of the infant's needs. For Ainsworth, these were key to shaping infants' secure base behaviour, and to meeting their biological and relational needs. Although rarely used today,[1] we believe that these scales are particularly relevant to the clinical process.

In the sections below, we will consider extracts from the text of each scale before turning to parallels with the patient–therapist relationship. Key phrases in her account are in bold.

Receptivity to signals

This variable deals with the mother's ability to **perceive and to interpret accurately** *the signals and communications implicit in her infant's behaviour, and, given this understanding, to respond to them appropriately and promptly. Thus the mother's sensitivity has four essential components: (a) her awareness of the signals; (b) an accurate interpretation of them; (c) an appropriate response to them; and (d) a prompt response to them. ... Sensitive mothers are usually accessible to their infants and are aware ... of their more subtle communications, signals, wishes, and mood. ... These mothers accurately interpret their perceptions and show empathy with their infants. ... The sensitive mother, armed with this understanding and empathy,* **can time her interactions** *well and deal with her baby so that her interactions seem appropriate ... in kind as well as in quality – and prompt.*

In contrast, mothers with low sensitivity are not aware of much of their infant's behaviour, either because they ignore the baby or they fail to perceive in his activity the more subtle and hard-to-detect communications. ... A mother may have somewhat accurate perceptions of her infant's activity and moods but may be **unable to empathise** *with him. Through either lack of understanding or empathy, mothers with low sensitivity improperly time their responses, either in terms of scheduling or in terms of promptness to the baby's communications. Further, mothers with low sensitivity often have* **inappropriate responses in kind** *as well as quantity (i.e., interactions that are fragmented and poorly resolved).*

Receptivity is an essential precondition of therapeutic work. Therapists intuitively note their clients' posture, gesture, tone of voice, dress-style, facial nuance, and feed these into their preconscious responses. They use all their senses – sight (gesture and body posture), sound (tone of voice), overall 'feel', even smell (anxiety-provoked sweat; residual alcohol; unbathed self-neglect) as information-channels suggesting how the client might be feeling. Empathic therapists are attuned to shifting mood states as they arise in sessions and that underlie whatever 'story' or narrative is being told. Just as mothers intuitively know when their child is not 'right', therapists are alert to 'anomalies' – departures from normal, discrepancies between the content and tone of a narrative, stories that don't make sense, or sections that 'don't quite fit'.

Others – like some of Ainsworth's mothers – may at a cognitive level be accurate observers, but fail to empathise, in the sense that they are not alive to the patient's feelings and fail to be guided by these in their interventions. The results are stilted or forced interpretations, which discount patients' emotional states, fall on deaf ears, or evoke other forms of defensiveness.

Cooperation vs. interference

*The central issue is the extent to which the mother's **interventions break into, interrupt or cut cross** the baby's ongoing activity rather than being geared in both timing and quality to the baby's state, mood and current interests. … Mothers at the [cooperative] end of this continuum seem to **guide rather than to control** the baby's activity. Such a mother integrates her wishes, moods, and household responsibilities with the baby's wishes, moods, and ongoing activity. Their interactions and shifts of activity seem **co-determined**. Rather than interrupting an activity that the baby has in progress, she delays her intervention until a natural break in his activity occurs. Or through mediating activities, often of a playful sort, she can gradually divert him from what he is doing toward something she wants him to do.*

*Such a mother uses **mood-setting techniques**. At bed-time, for example, she gradually slows down the pace and vigour of their interaction until he is relaxed and calm and more ready for bed than he could have been at the peak of excited play. She invites him to come and cooperate with what she has in mind rather than imposing it on him.*

*[Controlling] mothers are highly interfering in an overwhelming physical sense. Such a mother snatches the baby up, moves him about, confines him, and, indeed, releases him with utter disregard for his activity-in-progress. When she restricts and restrains his movements it tends to be by direct physical intervention or force. She may also try to use force in instances in which the baby's cooperation is required if the intervention is to be effective – for example, in feeding, in play, and (although this usually comes later) in toilet training. Other[s] … must be considered highly interfering because they are 'at' the baby most of the time – **instructing, training, eliciting, directing, controlling** …*

In either case it is clear that the highly interfering mother has no respect for her baby as a separate, active, and autonomous person, whose wishes and activities have a validity of their own....

A 'co-determining' mother capitalises on spontaneity. She responds to the baby's vocalizations, and does a minimum of trying to elicit specific sounds. She tends to pick up something the baby does as the beginning of a play sequence, and responds to his initiations of play. She may attempt to initiate play, but if the baby does not respond, she either desists, or shifts her approach.

*An interfering mother tends to play ... by **doing something** to the baby, or by getting him to do something she wishes. Such mothers instruct the baby in tricks or stereotyped games, persisting even when the baby is in an unresponsive mood. ... Similarly, with vocalization. The interfering mother persistently tries to elicit specific vocalizations (or gestures) regardless of the baby's current interest in vocalizing or lack of it.*

There are many relevant resonances here for therapists. In sessions, the timing of the responses is all-important: sensing when to speak and when to hold back and let the client 'get there' for herself.

A sensitive mother adjusts her expectations of her child, depending on age and stage and temperament, and will help by proffering a grasped-for object, or concept that is just – but only just – out of reach. So too therapists gauge their interventions at this 'bootstrap' point where the client, with a little help – or nudge – from his 'friend' can make a significant developmental step forward. Therapists sensitively pick up on the client's phrases, mini-narratives, and initiatives and develop them in concert with the client.

Being alert to the patient's spontaneity is another clear parallel with therapy. A spontaneously arising memory, thought, dream, or account of a new extra-therapeutic departure will be treated with great respect and validation. *Freshness* of expression on the part of both therapist and patient is vital. Good therapists are able to pick up and use clients' language and metaphors in their turn-taking side of the conversation. They also use the language of safety and survival when – in their 'right-brain' mode – they sense the attachment dynamic has been activated. In addition, therapists are aware of the arc of a session; they hold back near the beginning, allow intensity to build up, and wind things down as the end comes into view.

When therapy is in trouble, therapist and client seem to be on parallel tracks, each with their own agenda. There is no meeting of 'bodyminds'. The therapist becomes an omniscient know-all who can see through clients' defences to what is 'really' going on. Therapists feel – especially in the early stages of training – they must maintain stony-faced 'neutrality', and may mistrust their intuitions. This may engender feelings in the client of diminishment and invalidation. Or therapists' anxiety leads them to cram in interpretations or instructions; the client is not receptive and cannot 'hear' what is being said. Timing goes awry. Therapist comments take the form of 'lectures' or are jargon-ridden, rather than using the client's vernacular. As with Ainsworth's insensitive mothers, the therapist tries to impose her own agenda rather than following the client's lead. The didactic or controlling therapist moves from collaboration and responsiveness to a 'life-coach' role. A useful mantra is that therapists, like mothers of secure children, should be always in control – in the sense of protecting the material, temporal, and emotional boundaries of the therapy – but never controll*ing*.

Availability vs. neglect

'The central issue ... is the mother's **accessibility** to the baby, with emphasis upon her responsiveness to him. Although the essential component of psychological accessibility is that the mother be aware of the baby, she is not truly accessible unless she also **actively acknowledges and responds to** him. ... A highly accessible mother has her baby in her field of perceptual awareness at all times so that he is within reach. ... She can divide her attention between the baby and other persons, things, and activities without losing awareness of the baby. She is **never too preoccupied with her own thoughts and feelings** or with her other activities and interactions to have him in the background of her awareness and to sense where he is and what he is doing....*

The highly accessible mother not only is aware of her baby's activity and signals, but she responds to him readily. She can switch her attention to him easily if he needs her supervision or protection or if he approaches or tries to catch her attention. To be accessible, the mother does not necessarily understand and interpret the baby's behaviour nor does she necessarily respond appropriately to the baby's signals – nevertheless, the accessible mother is perceptually alert and responsive to her baby most of the time.

An inaccessible mother ignores her baby and in this sense she neglects him. 'Neglect' in this context does not necessarily imply physical neglect. The neglect is psychological for the most part – although mothers in inaccessible moods may sometimes show surprising lapses in failing to protect the baby from danger. There are two major types. ... First, there are mothers who are unaware of much of the baby's behaviour; they do not perceive his signals and communications and therefore cannot respond to them. Second, there are mothers who perceive the baby's signals well enough, but do not acknowledge or respond to them, and hence must be to the baby just as inaccessible as if they had been unaware.

The issue of availability may seem remote from psychotherapy practice, since therapists explicitly and contractually make themselves available to their clients. But this passage reminds therapists how important it is to look after themselves as well as their clients. If they are unable to give their clients their undivided attention – for example, through illness or an emotional crisis in their own lives – they should take time off. They need also to make sure that therapy does not impinge negatively on their own lives – for example, by taking appropriate breaks and holidays, not seeing clients at unsocial hours, etc.

Ainsworth's approach also emphasises the importance of therapists noting and being unafraid to bring up things that they don't understand.

The question of 'danger' is also relevant to therapy. Psychotherapy patients are sometimes literally 'dangerous' – suicidally to themselves, and occasionally to others. Most, at times, are up against their inner dangers – thoughts of despair, hopelessness, emptiness, or violence. Sensitive therapists are intuitively in touch with the deepest and most terrifying of clients' emotions. If they have a strong feeling that the client might be suicidal or about to act in a self-injurious way (e.g., with drugs or alcohol), they will find ways to talk about this. They know when to intervene to forestall danger – explicitly raising the issue of suicide and instigating practical measures (e.g., between-session phone calls, contacting a key worker, admission to hospital, etc.) to help tide clients over until they feel safe. Bureaucratic insistence on protocols and tick-box questionnaires to identify 'risk', though they have their uses, can undermine therapists' capacity to follow their responsive instincts. Even if aware of danger, over-passive therapists may, like Ainsworth's mothers, be paralysed and inhibited in their responses (cf. Lyons-Ruth & Jacobvitz, 2016) or unable to comprehend just how difficult it can be for clients to face their inner demons.

Acceptance vs. rejection of needs

*This ... deals with the **balance between the mother's positive and negative feelings** about her baby – about having a baby and about this particular one – and with the extent to which she has been able to integrate these conflicting feelings or to resolve the conflict. At the positive pole there is love and acceptance over-riding frustrations, irritations, and limitations – or perhaps more accurately, encompassing and de-fusing the negative feelings. At the negative pole anger, resentment, hurt, or irritation conflict conspicuously with and limit positive feelings and result in more or less overt rejection of the baby....*

*The arrival of a baby poses a potentially ambivalent situation ... for all mothers there are positive and negative aspects. Among the negative aspects is the fact that the new baby impinges on and limits the mother's own autonomy and interferes with other activities. ... Furthermore, there are **inevitable irritations and frustrations** in interacting with this particular baby from day to day. Among the positive aspects is the undeniable appeal a baby makes to his mother – evoking tenderness, protectiveness, and other positive reactions....*

*At the desirable, accepting, positive end of this continuum, negative components are not so much absent as somehow subsumed within the context of the positive relationship. ... At the undesirable, rejecting, 'negative' end ... positive components are not so much lacking as not integrated with the negative, rejecting components, so that there is an alternation between tenderness, nurturance, and delight on the one hand, and anger, resentment, irritation, hurt, and rejection on the other, without any adequate meshing of the two together. There is a good and lovable baby and a bad and infuriating baby, but **the real baby as he actually exists is somehow lost** between the two.*

Despite espousing neutrality and even-handedness, most therapists would admit that they favour some clients over others. Indeed, most have or have had 'special' clients as well as a few who evoke dread or 'heart-sinkness'. The essential issue here is being able, with help from supervision, to be aware of, and understand this countertransference – i.e., the dispositions aroused by the client's affective states and how they may resonate with one's own feelings and shape one's behaviour. Ideally, therapists are in touch with their own negative countertransference, especially when working with 'difficult' clients who may be unreliable, hostile, unresponsive, blocked, or seemingly stuck. They are able to acknowledge, tolerate, and contain these feelings, rather than being driven by them to make covertly critical or demeaning comments. Ideally, therapists neither romanticise nor demonise their clients, but are able to maintain balance in which they see both themselves and their clients as a mixture of good and bad, strength and weakness, hope and uncertainty.

Sensitivity as the Key 'Common Factor' in Psychotherapy

It is hard not to be impressed with the clarity of Ainsworth's vision of what makes a good parent, even if the exquisitely sensitive mother she describes is, in reality, exceptional. For Winnicott (1965), the 'good enough' mother desirably falls short of perfection – *well* short, as any parent knows! In his vision, children learn as much about how to think and act for themselves from their parents' failings as from their virtues. Nevertheless, much of what Ainsworth describes is consistent with the Winnicottian vision of a facilitating, holding environment. Ainsworth's descriptions also match the qualities clinicians think crucial in a psychotherapist: sensitivity to the patient's signals; cooperation with the patient's 'going-on-being', as opposed to intrusions that lead to 'compliance'; psychological and physical availability; acceptance; the capacity to manage their own negative feelings or 'hate' in the countertransference (Winnicott, 1965).

Another psychotherapy 'common factor', applicable to Ainsworth's account, is therapists' ability to respond in a *contingent* way to patients' communications, both verbal and nonverbal. Contingency here refers to how therapists track, follow, and are guided by what the patient 'brings' – behaviourally, affectively, gesturally – into the therapy room. Contingency, responsiveness, and sensitivity are closely related constructs. Secure-making parents watch and watch over their children – directly when they are young, more telescopically when they are older – and base their responses on these observations. They meet the child where that child is – affectively, developmentally, existentially. Likewise, with therapists and their clients. The therapist tries – together with the patient – to *make meaning* of their emotional experience; as in good parenting, mirroring, mentalising, and empathy are all key elements of good clinical work.

In sum, sensitivity – with the complex and subtle patterns that Ainsworth highlights – is a core element of attachment-informed psychotherapy. But remaining sensitive becomes problematic with disturbed, provocative, or severely depressed patients. Therapists may find themselves, via 'projective identification', shaped into negative feelings and sometimes seemingly insensitive behaviours. Unravelling this process, and its obstacles, with the help of mentalising, will be a continuing theme throughout this book.

There is also a sensitivity caveat. Being sensitive, creating an atmosphere of acceptance and close attention to patients' needs has sometimes been conflated with being overly gratifying and creating too-permeable professional boundaries. From an attachment perspective, it is entirely possible to be a sensitive, responsive, accepting clinician without 'over gratifying' the patient or overstepping boundaries. Nevertheless, the fear of becoming over-involved with patients, which has its roots in the view that the analyst's distance is crucial to the psychoanalytic project, still pervades the field in insidious ways, inappropriately (in our view) sanctioning therapists' withholding warmth, concern, and emotional presence.

At the other extreme, boundary violations (Gabbard, 2016) in therapy vary from the grave and abusive to more subtle forms of transgression. Some models of therapy appear to legitimise 'co-construction', with clinicians intrusively disclosing their own reactions and history in ways that interfere with patients' need to be heard and discovered for themselves. While countertransference reactions are a vital source of information about the client's inner world, 'sharing' them must be done – if at all – carefully and with an utmost respect for the patient's autonomy. As with Ainsworth's insecure children, vulnerable patients can all too easily be colonised by the therapist's conscious and unconscious intrusions. The therapist's job is to help the patient develop the capacities for self-regulation, and never, implicitly or explicitly, vice versa.

Mirroring

Winnicott (1971) suggested that the *mother's face* is the mirror in which the baby first begins to see him or herself, and that when this process is impeded or obscured (e.g., by maternal depression), there can be long-term adverse consequences:

> The mother gazes at the baby in her arms, and the baby gazes at his mother's face and finds himself therein … provided that the mother is really looking at the unique, small, helpless being and not projecting her own expectations, fears, and plans for the child. In that case, the child would find not himself in his mother's face, but rather the mother's own projections. This child would remain without a mirror, and for the rest of his life would be seeking this mirror in vain. (Winnicott, 1971: 89)

Thanks to Winnicott's inspirational insight, primary maternal mirroring can now be thought of not in terms of a passively receiving still pool, or bronzed reflective surface, but as a *dynamic* aspect of the infant–maternal gaze. This has since been confirmed by studies of 'mirror neurons', where the notion of a 'mirror' is used as a metaphor for reflective physiology (Rizzolati & Sinigaglia, 2010).

A seminal attachment-influenced study (Gergely & Watson, 1996) confirmed Winnicott's clinical intuition that frequent periods of intense mutual gaze are a recurring and normal feature of mother–infant interaction in the early months of life; similar mother–infant gaze and mimetic moments are also found in macaque rhesus monkeys (Suomi, 2016). Gergely and Watson (1996) identify two key features of these interactions: 'contingency' and 'marking'. The mother *contingently* waits for the child to initiate an expressive communication. She then mirrors this in a *'marked'* fashion – i.e., amplifies, exaggerates, or even caricatures the child's facial expression. The child might be slightly miserable, or 'down at mouth'. The mother will then shape her own mouth floor-wards in a semi-lune, while saying – 'cross-modally' combining aural with visual input (see too Stern, 1985) – in high-pitched 'motherese', '*Oh we are feeling miserable today aren't we...?*' This feeds back to the infant a visual 'representation' of his or her affective state. Repeated internalisations of these interactions, it is hypothesised, form the nucleus from which understanding of oneself and one's emotions grows. In these secure mother–infant bonds the mother 're-presents' infants to themselves as thinking, feeling beings, and as having a mind (Fonagy et al., 2002). The intra-psychic (the child's 'representation') emerges from the interpersonal (the mother-mirror).

Exact mirroring is a feature of the earliest days and weeks of life. Babies can mirror caregivers' (and researchers'!) tongue protrusions 48 hours after birth (Meltzoff & Moore, 1997). This external mirroring parallels the self-mirroring needed to build up a sense of the body-self (Stern, 1985). Two-month-olds' exploration of the movement of their hands in their visual field provides one-to-one contingency, visual input exactly matching proprioceptive feedback, telling that 'this is *my* body, unlike external objects (including Mum) where exact contingency is lacking'.

Maternal mirroring is typically only 'partially contingent'. Up to 3 months, when faced both with an exact mirror of their own movements on a split-screen, or one in which partial contingency is programmed into the computer (e.g., a built-in time-lag before the image corresponds with the movements that stimulated it), babies' attention favours exact contingency; after 3 months, partial contingency wins out (Gergely & Watson, 1996). Now babies are beginning to know where, and what, if not yet who, they are. With an established body-self, attention moves to 'self-in-relation-to-another', where partial contingency predominates.

These delicate balances can go wrong, subtly or grossly. The Facial Feedback Hypothesis (Hennenlotter et al., 2008) suggests that mother–infant emotional resonance depends on the mother's capacity to mirror the child's expression by minute mimetic movements of her *own* facial muscles, and then to 'read' these as a guide to the child's feelings. Where subjects' facial muscles are paralysed by curare, as in Botox cosmetic surgery, their capacity correctly to identify feelings from eye expressions in photographs is impaired; this applies especially to subtle negative emotions (Oberman, Winkielman, & Ramachandran, 2007).

Applying this to mother–infant mirroring, mothers' capacity to provide their offspring with a springboard for self-understanding means putting their own affective states and preoccupations to one side, and making available an internal 'space' into which the *child's* feelings can be projected, held, and represented. This model is similar to Bion's (1970) concepts of 'containment' and 'communicative projective identification'. Mothers who cannot 'read' their own feelings (e.g., because of their own internal distress or disruption) will have difficulty in reading those of their infants. Such children may be compromised in their pathway towards self-knowledge, with potential adverse consequences for themselves, and *their* offspring's future mental health.

Clinical mirroring

Contingency and marking, although usually not so named, feature prominently in client–therapist interactions. Sometimes mirroring is confined to the eyes and the vocal tone, but can also be seen in the verbal and gestural give-and-take of therapeutic exchange. Therapists 'contingently' wait for their clients to initiate a topic before responding with a 'marked mirroring' comment such as: '*Wow, that was quite a week!*' or '*You're saying you ended up smashing one of your favourite plates over his head!!!?*' or '*Oh dear! That sounds* very *difficult and miserable.*'

As Winnicott famously put it:

> …Psychotherapy is not making clever and apt interpretation; by and large it is a long-term giving back to the patient what the patient brings. It is a complex derivative of the face that reflects what is there to be seen. (Winnicott, 1971: 158)

Drawing on the parallels between caregiver/care-seeker and therapist/client interactions, mirroring can be thought of in a number of ways: 'exact', 'inexact', 'playful', or 'distorting'.

At the start of therapy, when participants are getting to know one another, therapists may confine themselves to reasonably exact, albeit 'marked' mirroring comments, as above. But in order to engage the client's interest and trust, they will want to move the conversation forward towards inexactitude, introducing variety and novelty with now only 'partially contingent' mirrored comments.

Jane's hatred

Jane was in torment: her husband had left her for another woman and he was claiming custody of their only child. Brought up by a single parent, with no siblings, her father having died suddenly when she was a baby, Jane had devoted all her energies to bringing up her daughter. She faced the very real possibility of losing her child and the security of her mother-role.

At the assessment interview, Jane's misery was all too evident in her held-back tears and tortured face. Her well-worn avoidant strategy was breaking down. Attempted mirroring comments such as 'that sounds pretty trau-matic' (in response to her description of the unsympathetic judge favouring her ex-husband) bounced off, leaving the (male) therapist feeling excluded and strangely unmoved by her horrible predicament.

Jane then blurted out how she 'hated' the idea of her daughter being in her untrustworthy husband's care. Picking up, 'mirroring', and also marking with vocal emphasis but with a changed context, the word '*hate*', the thera-pist suggested that Jane was suffused with deep *hatred* and rage towards her ex-, but perhaps felt this had to be held back for her child's sake (not at this stage voicing the thought that similar constraints may have afflicted herself *vis-à-vis* her mother).

This seemed to hit a spot. Empathy deepened; Jane's face relaxed, becoming more interactive and engaged. The therapist then ('inexactly', 'exaggeratedly') ventured, '*I know it's absurd, but I was imagining how you'd love to have a father who could threaten your ex- with a horse-whip, like in Victorian times.*' She relaxed yet more at this, and acknowledged that she really needed help in standing her ground with this powerful man, and how her hopes had collapsed when the judge ruled in her husband's favour. The therapist, transferentially, was now momentarily occupying the role of the primary caregiving father she had never had.

Mother–infant studies describe 'mid-range' regulation (Beebe et al., 2012) or partially contingent mirroring (Holmes, 2014b) as characteristic of secure rela-tionships. Comparable considerations apply to therapist–patient interactions. Excessively silent or enigmatic therapists, or those who over-exactly mirror clients' utterances but fail to elaborate or extend them, are unlikely to engage successfully or make therapeutic progress. Intrusive therapists, ever-ready with an interpretation, however apposite, but unleavened with a mirroring reso-nance of troubling feelings, may evoke threat rather than security, leading to drop-out or the entrenched defensiveness that underlies stuckness/impasse.

The Play's the Thing

Play is another bridge between secure attachment in infants and effective psy-chotherapy. The word derives from the Old English *plega*, meaning 'brisk movement', and Middle Dutch *pleien*, 'to leap for joy, dance'. Play is pleasurable, spontaneous, 'in motion', without an instrumental goal, the starting point for creativity and for the emergence of new thoughts, structures, and patterns. At the same time – from a developmental standpoint – play can be purposeful, and even serious. A toddler repeatedly rolls a truck back and forth, her gaze intent and focused. She pushes it into another truck, which is thereby propelled forward. She is actively learning the physics of motion, about wheels, the nature of 'billiard ball' causality. A preschooler pulls the stethoscope from his doctor's kit and listens to his teddy bear's heart, 'practising' next day's scary visit to the paediatrician. Play here is helping her to regulate emotion.

Playfulness is in evidence from the earliest to the last days of life. An infant wiggles her toes in the sunlight, traces arcs on her mother's cheek as she nurses; an elderly man jokes with his grandchildren, or playfully imagines a different outcome to a romantic encounter long ago. Optimally, and in a variety of ways, playing offers a means to 'relaxed self-realization' (Winnicott, 1971), discovering and elaborating what is in one's mind. Play in the earliest months of life is primarily 'practice' or 'functional' play, with the child experimenting with the multiple properties and functions of body parts, or physical objects – spoon, paper cup, or bucket of sand. The second year of life ushers in *pretend play*. The baby doll whose arms and legs she has been exploring, chewing on, and tossing in and out of sight, slowly comes to symbolise a 'real' baby that can be cuddled, whose 'hair' can be 'combed', and that can be 'fed' with a baby bottle or toy spoon. It can also represent a hated sibling, thrown out of the crib as far away as possible, or bitten and hit with great force.

Next comes language, and the accompanying 'story', taking pretence to yet more complex levels. The development of the capacity to symbolise, to understand that one object can 'stand for' another, is of enormous significance. Representational intelligence is fundamental to human communication, to shared symbolism and meaning systems. Pretend, used as an adjective, derives from the Latin *prae*, meaning 'forward', and *tendere*, 'to stretch'. It contains the idea that pretence takes a child forward developmentally, and is an exploration of their physical and emotional universe. (Much of modern physics, including Einstein's General Relativity, started off as 'pretend' or 'thought experiments'.)

'Pretending' allows children to imagine stories, scenarios, and outcomes, without concern for their reality, and to 'play' with thoughts and feelings without consequence. Latency children know full well that the world of dragons and heroes is not the real world, but the playspace of computer games is a safe location to explore their courage, strengths, and fears. Play is a sanctuary. Children who lack the gift of play, through genetic or environmental adversity, come – body and mind – up against a cruel world, naked and unbuffered.

As Winnicott (1971) noted, one of the striking things about many children entering psychotherapy, and indeed many adults too, is a paucity of play. This can manifest as barren, desultory exploration of toys, impoverished imaginal life, or sometimes as compulsive and unrelated play that keeps the therapist isolated and excluded. In adults, *play deficit* manifests itself in limited imagination and an emphasis on the concrete, or conversely as an inability to distinguish the limitless play of fantasy from the restrictions and requirements of reality (Fonagy & Target, 1996).

From the earliest moments of life, play emerges within a relational matrix. Winnicott noted that the 'good enough' mother 'meets' the child's 'spontaneous gesture' and 'makes sense' of it (Winnicott, 1965: 145). Winnicott's 'false self' child *complies* with the demands and needs of the caregiver at the expense of his own sense of reality and agency – the 'true self'. There are obvious parallels here with the Bowlby-Ainsworth model of insecure attachment. But by using the terms 'true' and 'false', Winnicott imports a normative quasi-moralistic tone. In the attachment model, insecure attachment represents needs-must adaptation to a specific environment in which the imperative for survival and security override the comparative 'luxuries' – in the short term at least – of spontaneity and exploration.

Winnicott was a master-clinician, pioneering the role of play in psychotherapeutic work. Here he is describing a 'therapeutic consultation' – i.e., a one-off meeting rather than ongoing therapy – with a baby who suffered from 'fits':

> [She] bit my knuckle very severely, this time without showing any guilt feelings, and then played the game of biting and throwing away spatulas; while on my knee she became able to enjoy play. After a while she began to finger her toes, and so I had her socks and shoes removed. The result of this was a period of experimentation which absorbed her whole interest. It looked as if she was discovering and proving over and over again, to her great satisfaction, that whereas spatulas can be put to the mouth, thrown away, and lost, toes cannot be pulled off. (Winnicott, 1971: 47)

A number of ideas are implicit in this vivid account. First, play is inherently interactive; for infants and small children, the parent's – in this case therapist's – job is to provide a safe, boundaried 'playspace'. This enables the child to play 'alone in the presence of the mother/therapist' (Winnicott, 1971), who neither neglects nor intrudes, but is just *there*, available for scaffolding, stimulus, and support (in this case sock-removal) when called upon. Here the focus of the baby's attention was exploring the difference between self and non-self. Winnicott observes that a play precursor may entail aggression (in this case knuckle-biting), testing the 'as if-ness' of the playspace for safety. The caregiver needs to be able to hold in her mind the simultaneous and apparent contradictory thoughts that biting ('very severely') is both real ('*I really hate you Mummy when you're not there for me the instant I need you*'), *and* pretend ('*this is only a play fight and my love for you totally subsumes any temporary feelings of hatred*').

As Winnicott repeatedly emphasised, play 'plays with' reality, in that it has a real/not-real quality that enables novelty to be tried out 'for real' in a safe 'unreal' setting. This applies as much to the mind of a mathematician, the language of a poet, or the physical playspace of nursery or sports arena.

In the example, the affect-regulatory aspect of the caregiver's social brain – here Winnicott's – is fully occupied by thought processes that the child is not yet mature enough to encompass herself. He *holds* the child's 'ruth'[2] and ruthlessness, her concern and love as well as her hate. We can imagine a different caregiver, perhaps 'disorganised', becoming enraged at such a moment, and imagining that the infant 'really' *means* to attack her. A frightening or frightened caregiver mistakes 'pretend' for the 'real' thing, seeing 'as-if' aggression as an actual assault, triggering retaliation or retreat, as though the damage were more than metaphorical. The child's capacity to use play for self-exploration and affect regulation will thereby be curtailed.

A literary example of this confusion is the play-within-a-play scene in Shakespeare's *Hamlet*. The usurping King Claudius is tricked by Hamlet into revealing his murderous guilt by the actor's *depiction* of enacted fratricide. In psychotherapy, early trauma will, one way or another, be 're-played'. Unavoidable or inevitable holiday breaks, minor mistakes and failures on the part of the therapist will re-evoke egregious traumata from the patient's past (absence, exploitation, neglect, seduction, etc.). As for a theatre audience, this helps patients 'see', mentalise, re-work, move on from, forgive, and contextualise 'effigies' from the past' (Freud, 1900).

Attachment and play are inextricably linked. Secure infants play more uninhibitedly, with greater complexity, and for longer than their insecure peers. Mothers of secure children are more likely to involve themselves in their children's play, and are better able to facilitate and scaffold their children's explorations (Slade, 1988). Secure play is inherently pleasurable. As we will discuss in the next chapter, this is likely to be mediated via hormonal 'cross-talk' (Feldman, 2015b) from the oxytocin (security mediating) to the dopamine (pleasure and reward) systems.

Play in secure attachment relationships suggests a snug fit, but also sufficient 'play' in the caregiver and care-receiver bond: a close connection but one that allows for movement and a mutual mid-range 'dance'. In adulthood, couples who, on the one hand, are not 'in sync' or, on the other, are 'joined at the hip', may have less creative relationships than those in which playfulness in this sense prevails. Play entails *movement*, both literal and metaphorical: overcoming physical stasis ('doing things' together), untrammelled by rigid patterns of thought and behaviour. Play is not all saccharine: the joy of play co-exists with protest, aggression, and competitiveness (especially in sports play), together with their containment and alleviation. At best, play epitomises the ability to explore the world from a position of safety, satisfying curiosity and hunger for understanding and new experience.

Psychotherapeutic play

From an attachment perspective, therapy is a crucible in which the patient feels safe enough to discover and make meaning of what is in his mind. The therapist provides the playspace and the facilitating environment for such discoveries, and a vantage point for thinking about them. An interactive pattern or 'dance' is established, in which each participant, based on their role as caregiver or care-seeker, influences and shapes the other's thoughts and behaviours. The essence of a 'good session' is one in which these moments of mutual movement result in a 'third' (Ogden, 1994), a jointly produced affective event or thought-sequence. 'Good' sessions are not necessarily those that are obviously happy or hopeful; misery or sadness or rage may surface, but in ways that feel satisfying, worked through, co-regulated, as though something important has been accomplished. The affective envelope of unearthing a feeling-pattern, of 'playing' with it by examining it from all sides, and then resolving it, constitute therapist's and client's joint task, or 'work' – work that is, in fact, play. All this requires a context of secure attachment: the foundation for effective and enduring psychological treatments. Relational safety is the precondition for co-regulation and meaning-making.

In this model, the therapist is not 'the one who knows' (Lacan, 1997), but has an 'open mind', is deeply curious, working on the assumption that there is meaning to be made and found, however provisional and subject to revision. Out of Kant's 'crooked timber of humanity' and the 'tangled web we weave', therapists try to find ways to make sense out of inchoate feelings. Some clients have rigid stories needing to be reframed and broadened; others are flooded with affects beneath which the story is submerged. The therapist names the unknown, links the disparate, illuminates the dark, not with an eye to 'telling' the patient what is there, but to help her find the verbal structures needed to organise her inner world (Slade, 1994).

Returning to Shakespeare, this picture is reminiscent of Jaques' speech in *As You Like It*. Here he offers a melancholy Eriksonian perspective on the (st)ages of man, from 'mewling puking infant' to a 'sans everything' finality. Jaques asserts that 'all the world's a stage', and 'we' are merely players. This need not be taken as an attack on authenticity, or the validity of our intentions, but rather a reminder that the 'scripts' (Byng-Hall, 1991) that we enact were prepared for us long before our birth, and continue to be written by unconscious forces over which we have but partial control. A good way to tap into this in psychotherapy is to ask patients about their 'given' name – where it 'comes from', why their parents chose it, how they feel about it, what their nicknames were as children, etc. Therapists need to take into account the life-stage where clients find themselves, and/or to which they may have regressed. A mentalising perspective is encouraged in which clients stand back from themselves and observe their thoughts and actions 'objectively', just as an audience learns about itself through vicariously living and being able to stand back from the lives of others as depicted on stage or screen.

Some therapy models are self-professedly playful: sand-play therapy with small children, psychodrama, art, music or dance therapy, the creation of a 'family sculpt' in systemic therapy, etc. Conventional adult individual therapy sessions are perhaps less so. But if not in some sense playful, therapy is unlikely to succeed. Humour is important (Akhtar, 2009). Therapists need to cultivate a light touch, helping clients to see their miseries objectively, even with a degree of 'laughing through tears', while at the same time not being infected with denial and other manic defences.

Imagine a patient describing a childhood dominated by an ultra-controlling parent – perhaps a 'tiger mother' – in which the child was not allowed their evening meal until piano practice and homework were fully completed to the parent's obsessive satisfaction. The therapist might say, perhaps in a quasi-humorous tone: *'that sounds like torture'*. The client then might back-track, holding the therapist's thoughts at bay: *'well, it wasn't that bad – I suppose I wouldn't have got where I am today without that sort of discipline'*.

To which the therapist might say *'Hmmm … is there some denial of legitimate rage going on there? … for all we know, you would have done just as well with a more liberal regime, and your ambivalence about your career – your "fear of success" – might then not have jumped up to bite you.'*

Alternatively, the client might respond, *'It's no laughing matter. It really was torture. I often felt the only way out was to die…'* This might remind the therapist with a jolt that the client is still a long way from reaching the stage of acknowledging a parent's legitimate wish, arising perhaps out of their own constraints or 'failures', for their children to 'do well'. Here the response might be *'There was genuine cruelty there … and that feeling of wanting to die seems very real still today…'*

Gestalt therapists play with the 'empty chair', in which clients are encouraged to talk to a missing parent, an erring husband or a dead child, and get in touch with appropriate feelings of grief, sadness, resentment, rage, and love. 'Role play' can be useful, especially in helping unstick rigid patterns of relating if they pervade the consulting room. Balint (1968) famously encouraged a patient who said she'd always wanted to be able to perform a somersault, to get up off the couch and give it a try in the consulting room. Thereafter, supposedly, she never looked back!

For therapists – and parents – learning to foster play entails a combination of technique with a capacity for spontaneity and fun. And this needs to be contained within firm but flexible boundaries. Therapy that is all work and no play may end up in dire dependency; all play and no work an evanescent diversion. Ways need to be found both to validate clients' attachment-relational patterns, and to 'play' with them, rather than repeating them and thereby reinforcing defences. As we progress in our exposition of the philosophy and techniques of attachment-informed therapy we hope to show how this can be done.

Summary

- Ainsworth's model of maternal sensitivity is a crucial ingredient in secure attachment.

- 'Sensitivity' comprises receptiveness, availability, cooperation, and acceptance.

- Insecure attachments – in the nursery and consulting room – reflect deficits in parental care, either in gross or subtle form: lack of receptiveness, distractedness, controllingness, and rejection.

- Secure attachments in infants arise out of caregiver–infant mutual gaze, contingent and partially contingent mirroring, and playfulness.

- Analogues of these are to be found in the therapist–patient relationship.

Notes

1. Recovered by David Pederson from a mimeograph created by Ainsworth at Johns Hopkins University, dated March 10, 1969, and reprinted at psychology.sunysb.edu
2. That is, companionship or connection: a now archaic term, persisting only in its opposite.

6

The Neuroscience of Parental Sensitivity

In this chapter we will show how Ainsworth's intuitions can now be buttressed with findings from cutting-edge neuroscience. The evidence for the role of sensitive maternal care in supporting positive developments in children is very strong (Feldman, 2015a, 2015b). So too is that demonstrating the lifelong impacts of its disruption. We start with some general observations, before looking in more detail at mother–infant synchrony and its psychotherapeutic analogues.

Evidence for the profound influence of early parental care is provided by the Adverse Childhood Experiences (ACE) studies (Felitti et al., 1998), in which 17,000 adults were screened for adverse experiences (abuse, neglect, parental mental illness, etc.) in childhood. The results were devastating: *the more out of a possible 10 adverse events were experienced, the more likely a person was to suffer negative long-term health and mental health effects*. These include heart disease, forms of cancer, musculoskeletal problems, autoimmune disorders, and early death. The number of psychiatric diagnoses also increased with each type of adverse event, as did rates of substance use and suicide (Putnam, Harris, & Patnam, 2013). Shonkoff (2012) has broadened the concept of early adversity to include 'toxic stress', adding other environmental stressors such as poverty, racism, and community violence.

The brain and hormonal mechanisms that explain these findings are beginning to emerge. Early maternal care has both immediate and long-term impacts upon: the capacity for stress regulation and the functioning of the Hypothalamic-Pituitary-Adrenal (HPA) axis (Francis et al., 1999); the development of emotion circuitry and cortical functioning (Callaghan & Tottenham, 2016); the activation of hormone systems, especially oxytocin, which facilitate attachment in both mother and infant (Feldman, 2015b; Strathearn et al., 2009); the activation of dopaminergic reward systems (Feldman, 2015b); and the quality of caregiving in the next generation (Champagne, 2008; Kundakovic et al., 2015;

Meaney, 2001). Maternal care helps regulate infants' fear circuits in the brain. Parental sensitivity, emotion regulation, empathy, and mentalising networks all support the development of secure and flexible attachments.

Where maternal care is disrupted, survival, physical and emotional, becomes a priority. Organisms defend themselves in one of three basic ways: flight, fight, and freeze (Porges, 2011). As mentioned earlier, these evolutionarily-based modes of stress regulation map directly on to avoidant, resistant, and disorganised patterns of attachment (Slade, 2014). In the absence of a secure base caregiver, threat leads the child either to shut down and avoid, that is, to down-regulate negative affect; to become hyperaroused; or dysregulated. Hyper- *or* hypo-activation of the fear response (LeDoux, 1996) is reified in insecure attachments, and links early stress to poor outcomes across the lifespan. Being in a state of chronic fearful arousal over a range of developmental periods changes the body and the brain in innumerable ways (van der Kolk, 2014). Disorganised attachment, as well as signs of extreme avoidance or dysregulation, suggest that a child has been unable to turn to a caregiver to regulate fear, and is therefore vulnerable to its long-term effects.

Biobehavioural Synchrony

As Feldman (2015b: 387) puts it: 'Parenting is the process most critically implicated in the survival and continuity of life on Earth.' The 'entrainment' of baby and mother brains – i.e., correlations, correspondence, and mutual regulation of physiology, behaviour, and affect – begins *in utero* (Feldman, 2015b), with disruptions affecting basic physiological processes (Hofer, 1995) from the onset of pregnancy (Monk et al., 2016). Feldman describes these processes as based on *biobehavioural synchrony*.

> The exclusive parent–infant bond derives from the fine-tuning of the parent brain to inputs from each child via ... 'biobehavioural synchrony'. What is described here is a co-wiring of parents' and infants' brains and behaviour into a synchronous unit that supports the infants' brain growth and buttresses social competencies. (Feldman, 2015b: 387)

The concept of biobehavioural synchrony was first developed by entomologists looking at social species, or 'super-organisms', such as ant and bee colonies (Wilson, 2012). Via hormonal signals, the physiology of the individual 'sub-units' (in this case the bees or ants themselves) is coordinated with the behaviour (wing flapping, leg movements, etc.) of others in the colony. Comparable individual-to-individual entrainment phenomena are also prevalent in mammalian social species, including primates and humans, whose brains 'contain networks that resonate in real time to the states, actions and emotions of con-specifics' (Feldman, 2015b: 394). These processes are the neural substrate underpinning Ainsworth's maternal sensitivity.

Synchrony applies at many levels: neural (via mirror neurons), physiological (heart rates), and hormonal (oxytocin). At a behavioural level, synchrony is evident in mirroring and playful or mutually pleasurable interactions. The starting point for these complex mother–infant feedback loops is the release of maternal oxytocin in late-stage pregnancy and parturition. Oxytocin plays a key role in establishing and maintaining affectional bonds, priming the mother to interact with her baby in a number of sensitive ways: eye-to-eye contact, responding readily and accurately to cues, adjusting her voice and touch to the baby's needs, making close, soothing, and affectionate physical contact. Comparable hormonal processes in the infant mean that the child feels increasingly connected to and familiar with the parent.

Moment-to-moment behavioural entrainment, parent–infant proximity and touch set off a cascade of reactions in parental and child brains: 'Oxytocin functionality is transferred from parent to child via repeated experiences of social synchrony' (Feldman, 2015b: 388). Oxytocin is released in 'pulses', with maternal surges inducing oxytocin in the infant and vice versa. As a peptide hormone as well as neurotransmitter, via dendritic rather than synaptic secretion, oxytocin has distant and far-reaching effects, such as being responsible for coordination and tuning of neural networks, alongside more specific localised effects.

Oxytocin 'cross-talks' to other hormonal and neurochemical systems. The fear system (the amygdala), the oxytocin-producing hypothalamus, and the dopaminergic reward system are 'connected … to cortical networks implicated in empathy, embodied simulation, mentalizing, and emotion regulation' (Feldman, 2015b: 390). Oxytocin reduces activity in the HPA stress axis and enhances the reward-giving dopaminergic pathways.

As any parent or observer of parents and children knows, being with babies can be intensely pleasurable and rewarding. Heightened sensitivity to danger and the need for protection (i.e., the classic Bowlby model) *works synergistically alongside pleasure and reward* in bonding. At an endocrine and neurotransmitter level, the attachment system supports the higher-order social parental brain, which in term promotes social development, including playfulness and enjoyment in the child. A safe child is a happy child and a happy child is a safe child. Secure mother–infant physical contact, via breast-feeding, touching, and stroking, also instantiates in the child well-modulated ('mid-range') stress responses via the HPA hormonal axis. This has long-term positive consequences for physical as well as psychological health (Maunder & Hunter, 2015).

Biobehavioural synchrony is not confined to *mother*–infant relationships, but has also been demonstrated in both primary and secondary caregiving fathers (Feldman, 2015b) as well as non-biological parents: 'Seeing infants appears to elicit the motivation to care in all adult members of the species, which may have functioned to enhance survival throughout human history when many mothers died at childbirth, thus leaving infants to non-parental care' (Feldman, 2015b: 390).

With non-biological female carers, oxytocin release is triggered by the experience of hands-on caregiving, in the literal sense! Males access these synchronous states through different pathways. Fathers' testosterone levels decrease in the early months of their child's life, making them more available for interaction and close bodily contact. In mammalian species where fathers play a role, paternal care is mainly 'facultative', in the sense that it enhances infant survival through protection and support of mothers. But while, typically, fathers serve different, and later, roles in infants' development, their brains are sufficiently plastic to adjust to the demands of direct infant care if necessary, and, like females, will secrete oxytocin, especially if they become the primary caregivers.

Hormonal synchrony reveals itself behaviourally in the dyadic reciprocity and mutuality described by authors such as Beebe and Lachmann (2013), Sander (1977), Stern (1985), and Tronick (2007). Using video micro-analysis, Beebe and her colleagues studied the *rhythms* of synchrony and attachment. There can be too much (where the mother crowds – 'looms in on' – the baby), or too little (the mother is distant and disengaged). The Goldilocks position is 'just right', and supports both closeness and autonomy. The coordinated mid-range 'dance' of mother and infant gaze, vocalisation, and movement at age 4 months predicts secure attachment at 1 year, and later social skills (Beebe et al., 2012). This work adds nuance to the notion of synchrony and is consistent with the notion that hyper- and hypo-regulation are associated with avoidant and resistant attachment organisations, respectively.

Biobehavioural synchrony in the consulting room

Our species' physiological systems have evolved multiple pathways and buffering systems to ensure survival in a variety of differing circumstances and conditions. The biobehavioural synchrony typical of secure attachments can be thought of as adaptive responses to relatively benign environments, as well as providing a degree of resilience in the face of the inevitable adversities that life throws up, even to the most favoured. The organised forms of insecurity are best viewed not as pathological, but as 'adaptations' to sub-optimal environmental conditions. Nevertheless, biobehavioural synchronies are clearly vulnerable to dysfunction. Patients presenting for psychotherapeutic help are likely to have been subject to such disruptions.

The concept of neuroplasticity offers hope, however. This refers to the ways in which adverse developmental processes can be reversible. The psychological and social environment impacts throughout life, not just on brain function but even on the structural architecture of the brain, including grey matter density, especially in the prefrontal cortex (PFC) and amygdala (see Carvalho et al., 2014; Lebel et al., 2016). As with the ACE study, Caspi, Moffitt and co-workers' 30-year follow-up study showed that stressful life events in childhood are associated with enhanced risk of depression in adulthood (Caspi et al., 2003; Caspi et al., 2010). But not all children are similarly affected. Those with 'long' serotonin transporter genes (5-HTTLPR) are more resistant to adversity than those with the short variant. Primate (Suomi, 2016) and human (Caspi et al., 2010) studies show that 'short' allele individuals, *when in favourable environments*, flourish *more* than those with 'long' alleles. Thus, the very vulnerabilities that bring people for psychotherapeutic help may also make them susceptible to the benign influences of therapy.

Clients seeking psychotherapeutic help are often those damaged by early adversity. The differential susceptibility model (Belsky, Bakermans-Kranenburg, & van IJzendoorn, 2007) inspires therapists to feel confident that, given the right circumstances – not just the therapy itself but the client's environmental context – flourishing is possible. Therapists might also remind themselves that those clients who seem relatively impervious to therapeutic help – and they do exist! – may be genetically predisposed to minor rather than damascene improvements.

It may seem a long leap from hormonal studies of mother–infant physiology to speculations about the therapist–patient relationship. Yet there is evidence that familial and other dyads (parent–child, siblings, romantic partners, friends) also synchronise with and mirror each other's biology and behaviour (Saxbe & Repetti, 2010). There is as yet no specific experimental evidence on therapist/patient biobehavioural synchrony, but efforts are underway to measure oxytocin release between patient and therapist (R. Feldman, personal communication, August 8, 2016).

However, a note of caution is needed. Administration of intranasal oxytocin, which might be expected to enhance pleasurable sociability and reduce antisociality, appears to be least effective in those individuals in whom early emotional trauma seem most to call out for it (van IJzendoorn & Bakermans-Kranenberg, 2012). Biobehavioural synchrony may be a laudable objective in the consulting room, but with disturbed patients, at least, it may be hard to achieve. As we shall see, working on the tension between client adverse expectations and therapeutic moves towards greater synchrony can be used as a lever for change. At this stage we would merely emphasise the importance of *therapeutic process at a physiological* – not just cognitive – level; the dynamic to-and-fro of therapist–patient interactions; and the overriding importance of Ainsworthian sensitivity – parental and therapeutic.

Diana's phone calls

AS had an emergency phone session with a long-time patient during her summer break. Diana, who was in her early 60s, had been beset by panic at applying for a new job. Typically avoidant, the only clues to Diana's fear

(Continued)

(Continued)

and anxiety were recurrent stomach pains and digestive problems. But as her therapy progressed, affect moved from body to mind. She had begun to actually *feel* anxious, which she found intolerable. Therapy was making things better – and worse.

In the phone session, the therapist focused on two things: What Diana might do to calm herself down in moments of panic (deep breathing, relaxation) and why she was so terrified of this much-needed and potentially positive change. She also – as she had many times before – reiterated her certainty that Diana, a very talented professional, would shine in the new job. (The therapist might also have addressed the timing of the patient's panic attack relative to her vacation, but opted not to.) As the session was winding down, Diana said: 'You know parts of me that no one knows.' Minutes later, she noted that she felt much better, and said 'I find it soothing to hear your voice, and [joking] not only because of the brilliant things you say, but it's something about just talking to you.' The therapist acknowledged and reflected this back, suggesting that it probably had to do with the sound of her voice, the association between calming down and their regular, weekly, monthly, and yearly efforts to understand.

What the therapist was thinking, but not saying, was that 'just talking' was probably a form of 'biobehavioural synchrony' between the two of them. As they began to connect, the agitation of the early minutes of the session subsided. The sound of a familiar, soothing voice, the therapist's effort to mirror and extend what Diana said, and the therapist's implicit belief that she could 'hold' – and Diana could tolerate – her fear and understand it, all played their part. Arguably these led to, and were facilitated by, the reciprocal release of oxytocin in both of them. No doubt more cortical processes took place too but without these non-verbal subcortical elements, it is unlikely Diana would have found the session as helpful as she did. A week later, after another briefer call to assuage her anxiety en route to signing her job contract, she texted the therapist: 'During vacation I think I need a tape of your voice.'

Synchrony – in a more general sense – is built into the parameters of the patient–therapist relationship. A 'common factor' of most therapies is a warm, calm, quiet, interruption-free, consistent, predictable, regular, reassuring therapeutic ambiance and therapist persona. It is reasonable to speculate that these features reproduce and evoke some of the biobehavioural aspects of secure mother–infant relationships, and that therapists provide, metaphorically at least, the sensitive 'touch' which is often so lacking in their clients' developmental experience.

Sensitive Periods

We will now turn briefly to another cutting-edge theme in contemporary social neuroscience: that of *critical* or *sensitive periods* (Feldman, 2015a; Tottenham, 2014). These are windows in developmental processes when environmental influence and therefore neuroplasticity are most salient. Classical imprinting, as described in prosocial birds by Bowlby's mentors Lorenz and Tinbergen (Burkhardt, 2005), is less clear-cut in humans. Nevertheless, there are sensitive periods in the developmental process in which infant and maternal physiology and behaviour are closely entrained. These have long-term implications for psychological and physical health, and contrast with periods in which individuals are much less open to environmental influence.

Neuro-hormonal components in sensitive periods include the PFC, the amygdala, and the HPA axis and cortisol system. The mother's presence influences both the development of the amygdala and the infant's exploratory behaviours. Rat pups in the presence of their mothers find new odours interesting and attractive. Mature rats become odour aversive. Mother-deprived rats are odour-aversive from the start, and as adults are generally less exploratory and more reactive to novelty (Tottenham, 2014). The presence of the mother in the sensitive period enables these infants, when mature, to be more mature and exploratory.

Comparable processes have been found in humans (Davidson & McEwen, 2012). Securely attached infants in the presence of their mothers are less frightened by a 'visual cliff', and have lower salivary cortisol levels, compared with insecure or mother-absent counterparts. During sensitive periods, the presence of the mother strengthens and tones the PFC–amygdala link. If the mother is stressed, or the children are parent-deprived (e.g., Romanian orphans), the buffering and cortisol-level lowering impact of parental presence is reduced. Their neuroplasticity diminished, these children are more anxious, less adventurous, and more prone to anxiety disorders (Rutter, 2012).

Children whose parenting has been interrupted or sub-optimal may appear more 'mature' than those where continuous and consistent parenting has prolonged the sensitive period in which these relational buffering effects are active. Such children may have a preternatural sense of self. Their accelerated development is 'adaptive' in that caution and threat-aversive strategies are needed in the absence of a buffering caregiver, but can have long-term negative consequences of impaired emotion processing.

Effective therapy, we argue, entails re-establishing a sensitive period in clients' lives so that the suffering patient is open to the anxiety-modulating presence of a caregiver. Under the aegis of entrainment and biobehavioural synchrony, the neuroplasticity needed for new relationship constellations – the ultimate objective of psychotherapy – can be achieved. The 'borrowed brain' of the therapist begins to modulate unstable PFC/amygdala cortisol-mediated flight/fright tendencies, so that a playful inner dialogue becomes possible, sometimes for the first time. Emotion-processing and cortical-mentalising networks are activated and reworked. However entrenched a person's IWMs, the malleability of the bodymind – and hence the sense of self – is ultimately retrievable. This is Kris's (1952) 'regression in the service of the ego', that provides an opportunity for reworking the self so that it becomes more comprehensive, more coherent, and imbued with a greater and more authentic sense of agency.

Summary

- Secure attachments in infants arise out of biobehavioural synchrony affecting the endocrine and brain limbic systems.

- This is likely to apply also to the therapist–patient relationship.

- There is evidence for sensitive periods in human development, where mother–infant synchrony is at its height.

- Psychotherapy entails reawakening a sensitive period and re-establishing biobehavioural synchrony.

- Both biobehavioural synchrony and the reawakening of a sensitive period can lead to the functional and structural brain changes that are the ultimate objectives of psychotherapy.

7

Mentalising

Mentalising is absolutely central to attachment-informed therapy, permeating almost every aspect of therapeutic work. Indeed, if analytic therapists were to claim a unique skill, they could argue that, as expert mentalisers, they have taken the everyday process of understanding what goes on in people's minds, their own and others, and refined it to an art – or craft. Mentalising is what therapists 'do', subsuming such familiar themes as psychological mindedness, insight, and reflexivity, but locating them in an evidence-based, philosophically subtle, and developmental context, each of which will be touched on in what follows.

What exactly *is* mentalising? It is the capacity to envision mental states in oneself or another. As Bateman and Fonagy (2004: xxi) put it:

> the *mental process* by which an individual implicitly and explicitly *interprets* the actions of himself and others as *meaningful* on the basis of *intentional mental states* such as personal desires, needs, feelings, beliefs and reasons. (emphasis added)

Another definition from Fearon and his colleagues (Fearon et al., 2006: 207):

> ...the heart of good mentalising is not so much the capacity to always accurately read one's own or another's inner states, but rather a way of approaching relationships that reflects an expectation that one's own thinking and feeling may be enlightened, enriched and changed by learning about the mental states of other people...mentalising is more like an attitude than a skill, an attitude that is inquiring and respectful of other people's mental states, aware of the limits of one's knowledge of others, and reflects the view that understanding the feelings of others is important for maintaining healthy and mutually rewarding relationships.

And a portmanteau version: 'the ability to see oneself from the outside and others from the inside' (Holmes, 2015). Here is a literary illustration. In Zadie Smith's (2016) novel *Swing Time*, the protagonist discovers that, when watching himself on film, the dancer Fred Astaire always referred to himself in the third person.

> [Astaire said] '*he isn't doing that right*' … it echoed a feeling I … had that it was important to treat oneself as a kind of stranger, to remain unattached and unprejudiced in your own case. I thought you needed to think like that to achieve anything in this world. (Smith, 2016: 117)

As we described earlier, the current concept of mentalising starts from the work of Fonagy and colleagues Miriam and Howard Steele studying the intergenerational transmission of attachment security (Fonagy, Steele, & Steele, 1991). Noting that adults varied in their capacity to reflect upon their own and others' internal experience, they coded Adult Attachment Interview transcripts for what they first termed 'reflective self-function', later shortened to 'reflective functioning' (RF), and eventually subsumed into the more general category of 'mentalising'. Mothers who were high in RF were much more likely to be secure on the AAI, and their children more likely to be secure in the SSP, whereas low levels of maternal RF were associated with both organised and disorganised insecurity (Fonagy et al., 1995; see too Grienenberger et al., 2005; Slade et al., 2005).

There are several interrelated aspects to mentalising. First, it is 'meta-cognitive', in that it refers to the capacity not for thinking as such, but to the *interpretation* of thoughts and actions – thinking about thinking (Fonagy, 1991; Main, 1991), or 'mind-mindedness' (Meins, 1999).

Second, mentalising is not primarily an intellectual or rational phenomenon. Full-blown *explicit* (i.e., conscious or self-aware) mentalising is a three-stage process. It is *experiential* in that its starting point is an 'automatic' affective response – a 'thought' often accompanied by somatic sensations and/or images. This is followed by *awareness* or 'noticing' what one is thinking. Lastly, and only in explicit as opposed to implicit mentalising, *thinking* about what one has found oneself thinking about (cf. Holmes, 2014b).

In *implicit* mentalising these processes also occur, but 'pre-consciously', or below awareness (see Shai & Belsky, 2017). People mostly manage to walk down the street without bumping into one another. The mind 'computes' others' and one's own intentions in order to guarantee safe passage. We are continually predicting the mental states of others without especially being aware of how, or indeed why, we do so – whether they are sad or angry or off-hand, bored, preoccupied, etc. It is only when our predictions go wrong, or conflict, or unhappiness arises, that the explicit mentalising with which therapists are concerned becomes necessary.

Third, mentalising is concerned with the *meanings* we attribute to our own and other's actions – that is, to the hypotheses we use to understand why one might have thought or done such and such a thing. This links with a fourth aspect: mentalising as a key attribute of *persons* – and other 'sentient beings' – as opposed to the pre-primate and inanimate world.

Central to mentalising is Dennett's (1987) *'intentional stance'* – the capacity to have projects, desires, and wishes. Mentalising is also related to empathy in that it implies the ability to put oneself in another's shoes, which means seeing the other as a sentient person, as opposed to a 'thing'. Finally, mentalising is not a fixed property of mind, but a *process*, a skill, which at any given moment may be present or absent to a greater or lesser degree. One of the significant ways in which therapy induces change is by helping its subjects – adults, parents, children – develop mentalising skills (Bateman & Fonagy, 2004; Sadler et al., 2013; Slade, 2006).

Abigail and the 'baby-sitter'

While her lone-parent mother was doing an evening shift at the local super-market, 10-year-old Abigail was left with a seemingly helpful and friendly neighbour, who in fact was sexually abusing her. When Abigail refused to go to the babysitter any more, her mother flew into a rage, threatening to 'put her into care'. Abigail said that the man was 'not very nice', but this again provoked a furious response, and she was told that she had no right to say such things about such a kind man.

Abigail's mother, no doubt stressed, and therefore with her mentalising capacities inactivated, ablates the validity of her daughter's experience. Abigail is twice invalidated here, first by her abuser, and second by her mother, who failed to respond to her distress cues. Had Abigail's mother been able to mentalise, she would have interpreted her daughter's refusal to go to the babysitter as meaningful and motivated by fear and the need for safety. She might have been stimulated to self-mentalise, and consider the feelings *she* had about his man – that there was indeed something 'creepy' about him – feelings hitherto pushed to one side in order to survive economically. Stress is the enemy of mentalisation: when anxiety reaches a certain level the mentalising brain goes 'off line', and the mind moves into 'survival mode' (Allen, 2012b).

Measuring Mentalising

Fonagy et al.'s (1998) AAI 'reflective function' scale assumes a spectrum of mentalising skills. Transcripts of the AAI, which can be used to measure general RF, or the Parent Development Interview (PDI; Slade, et al., 2003), used to measure parental RF (Slade, 2005) are rated (from 1–9) using a number of criteria listed below (Fonagy et al., 1998) (hypothetical examples of high-level mentalising in the therapy context are added):

- Awareness of the nature of mental states ('Sometimes I wonder if I'm not just making all this up…').

- Explicit efforts to tease out the mental states underlying behaviour ('I suppose my mother was pretty sad and overwhelmed at the time and didn't have much space to think about us children').

- Recognition of the developmental aspects of mental states ('I was so young at the time I didn't realise that the things my step-Dad asked me to do weren't quite normal').

- Showing awareness of mental states in relation to the therapist ('I realise that hearing this story is probably very painful for you').

Let's turn to three versions of our now familiar scenario. The first represents high-level mentalising, the second moderate, and the third deficient.

> A 6-month-old baby cries in the night, waking her parents. Her mother, still in bed, turns to her partner. She says: 'Oh, the little fiend, she knows I've got to get up really early tomorrow to go work. I'll be really washed out. She's just doing it to punish me.' She then goes to her child, saying to herself, or out loud to the baby: 'You poor little thing … I wonder what it can be this time? … Are you hungry, too hot, is your nappy wet? … Did you have a bad dream?' She picks the child up, soothes her, does what is necessary. In a few minutes the whole family is asleep again.

The mother's mentalising here is generally implicit in that she intuitively 'knows' what is likely to be wrong and acts accordingly. But if she gets it 'wrong' (e.g., mistaking the need for a feed, or being too hot), the baby will, via continued crying, soon 'tell' her, and she will try a different tack. Sometimes, however, she may have to resort to explicit mentalising, talking to herself – or even recruiting her partner's opinion and support:

> 'I really don't know what wrong with her. I've tried giving her a feed, changing her, taking blankets off, but she still doesn't seem right. What do you think? Maybe she's ill. I'm getting exhausted and near the end of my tether. Could you take over for a while? Maybe I should take her to the doctor in the morning.'

Throughout, the mother is using her mentalising to 'regulate' the baby's distressed affect, empathising with it, mirroring it in her own mind, naming it, modifying and modulating it, turning blue-murder screaming into describable and manageable hunger or over-heating or fear or illness.

Here's another example with the mother attempting to mentalise in the face of intense negative affect:

Responding to a research question about whether she ever feels guilty as a parent, a mother replies: 'A couple of times in the middle of the night when he's had a bad bout with teething, and he wants to nurse a lot, he puts his little fingers in my mouth. I feel so guilty because all I want to do is just snap those little fingers up with my teeth, and it takes every ounce of control I have not to bite those annoying little fingers.'

And a clearly non-mentalising scenario:

The caregiver might be alone and/or stressed or intoxicated. Mother, eventually, goes to the crying baby, but now shouts at her, handling her roughly: 'You little devil … you're just doing this to annoy me. You know I've got to get to work early tomorrow. How dare you wake me up like that? Now *get back to sleep*.' At which point she almost slams the baby back into the crib, and slams the door.

In the first illustration, the mother starts with a lapse of mentalising – in her sleep-deprived state she cannot differentiate between her feelings and those of the baby ('equivalence mode', see below). Her experience of her child's crying is seen from the perspective of her own feelings of panic and paranoia. But her developmental history, buttressed by the presence of her partner, enables her to retrieve a mentalising stance and to reflect about her own state of mind and that of her child. She contains her irritation and resistance to being woken, brackets them off, sees them for what they are – *her* feelings, not those of the baby. This clears the way for a secure attachment response to the distressed child, responsive, empathic, and effective. Therapists, too, like all ordinary mortals, have good days and bad, life difficulties and problems, but if these are not too pressing or overwhelming, they can be placed to one side while working.

In the second example, the mother is able to identify her own guilt, and is thus 'mentalising', but can barely contain her rage, and one has the sense that she is only just able to keep from acting on her impulses, and we suspect that these are communicated in some way to the child. In the third example, the mother is either highly aroused, or out of it, both of which are inimical to mentalising (Bateman & Fonagy, 2004). She is slow to respond, and when eventually she does, she sees the baby's distress in terms of her own feelings rather than those of the child, and handles the baby harshly. This self-referential response is what Lyons-Ruth describes as 'hostile/intrusive' (Lyons-Ruth & Jacobvitz, 2016), a common feature in disorganised attachment. Another is the 'fearful' parent, who might lie in bed in a terrified and helpless state, emotionally frozen and unable to respond to their child's distress.

Comparable patterns are sometimes found in the reactions of mental health professionals when confronted by disturbed behaviour in hospitalised patients. Like the third mother, reactions are often dominated by overwhelming countertransference feelings of aversion, high anxiety, and compromised mentalising. The patient may be seen as deliberately 'winding us up', malevolent, or dangerous. This in turn can drive non-mentalised responses such as instant discharge, or, conversely, over-protective use of restraint. But with the help of staff support and supervision, these reactions, like those of the sleepy mother and her partner, can be defused and more mentalising attitudes regained.

Conceptual Basis of Mentalising

Summarising the discussion so far: mentalising starts from the capacity to be able to put oneself in another's shoes; entails the ability to see and evaluate oneself and one's feelings from the outside and those of others from the inside; differentiates feelings *about* reality from reality itself; is a graded rather than all-or-nothing; is related to arousal; determines responsiveness; is enhanced by the presence of a secure soothing partner or other intimate.

In addition to mentalising's attachment legacy via the AAI and reflective functioning, three other intellectual roots (cf., Choi-Kain & Gunderson, 2008) need brief discussion: cognitive psychology, Kleinian Object Relations, and francophone psychoanalysis.

Cognitive psychology

Children normally are able to distinguish between animate and inanimate objects, and among the animate, between persons and non-human living creatures, from a very early age. Around age 4 to 5, the child begins to demonstrate 'theory of mind', the knowledge that what is in one person's mind can be and often is different from what is in another's. In the classic 'false belief' experiment (Wimmer & Perner, 1983), children are asked to predict where someone who has gone out of the room will look for a missing object on their return. Unbeknownst to the absentee, but not to the observing child, the object is moved from one container to another. Until around the age of 3, children assume that the other's view of the world is identical to their own and therefore that the 'deceived' subject will know where to look for the missing object despite its translocation. By 5 years, children can understand that deception is possible, and that a person's view of the world depends on the information available to them. The searching adult will therefore be likely to look in the wrong place. It is only a small step from this to mentalising – i.e., seeing that 'the world' is filtered through a perspectival mind, and one's model of reality depends on one's viewpoint.

This ingenious experiment also links children's cognitive capacities with their ability to understand, predict, and negotiate social relations. Armed with a theory of mind, a child can begin to understand the part played by deception, possession, competition for resources (the 'object' is usually something desirable to eat) in social groups, and to know when these are playful and when they are 'for real'.

Bion and object relations

The psychoanalyst Bion is famous for his theory of thinking (Bion, 1962, 1970). He proposed a general theory of the origins of thought, rather than the specific mind-reading skills that the term mentalising attempts to capture. Nevertheless, his ideas help us look more deeply into the essence of mentalising.

Bion starts from Freud's idea that, ultimately, thinking – the 'mind' itself – is a response to, and a bulwark against, absence and loss. Thinking bridges inevitable gaps in attachment continuity: the 5-year-old child goes happily to school because he carries with him a thought/memory/image of a loving parent/secure base in his mind to whom he can turn in times of stress or danger. For Bion, thinking – which might also be called 'image-ination' – arises in response to absence: 'no breast, therefore imagine a breast'. Bion differentiates between 'thoughts' and the 'apparatus' (his word) that thinks them. Thoughts must be 'contained' by a thinking thinker. Bion was fond of quasi-mathematical terms. He called the capacity to think thoughts 'alpha function'. Alpha function transforms 'beta elements' ('thoughts without a thinker') into 'alpha elements' that are then available for being thought about (i.e., mentalised).

Bion postulates a conflict between (a) the desire to rid oneself of 'bad' thoughts that are inherently disturbing (our crying-in-the-night baby's screams arise out of undifferentiated 'pain' to which, at this stage of development, no specific 'meaning' can be attributed) and (b) the capacity to modify them so that they can be held onto and so 'thought'. He sees the outcome of this conflict as depending on the ability of the 'breast' (i.e., Mum) to help the infant with his frustrations, to accept projections, and gently to return them in a form in which they can now be tolerated. This process is closely linked with the *naming* of feelings: for example, *'mummy's going away for a minute, but don't worry because she will be back soon'*. Explicit mentalising/alpha function involves words; words help us bridge the gaps in existence caused by separations, whether involuntary or willed.

In Bion's view, a non-containing mother sows the seeds for later deficits in mentalising. In the third example above, the stressed mother sees her infant as a persecutor; she cannot mentalise herself into a receptive state of mind. This interferes with the *infant's* developing capacity to mentalise, since his feelings have not been 'real-ised' (another of Bion's formulations) by the mother. Instead, the *mother's* feelings (*'you just want to wake me up to wind me up'*) invade the infant self as an 'alien' nidus (a malign 'nest', Fonagy et al., 2002), forming the basis of a persecutory, self-hating inner object in disorders such as psychosis, borderline pathology, or major depressive disorder.

In Bion's model, the transformation of 'beta' into 'alpha' elements leads to the establishment of a 'contact barrier' between unconscious and conscious thoughts. This means the subject can differentiate between the somatic sensations, un-named desires, and proto-feelings that comprise 'pre-conceptions' (beta elements), and thoughts or 'conceptions' (alpha elements) which form the stuff of rational thought. This enables an individual to differentiate reality from phantasy and imagination from perception, both key components of the ability to mentalise. Where the contact barrier is weak, phantasy can invade rational thought, leading to distorted perceptions of reality, and an inability to 'factor in' one's own emotional states in any situation. The extreme end of this is seen in delusional and hallucinatory thinking.

Bion's quasi-mathematical term for mentalising is 'K' (i.e., knowledge or knowing). 'Minus K' or 'not-knowing' is an 'attack on linking'. Tendentiously – determined to stay faithful to his Freudian allegiance – for Bion this is a residue of Oedipal resentment of the parent's sexual relationship. In attachment terms, this is not as envy or hate-driven destructiveness, but as a way of 'not thinking' – and so not experiencing the associated pain and danger – about the traumas to which one has been subjected. Bion's K equates to the attachment notion of 'exploration'. The precondition of K is a mentalising secure base – in children a real-life caregiver, in adults the 'inner secure base' which is able to ensure that whatever horrors or monsters one encounters in the inner or outer world, one will survive emotionally.

Francophone psychoanalysis

The French word *le mentalisation* was current in francophone psychoanalysis long before it became popular in the Anglo-Saxon world. Luquet (1981) and Marty (1991) start from the clinical phenomenon of somatisation disorders, conceived in terms of 'operational', robot-like thinking, devoid of affect; i.e., alexithymia – the inability to put feelings into words.

Mentalising represents alexithymia's antithesis: the capacity to transform primitive impulses into feelings, and to represent, symbolise, sublimate, abstract, reflect, and make meaning out of them. Lecours and Bouchard (1997: 862) formulate a sophisticated hierarchical classification of *degrees* of mentalisation. At one extreme lie 'somatisations, crude violent behaviour and self mutilation'. Sophisticated mentalisers, at the other pole, might say to their therapists something like: '*I know that whenever I feel this tired-exhausted feeling, I'm keeping something out, that I am angry but cannot somehow feel it.*'

Seeing mentalising as a spectrum is compatible with Stiles' 'assimilation model' (Stiles et al., 1990), in which 'problematic experiences', ranging from those indistinctly felt, if at all ('unthought knowns'; Bollas, 1989), to problems that can be clearly articulated and worked on. Psychoanalytic approaches that help clients to translate their inchoate feelings and actings-out into 'mentalised affectivity' (Fonagy et al., 2002) work at the dimly sensed 'unconscious' end of this spectrum. Cognitive therapies deal more comfortably with the 'known knowns'.

Developmental Origins

Mentalising is a developmental achievement, nascent in infants and small children, gathering pace gradually in the course of childhood and adolescence (Dumontheil, Apperly, & Blakemore, 2010), but not fully fledged until adulthood. For Fonagy et al. (2002), psychopathology can be seen in terms of the persistence into adult life of pre-mentalising stages. In their model the route to mentalising passes through three precursors: *teleological*, *equivalence*, and *pretend* modes. All three co-exist with mentalising in adult life. Reversion to pre-mentalising phases typically occurs under stress or threat, especially in the absence of a 'buffering' intimate.

Teleological mode

This is 'end-oriented' thinking in which behaviour is understood not in terms of desires, plans, and projects, but based on a consequential, 'if this, then that' pattern. A domestic dog thinks teleologically: leash taken up 'means' walk. Most, but perhaps not all,[1] dogs are unaware – blissfully perhaps – of whether their 'master/mistress' is skulking off after a spousal row, drawn to the beauties of a spring day, or seeking solitude in order to think about a new book. Similarly, preverbal, pre-mentalising children 'know' a huge amount about their world, and the causes and consequences of actions, without being able fully to read other people's minds.

Peter and the nurse

Teleologically, in-patient Peter would typically harm himself when thwarted. He found it hard to grasp the emotional states driving these deliberate self-harm episodes. Rather than 'My cutting arises out of feelings of rejection', he would say: 'Of course I cut myself, they didn't give me the medication I asked for.'

He was referred for assessment in a specialist psychotherapy clinic. Towards the end of a difficult interview, he was asked if he felt any of the staff understood him.

'Nope, no one', came the reply.

'What about your "key-worker"?'

'Oh, she just thinks I'm a waste of space like everyone else', he replied.

'Do you really mean that?'

'Well, I don't suppose she *really* does, that's just the way I feel about it most of the time.'

Here, momentarily, is Peter mentalising. He moves from teleology to fragmentary mentalising – it's not that the nurse really rejects him; he can see that it is his *perception* of her attitude that is the problem. Coming to that point entailed a combination of mild challenge with therapeutic 'holding' so that his typically hair-trigger arousal was in abeyance. The buffering effect of the therapist as secure base held the amygdala in check sufficiently for the PFC to do its regulating and mentalising job.

Equivalence mode

Here the world as it appears to the subject is seen as 'equivalent' to the world as it is. There is no distinction between thought and reality, one just 'knows' something to be the case, irrespective of evidence or 'triangulation', such as checking out perceptions with a trusted other.

Cognitive therapists work hard to help their clients counteract equivalence mode thinking. Peter in the example above might say: '*I know perfectly well why they don't give me the medication I need – they hate me.*' He will be helped to consider alternative possibilities: maybe they want to reduce his dependency, or are required by their superiors to stick to a rigid medication regime, irrespective of patient need.

Mentalising strengthens the boundary between fantasy and reality, between what is and what is imagined to be the case. This moves therapeutic discourse from the concrete to the *metaphorical*. Metaphor is inherently mentalising in that an image, while containing an important psychological truth, is by definition in the mind rather than 'out there' in reality. Peter's complaints about the staff not giving him medication, mentalising and metaphorised, led on to his talking about more general feelings of not being understood or not having his needs met – currently and in the past.

Pretend mode

Here the external world is pushed away; the child retreats into an exclusively imaginary space, un-tempered by reality. Picture an adolescent boy shut away in his bedroom, playing endless computer games. In contrast to equivalence mode, where the 'contact barrier' between reality and fantasy is too porous, in 'pretend mode' reality is rigorously excluded.

At its worst, therapy itself can reinforce 'pretend' modes of thinking, becoming, in the classic anti-analytic jibe, 'the disease of which it purports to be the cure' (Reik, 1948). Clients may, in fantasy, withdraw from the world into the therapy space, imagining a blissful exclusive relationship with an idealised therapist. The realities of the client's life are sidelined or, if mentioned, are without real affective involvement.

Tom's dreams

Tom's life was a mess. He drifted from one superficial relationship to another, feeling depressed and cut off from his children, who lived with his divorced wife. Little of this was discussed in therapy. Prior to each session he would consult his dream-diary, memorise it, and then regale the therapist with endless and complex dreams, full of portentous themes. Eventually the therapist, normally rather adept at dream interpretation, said, '*I really can't make head or tail of these dreams – they seem to me as confused as your life is at the moment … perhaps* that *is what we should be focusing on.*' Shame-facedly, Tom began to voice his feelings of helplessness and vulnerability, and his conviction that were he to describe the reality of his everyday life the therapist would deem him stupid and inadequate.

Learning to Mentalise

Learning to mentalise holds the promise of freedom from the psychological impact of past trauma. Facts cannot be altered, but how they are 'processed', i.e. felt, and thought about, can. Trauma not only inflicts mental harm but inhibits the mentalising that is integral to recovery. The role of attachment-informed therapy is to counteract that process *in vivo* through the therapeutic relationship. But there is a caveat. Faced with acute danger, mentalising can be disadvantageous. About to be eaten by a lion, one doesn't want to spend too much time imagining what's going on in the feline's mind. Mentalising is inherently 'slow'; arousal activates fast thinking and inhibits mentalising (cf. Kahneman, 2011).

Although children brought up in secure families succeed in theory of mind tasks at a younger age than those from less favourable backgrounds, the latter also achieve a degree of mentalising capacity by the age of 6 (Fonagy, Gergely, & Target, 2007). It is not that those destined for psychological illness lack the capacity to mentalise; rather, the problem is that mentalising is on a knife-edge and easily prone to disruption.

This takes us back to affect regulation. Affect regulation is intimately connected to mentalising – only when feelings are held within manageable limits can one begin to think about them. Relative calmness in the face of distress fosters mentalising; clinical, developmental, and neurophysiological studies all show that excessive arousal and mentalising are mutually incompatible (Bateman & Fonagy, 2004). Caregivers' mentalising helps children acquire an internal image of themselves, introjected from their parents' responsive and accurate reflections of their moods, feelings, and desires. Secure attachment entails modulation and down-regulation of painful affect, aided by a caregiver who is not unduly upset by the infant's distress, and knows not to 'take it personally'. The problem for people suffering from personality disorders is not that they cannot mentalise, but that their propensity to hair-trigger arousal means that the space and time to think about their thinking is narrowed.

Mentalisation encourages therapists to subject their ideas and feelings to constant scrutiny. 'Countertransference' exemplifies high-level mentalising – therapists must always be asking themselves: 'what am I thinking and feeling at this specific moment with this particular person?' From the integrative perspective, every theoretical viewpoint (not excluding attachment-informed therapy!), is subject to question. Why am I so passionate about this or that position? What and whose conscious and unconscious interests do my reactions serve? What are my justifications, and how do I know they are not merely rationalisations? Complex mentalising is hard work: there are few therapists who don't from time to time end their day feeing tired or drained. But it is also hugely rewarding – offering an escape from surface living. Rising above suffering means liberation from enslavement to a restricted vision of one's self and life's opportunities. The next chapter centres on a specific example of this.

Summary

- Mentalising: to see oneself from the outside and others from the inside.

- The concept's origins include cognitive developmental psychology, Kleinian object relations, francophone psychoanalysis – and attachment research.

- Maternal 'holding' and awareness of children as having minds and projects of their own sets the mentalising process in motion.

- Pre-mentalising modes include teleological, equivalence, and pretend thinking.

- Arousal inhibits mentalising – this is especially problematic in people suffering from personality disorders.

- Mentalising is a central therapeutic skill. 'Being understood' in therapy is a first step towards self-understanding.

- Therapists' mentalising can be compromised, too, and should be monitored as closely as disruptions in patients' mentalising.

Note

1. This assertion often evokes a flurry – and fury – of disagreement, usually citing the owner's own much-loved and psychologically co-evolved pet.

8

'Earned Security'

Attachment and Resilience

In this chapter, we use a case example to illustrate the phenomena and problematics of 'earned security', its central relevance to psychotherapy, and how it overlaps with the current psychological hot topic of resilience (Rutter, 2012; Southwick et al., 2014). We start with a brief discussion of earned security, before considering its relevance to resilience and how psychotherapy helps foster both.

Earned Security

Earned security was first described by Main and Goldwyn (1989), who noticed that some subjects show a high degree of coherence and collaboration in their AAI transcripts, pointing to secure attachment, despite having had apparently unloving and even traumatic relationships with parents, typically associated with insecure attachment (Hesse, 2016).

Two explanations for the discrepancy have been put forward. The first, (unsurprisingly) favoured by clinicians, is that, despite childhood adversity, adult security *can* be achieved – earned or learned – through positive relationships with other significant individuals, such as grandparents, older siblings, teachers, etc. (Egeland, Jacobvitz, & Sroufe, 1988; Fear, 2016). Lieberman and her colleagues (Lieberman et al., 2005) referred to these as 'angels' (as opposed to ghosts) in the nursery: benign figures who provided safety when primary caregivers did not. The opposing view, championed by Roisman and colleagues (Crowell, Fraley, & Roisman 2016), is that earned security is an artefact of retrospective studies, and that objectively adequate parental care, seen 'backwards' through the dark glass of depression, is often wrongly described in negative terms by those who are currently unhappy.

In an attempt to resolve this impasse, Saunders et al. (2011) analysed the methodological difficulties raised by the earned security concept. First, there are relatively few earned secure individuals in high-risk samples, which makes statistical analysis difficult. Second, there is no generally agreed upon method of measuring 'adversity' – e.g., whether coding 'un-lovingness' is required from one parent, or both (cf. Pearson et al., 1994). In an attempt to circumvent these problems, Saunders et al. (2011) chose a low-risk sample of pregnant women, of whom 16 out of 121 fulfilled the criteria for earned-secure using the AAI as a measure. This group had coherent narratives, despite *both* parents being deemed neglectful, rejecting, role-reversing, or success-pressurising, albeit from retrospective accounts.

From a psychotherapeutic perspective, their significant findings were: (a) the earned secure group had had higher levels of emotional (but not instrumental) support from *non-parental figures* in childhood (i.e., 'angels'), whether familial (e.g., grandparents) or non-familial (e.g., teachers); (b) this extra-parental support was beneficial *throughout childhood and adolescence*, not just in the early years; (c) the earned security group's *children*, when subsequently rated in the Strange Situation, were more likely to be judged secure than children of insecure; and (d) the earned secure group were more likely to have been *in therapy, and, if in therapy, for longer*, than their insecure counterparts.

These findings speak directly to psychotherapists whose work aims to provides non-familial, non-instrumental, emotional support, while the benefits of time spent in therapy are incremental and cumulative (cf. Wampold, 2015). The Saunders et al. (2011) study, especially if replicated prospectively, strongly suggests that psychotherapy can help transform childhood adversity into more secure attachment dispositions, enhancing resilience, possibly cross-generationally. Helping clients move from established patterns of insecurity to earned security, sharing feelings, and trusting another to help modulate and regulate them, is the essence of what psychotherapists do.

Resilience

The term 'resilience' comes from the Latin *resilire*, 'to rebound or spring back'. Implicit is the idea of a traumatic or adverse force impacting on a system which, rather than shattering, has sufficient flexibility and elasticity to 'bounce back'. Resilience in the physical sciences implies both strength and 'ductility' – i.e., the ability to stretch without snapping or falling apart. As a psychological construct, Rutter (2012) defines resilience as '*patterns of positive adaptation in the context of significant risk or adversity*'. Note his characteristically careful qualifiers: 'patterns' (i.e., processes rather than fixed properties), 'context' (resilience applies to specific situations rather than being an inherent feature of the individual), 'significant' (prolonged and multiple adversity leads to worse outcomes than single traumatic episodes).

Resilience and secure attachment abut, overlap, and sometimes conflict in a number of ways. As we hope by now to have convinced our readers, attachment makes clear distinctions between secure, sub-optimal, and pre-pathogenic developmental pathways. But we have also insisted that insecure patterns are not to be conceived as unhealthy or undesirable in themselves, rather as *resilience-promoting adaptations* to specific environments, enabling survival under adverse circumstances. From an evolutionary perspective, this range of attachment patterns provides the variation that natural selection needs to 'work on' in order to maximise the chances of species survival (Laland, 2017).

Clinicians need to understand the context of their clients' seemingly sub-optimal attachment strategies. Psychotherapy, in aiming to install earned security, may temporarily *decrease* resilience, as defences are stripped away and more healthy modes of attachment have not yet matured. As Gramsci (1999: 67) put it, 'the crisis consists … in the fact that the old is dying and the new cannot be born; in this interregnum a great variety of morbid symptoms appear'.

We shall see later how therapists must be able to hold and help manage this 'variety of morbid symptoms'. The attachment-informed therapist has to strike a balance between support, in which defences are upheld, and the ultimate aim of dismantling anachronistic modes of relating, replacing them with more adaptive ways of being.

Contemporary societies see it as their role to foster resilience in their members. Inoculation programmes strengthen the immune system. As newborns borrow mothers' antibodies via the colostrum, so infants draw on ('borrow') the maternal brain, especially the left PFC, to help co-regulate their emotions. Attachment-informed parenting programmes such as 'Child–Parent Psychotherapy' (Lieberman & Van Horn, 2008), 'Minding the Baby' (Sadler et al., 2013; Slade, 2006) build on this, aiming to counteract the negative impact of trauma, poverty, stress, and social disruption on physical and psychological development.

Let's now look at a 'case history' of resilience, based on the autobiography of an early twentieth-century writer, William H. Davies, whose overcoming of adversity illustrates many aspects of resilience and earned security in ways that are relevant to psychotherapists.

'What is this Life?': W. H. Davies' *Autobiography of a Supertramp*

W. H. Davies (1871–1940) is best known for his poem *Leisure*, and its lines:

> …What is this life if full of care
> We have no time to stand and stare?

Through his poetry and autobiography, Davies enjoyed literary success in the early part of the twentieth century. The middle of three children, he was born in the coastal fishing port of Newport, Wales. His father, a craftsman, died when he was 3. His mother immediately remarried and handed the children over to their paternal grandparents, cutting off all contact with them. Davies was close to his grandmother. Although an avid reader and a good sportsman from an early age, he was a difficult child. Aged 10, he was arrested for theft and given twelve lashes in punishment. His delinquency continued, and he left school at 14. Soon afterwards both grandparents died. For the next seven years he became a 'supertramp' (his phrase), first in the UK and then on the US East Coast, finding companions with whom to travel, begging, taking casual work on rough transatlantic cattle boats, and engaging in petty crime, which, ironically, spared him the harsh New England American winters through spending them in the comparative comfort of jail.

1899 was the year of the Klondike 'gold rush'. Davies set off to make his fortune in the American West, but, in attempting to 'jump' a West-bound freight train, he slipped, severely injuring his leg, which then had to be amputated. He spent three months in hospital in Ontario. Eventually rehabilitated and equipped with a wooden leg, his tramping days over, he decided to become a writer. He returned to the UK, and lived in a Salvation Army Hostel in the East End of London for the next two years, regularly sending poems and articles to publishers and newspapers, signally without success. Eventually he was 'discovered' when the literary giant George Bernard Shaw received the manuscript of his *Supertramp* autobiography (Davies, 1908/2011), and agreed to write a preface. He was embraced as a 'working-class hero' by the metropolitan literati, such as Pound and Sitwell, who praised (perhaps a touch patronisingly) his John Clare-like[1] naïve profundity.

Davies' account of life at the margins at the end of the nineteenth and start of the twentieth centuries has a fresh and original timbre. He tells the story of his possibly autistic older brother, instructed by their grandmother, who was going out, to 'watch the fish' cooking on the stove for their supper, at risk from a hungry cat. The cat duly ate the fish, much to his grandmother's fury on her return. 'But Granny', said the brother, 'I did watch the fish – all the way down into the cat's stomach'! Davies similarly laughs at himself and his early literary efforts.

Davies' account illustrates many of the features identified in the early research on resilience. Using a 10-year qualitative 'follow-back' methodology, Hauser, Allen, and Golden (2006) studied delinquent boys who had been admitted to a children's home. Those demonstrating *self-reflection, agency, self-complexity, persistence, ambition, good self-esteem*, and the ability to create a *coherent self-narrative* were least likely to re-offend.

Davies was determined and persistent, despite setbacks. He had significant assets – intelligence, an interest in reading, sporting prowess; he was companionable and 'pluripotential' in the sense that he could switch from one path, tramping, to another, writing; his writing demonstrates 'reflective capacity', i.e., the ability to stand back from and laugh at himself and others, and to develop a coherent narrative about his life. He demonstrates three key psychotherapy-relevant features of resilience: *agency, relationship-competence*, and *mentalising*.

But the resilience, especially when it is built around avoidance, as in Davies' case, is a mixed blessing. Despite being an account of a young man's life, there is virtually no mention of women or sex in Davies' autobiography. It is a reasonable hypothesis that, for survival's sake, Davies suppressed his emotional needs, breached only on one occasion. When he was about to leave the hospital with his wooden leg, the hospital matron came to bid him goodbye, and kissed him on the cheek. Davies comments: 'I felt my voice gone and my throat in the clutches of something new to my experience' (1908/2011: 43).

This breakthrough of unmet craving for love and closeness is also evident in the poignant poem, *A Fleeting Passion*, in which he describes the aftermath of a night spent with a prostitute:

Let's grimly kiss with bated breath;
As quietly and solemnly
As Life when it is kissing Death
Now in the silence of the grave
My hand is squeezing that soft breast...

Davies is describing his devastating experience of the juxtaposition of love and separation, attempting through his verse to create a coherent narrative out of the attachment paradox that with love goes the ever-present possibility of loss. His resilience was founded on extreme emotional self-sufficiency. The tenderness of the mother-matron – evoking un-mourned grief for the mother who had abandoned him, and the grandmother who had died – penetrated his hitherto adamantine defences.

Attachment and Resilience

Different developmental environments call forth different relational strategies. Each in its own way represents an 'adaptation', always attempting to maximise security, and with it resilience in specific circumstances. Schematically, these strategies can be characterised as 'horizontal', 'vertical', and 'circular'. In secure attachment, parents and children see one another on a level, or 'horizontally'. There is a fundamental equality, despite obvious differences in maturity and competence. The 'horizontal' caregiver holds in mind the developmental dimension of life and knows in his or her bones that the child is father of the man. In 'vertical' child-care the parent is always the one who knows best. Competence is located exclusively in the parent and flows unidirectionally downwards. A degree of security is guaranteed, but creativity and independence are at risk. 'Circular' patterns are seen in disorganised attachment, where the unparented or abused child attempts to exclude external influence and be sufficient unto him or herself. In adults, borderline and narcissistic personality disorders evince a comparable impregnable circularity.

Secure attachments

Secure attachment is 'horizontal' (and 'democratic') in the sense that mentalising, mind-minded mothers view their children as sentient beings with projects, desires, and thoughts of their own, as well as recognising and reinforcing their children's autonomy. The autonomous child is an active child, who is able to tackle and overcome minor stresses and setbacks. The capacity to tackle danger and stress – whether from without or within – rather than to passively succumb is a crucial aspect of resilience. Davies' tramping may be an extreme example of an active form of denial, but his ability to turn his life around, rather than to collapse following his amputation, is testament to the importance of the activity principle. This may have had its origins in the way that his grandmother, an 'angel' (Lieberman et al., 2005), or in Saunders et al.'s (2011) terms a non-parental, non-instrumental, emotionally supportive figure, undertook the caregiving role with her grandchildren. This often applies in communities where mothers – as the result of poverty, substance use, illness (such as AIDS) – are unable to care for their children, who are then raised by grandparents and other family members.

Secure attachment does not equate to continuous uninterrupted mother–baby harmony and proximity. Tronick (2007) found that alongside periods of intense physical and emotional intimacy, normal secure parent–child interactions include 'ruptures' in which parents are regularly *out* of tune with their infants. In secure attachments these ruptures are readily and regularly 'repaired', triggered by the attachment dynamic in which the parent soothes the distressed infant until peace is restored. The infant goes through many rupture/repair cycles throughout the day.

This observation is consistent with early animal experiments (Levine, 1957), suggesting that 'stress inoculation' has a strengthening or 'steeling'[2] (Rutter, 2012) impact. When mature, rats who as pups were separated from their dams for short periods show less fear response and wider exploration compared with those deprived of this mild stress. After these brief separations, rat mothers show enhanced 'high-arched licking and grooming' that may contribute at physiological and possibly epigenetic levels to the pup's resilience (Meaney, 2001). By contrast, *prolonged* separation of pups from their mothers has the opposite effect, enhancing anxiety and weakening resistance to stress and disease in adulthood.

Similar findings have been found in primates (Suomi, 2016) and probably apply to humans. It could be argued that Davies' harsh childhood primed him to cope with the physical and social adversity he experienced in pre-welfare Britain and the USA. Goransson (2009) has argued that today's middle-class 'helicopter' or 'curling'[3] parents, ever-ready to over-protect their children from stress, may be doing them a disservice, depriving them of the 'Captains Courageous'-type (Kipling, 1897/2014) maturation which overcoming mild adversity engenders.

In sum, the capacity to 'extend' the self to include significant others, to nurture and open up a new sensitive period, along with mentalising and stress inoculation, are resilience factors arising out of secure attachment.

Insecure attachment

The two main 'organised' forms of insecure attachment adopt 'vertical' routes to resilience, typified either in avoidant individuals, like Davies, using a 'top-down' strategy based on affect suppression, or, in anxious attachment, 'bottom-up' patterns of clinging and affect augmentation, which draw in the caregiver as a protective shield. This is relevant to another psychobiological overlap – between social status/rank and attachment. Suomi's (2016) primate studies show that, like peer-reared and insecurely attached individuals, low-ranking members of a group are physiologically and socially disadvantaged. Vertical strategies to resilience can be understood as attempts to circumvent this, either by 'pulling rank', distancing from group pressures (a deactivating strategy), or latching on to a high-ranking other (a hyperactivating strategy).

Such 'vertical' strategies tend to be more fragile and less flexible than secure patterns (Bonanno & Burton, 2013). Avoidant children have high levels of stress hormones (Dozier et al., 2008); staying detached consumes psychic energy which is then not available for other cognitive tasks. Secure individuals can call upon help when needed, but otherwise remain independent and autonomous. The anxiously attached need the constant accessibility of a secure base via texting, telephoning, physical presence, etc. When stressed, the anxiously insecure are not able to transcend or metabolise their negative emotions, and therefore are more likely to respond in non-resilient ways – collapse, dependency, chronic depression, or anxiety.

Both secure and 'organised insecure' attachment strategies achieve resilience through the recruitment of a caregiver. By contrast, the disorganised have no choice but to find security in the closed circle of themselves. The disorganised pattern illustrates one of the tragedies of resilience: children raised in adversity, and therefore in most need of resilience, are least able to mobilise resilience-enhancing resources. Disorganised children's mothers tend to be poor mentalisers, and are therefore unlikely to transmit those skills to their children; their left PFCs are less accessible for modulating their children's affect than their secure counterparts. Children raised in conditions that engender secure attachment and foster resilience are to an extent buffered against adversity. To those that have, it shall be given.

In the developed world at least, the adversities that contemporary humans face derive not so much from the physical environment – predators, food scarcity, fire, flooding, and earthquakes – although of course all of these play their part,[4] but from our con-specifics. Neglect, separation, emotional abuse, environmental degradation, economic deprivation, physical and sexual predation, theft, gun crime, inequality, and injustice: these are the adversities to which today's children are principally prey. The 'others' to whom the traumatised child turns for comfort and help are often themselves afflicted by the same adversity and threadbare resilience. This irony is central to the Main-Hesse (Main & Hesse, 1990) theory of disorganised attachment in which the child is in a 'double bind', or approach–avoidance dilemma, and where 'fear without solution' leads to circular patterns of self-soothing.

Grounds for hope

Therapists will not at this point succumb to pessimism, however. First, attachment categories are necessarily broad-brush. Clinically, there is often a mixed picture (Holmes, 2010; Slade, 2014). Davies undoubtedly used 'vertical', avoidant, emotionally suppressive strategies to cope with the loss of his mother and grandmother, and to maintain his independence. But he was also a good mentaliser, formed male friendships easily, had intellectual and sporting skills, was determined, and endowed with buoyant self-esteem. He fulfilled many of the features of resilience identified in the research literature (Southwick et al., 2014). He was resilient in the original sense of being able to bounce back after setbacks rather than shattering. Despite his traumatic accident, he was not entirely emotionally disabled by his amputation.

Second, attachment categories, while tending to be stable over time, are not immutable, and are responsive to context. Depressed mothers tend to have children classified as insecure, but if their depression remits, either spontaneously or through therapy, their children revert to secure attachment (Cooper et al., 2015). As measured by salivary cortisol responses, secure attachment mitigates the effects of stress on children growing up in poverty (Fearon et al., 2016).

A third relevant theme is that of 'positive life events' and their role in changing a life-course and contributing to resilience. Brown and his co-workers (see Bifulco, 2009) have charted how depression in working-class mothers is triggered or exacerbated by negative life events, such as separation, bereavement, housing difficulties, and unemployment. But the converse also applies: starting a new relationship, getting a job, finding stable accommodation, or children's success at school, helps alleviate depression, especially in the context of a supportive relationship with a key worker or therapist. Sroufe and his colleagues (Sroufe et al., 2005) likewise found that a child's attachment classification could change from insecure to secure if the mother's life circumstances changed for the positive.

Clearly, both adverse and positive life events are to an extent random and unpredictable, but their cognitive appraisal – the meanings we attribute to them – is not. Davies' story illustrates how resilience entails seeing adversity as a challenge rather than a life-diminishing trauma. If taken as a statement of fact, Nietzsche's (1988/1900) much-quoted aphorism 'that which does not kill us, makes us stronger' is clearly false. But as a psychotherapeutic injunction and aspiration, it has merit. The capacity to respond and adapt to positive life events is part of the resilience armamentarium. Chance and accident test resilience; the capacity to respond positively to adversity is contingent upon positive attachment experiences.

This view is consistent with recent longitudinal attachment research. Studying the timing of menarche in secure and insecure girls, Belsky, Fearon, and their co-workers (Belsky, Houts, & Fearon, 2010) showed how attachment status at 12 months predicts the timing of the onset of menarche, with insecurely attached girls maturing earlier than the secure group. A later study (Sung et al., 2016) showed that even in the presence of economic adversity, daughters of mothers with good mentalising capacity have delayed menarche compared with the non-mentalising group. This fits with the finding that grandchildren of Holocaust survivors are in some circumstances more resilient than those without a trauma history (Barel et al., 2010). Taken together, these studies provide support for Belsky's (1997) evolutionary model of attachment, in which different environmental conditions call forth different psychobiological patterns. Adverse environments require 'insecure' (in our terms 'vertical') strategies, including early sexual maturation, in order to ensure survival into the next generation. Secure attachment in more benign environments leads to prolonged sensitive periods and so enhances learning, creativity, and stability.[5] Epigenetic processes (Meaney, 2001) suggest that these environmental effects impact the genome and can be transmitted to future generations.

An emerging picture is one of an ecological model of resilience, 'designed' (in the evolutionary sense) to maximise survival, physical and psychological, depending on environmental circumstances. Under normal circumstances, copying and learning as opposed to striking out one's own is the best strategy; but when faced with environmental disruption where 'normal procedures' no longer apply, the extreme independence associated with avoidant attachment fares best (Laland, 2017). This formulation challenges the implicit normative assumptions of the terms 'secure' and 'insecure'. 'Vertical', insecure attachments are not in themselves 'less good' than secure ones – indeed in adverse circumstances they may be life-saving – but they do imply a degree of disadvantageous inflexibility – at an individual, if not a group, level.

Implications for Psychotherapy

What are the implications for attachment-informed psychotherapy practice of these findings, as illustrated by Davies' story? As mentioned already, the resilience triad of *relatedness, reflection, and agency* (Parens, 2009) are central themes in most psychotherapies. But fostering these capacities in clients is often far from straightforward. As we have seen, insecure attachment is an adaptive response to sub-optimal environments. Relinquishing pre-existing resilience strategies in the hope of developing more flexible and salubrious ones requires trust, time, and courage, all of which are problematic for the insecurely attached. Davies' initial response to the matron's spontaneous offer of a loving kiss threatened his impervious emotional avoidance – and sent him hopping from Ontario to London's East End.

Faced with adversity, Davies *decided* to become a writer. His autobiography can be seen as a species of self-therapy, drawing on his well-developed capacity for self-reflection. In doing so, he remained an active agent, in charge, within fate-imposed limits, of his own life. Mentalising mothers – or in Davies' case his earned security promoting grandmother – validate their secure offspring's *agency*, seeing their children as active, choosing beings, with their own and unique minds, likes and dislikes, aims and objectives, and projects. This 'self-agency' (Knox, 2010) is integral to resilience. Psychotherapy clients' agency is typically undermined or underdeveloped: they feel collapsed, helpless, victimised, unable to find a way forward.

Helping to overcome this compromised sense of agency is a key psychotherapy task. However, interpretations that emphasise how patients 'actively' resort to helplessness may be 'heard' as criticism, and disparagement of entrenched, life-preserving resilience strategies. It is essential to avoid 'blaming the victim'. Initially, skilful therapists will emphasise the ways in which clients have been disempowered – how they felt compelled to comply with sexual abuse or accommodate to depressed parents' moods. Only gradually does it become possible to acknowledge and own their contribution to their dilemmas. Many steps backwards and forwards will be needed before seeing how their expectations of invalidation or abuse jeopardise the very longed-for closeness and security for which they yearn, including that with the therapist.

Liberating agency is a vital part of the psychotherapy process, and a marker of good outcome and signpost to future resilience. Therapists will be on the look-out for signs of extra-therapy agency and activities: making new friends, seeking employment, gardening or exploring nature, joining clubs, or planning home improvement projects, even tidying papers and belongings.

Resilience research draws attention to a number of other relevant aspects of psychotherapy. The rhythms of therapy itself – the weekly or daily 'hour' with its protected time and space, but non-negotiable periodicity, together with holiday 'breaks' – is a living embodiment of 'stress inoculation'. The quotidian finding/losing, to-and-fro of therapy is a school for surviving loss, and the instillation of hope that the good object, out of sight but not of mind, will once more be there when called for.

Conclusion

Let's return to Davies' famous couplet. The ability to 'stand and stare' emphasises the 'present moment' as an antidote to past trauma or future anxiety. Resilience entails the ability to let go of the past, however painful, to resist future worries, and to inhabit and embrace the here-and-now. Mindfulness meditation is increasingly incorporated into 'third wave' cognitive therapy (Kahl, Winter, & Schweiger, 2012), explicitly training clients to 'stand and stare'. Comparably, in Mentalisation Based Therapy (MBT) (Allen, Fonagy, & Bateman, 2008), therapist and client together 'press the pause button' – and, through 'action replay', put problematic experience under the microscope, momentarily damming the inexorable flux of feelings.

Davies' seemingly naïve and simplistic poem takes us a step further in the search for resilience. The poem goes on:

> No time to see, in broad daylight,
> Streams full of stars, like skies at night:
>
> No time to turn at Beauty's glance,
> And watch her feet, how they can dance:
>
> No time to wait till her mouth can
> Enrich that smile her eyes began?
>
> A poor life this if, full of care,
> We have no time to stand and stare.

Here Davies alerts us to two other crucial aspects of resilience. First is *connectedness*, not just to others and their dancing feet, but to the natural world of streams and stars (cf. Holmes, 2016). The second is the role of *the face*. A mirroring, smiling, mother's face is the starting point for secure attachment. The accepting, loving face symbolises the internal secure base needed to endure – to 'face' – the horrors, losses, guilt, vicissitudes, setbacks, and cruelties that at times life inevitably brings. Psychotherapists are guardians of that process. Helping clients assemble an internal secure base is, *pari passu*, a royal road to resilience.

Summary

- Children of mentalising mothers are more likely to show resilience in the face of adversity.

- Resilience is contextual and relational, rather than a fixed property of individuals.

- Components of resilience include a sense of agency, mentalising capacity, negative affect processing, and building relationships.

- Despite adversity, earned security is possible with the help of extra-familial emotional support, of which psychotherapy is an example.

- Insecure attachment strategies are best seen as adaptive responses to adverse circumstances.

- The role of therapy is to help clients move from 'vertical' to more 'horizontal' forms of resilience.

- This may entail periods of extreme vulnerability and need for support, of which therapists should be aware.

Notes

1. Another 'primitive' autodidact nature poet.
2. 'Steeling' is a metaphor taken from material science: subjecting metal to minor stress or heat strengthens it.
3. A metaphor drawn from the sport of 'bowls on ice', in which players 'curl' the 'chuck' by 'over-protectively' smoothing its passage, thereby ensuring the greatest possible distance of travel.
4. These too have their social dimension. Sen (1982) argues that widespread famine has never occurred in a democracy.
5. A phenomenon also seen in plant species – those shown on 'stony ground' lead to early seed-formation compared with those sown on more fertile soil.

9

'Organised Insecurity'

Fostering Security through Therapeutic Conversations

Making sense of symptoms, and of one's role, relationships, and destiny, is integral to effective psychotherapies and applicable to clients and therapists alike. The aim of this and the next chapter is to develop the *explanatory framework* underpinning attachment-informed psychotherapy. We hope to show how attachment theory impacts on practice in ways that are accessible and comprehensible for both therapists and patients.

Let's start with an everyday example.

Richard and Rebecca's 'non-rendez-vous'

Married couple Richard and Rebecca get on well most of the time, except for one 'shark-infested' arena: meetings. They have a long history of 'non-rendez-vous', stretching back to the early days of their relationship. On one occasion, they arranged to meet in a coffee shop at 3.00 pm. Rebecca was there at 2.50. By 3.01, when Richard had failed to appear, she gave up in despair and wandered off. At 3.02, he breathlessly arrived: no Rebecca. He went looking for her. After half an hour of fruitless searching they finally bumped into one another and an all-too-familiar row broke out – '*You said 2.45, where the hell were you?*' … '*No I didn't, it was 3.00, anyway I was only one minute late*', etc. Eventually peace was restored – until the next time.

Different psychological theories will have their own theoretical frameworks for thinking about this trivial yet telling episode. Psychoanalytically,

Richard's lateness might be seen as unconscious aggression, even echoing, at a stretch, protest at an over-rigid maternal feeding schedule dating back to infancy. Systemic therapists would point to the lack of executive decision-making, with neither party clearly in control, lateness being used as a 'distance regulator' to avoid intimacy except through the medium of argument. From an attachment perspective, Rebecca is anxiously insecure, unable to trust Richard as a secure base able to keep her in mind. Richard's lateness triggers this dynamic; she panics, assumes he has forgotten about her, and, as in the SSP, when they are eventually reunited she cannot easily be pacified, fearing she will be let down once again. Richard is clearly avoidant, assumes the only safe and sensible strategy is self-sufficiency, and fails to mentalise Rebecca's anxiety, which he dubs as 'stupid' and 'irrational'.

A number of authors use insecure attachment classifications, and the developmental experiences that lead to them, as an explanatory framework (e.g., Crittenden, 2006; Johnson & Whiffen, 2005; Liotti, 2004; Wallin, 2007). We too endorse this approach (Holmes, 2010; Slade, 2000) but are also aware of its clinical limitations. There is an inherent difficulty in reconciling research tools like the SSP and AAI, designed for studying and comparing populations, with the salience in therapy of specific life-stories and the uniqueness of the individual.

Here we focus on the obvious fact that most therapies, especially with adults, are essentially conversations, albeit of a specialised kind.[1] As T. S. Eliot's Sweeney says: 'I gotta use words when I talk to you' (1963: 29); or in Freud's version (1916: 17): 'nothing takes place in a psychoanalysis but an interchange of words between patient and analyst'.[2] Thus far we have emphasised the physiological and gestural aspects of secure attachment. We need now to consider attachment-influenced approaches to language and conversation in therapy. As Freud (1900) highlighted, 'the unconscious', despite being an essentially non-verbal 'right brain' phenomenon, continuously reveals itself through language (cf. McGilchrist, 2009). As well as slips, puns, double-entendres, etc., these linguistic phenomena encompass the silent (yet revealing) spaces 'between' words, as well as their tone, rate, emphasis, and syntax. We believe that attachment theory and research offer a particularly rich approach to understanding these dimensions.

We will first briefly describe the Adult Attachment Interview and its classification scheme, and consider the use of the AAI itself in psychotherapy. We will then use the AAI as springboard for informing therapeutic listening and making deeper sense of therapeutic conversations. We will focus specifically on illuminating and expanding inner speech; therapeutic conversations as 'speech acts'; making meaning of subject positions; and discovering metaphor and its origins in early relational experience. The focus here will mainly be on 'organised insecurity'. Dialogic and verbal aspects of disorganised attachment will be tackled in the next chapter.

The Adult Attachment Interview and Discourse Patterns

A distinctive feature of psychodynamic therapies is their longitudinal perspective, attempting to place current symptoms in a developmental/historical context. As we have said, for psychotherapists, as for Wordsworth (1802/1984), the child is father (and mother) of the man (and woman). We now embark on a brief recapitulation.

Ainsworth related the quality of infant/caregiver handling in the first year of life to secure or insecure classification in the SSP at 12–18 months. Children's behaviour upon reunion after parting reveals their expectations about care and comfort; these 'representations', derived from deeply felt, formative interactions, lead to the development of IWMs. These are inbuilt assumptions about self–other responses to threat, illness, or exhaustion, determining not just how we act, but also how we think, speak, and react emotionally when the attachment dynamic is activated.

It took the original mind and drive of Mary Main to find ways of measuring and developing these ideas. In the early 1980s, she and her colleagues became interested in how attachment dispositions might be transmitted from parent to child. The Adult Attachment Interview (AAI) (George et al., 1996) is a semi-structured, psychodynamically informed instrument that asks parents to describe their childhood relationships with their own parents. The interview elicits a general description of the relationship, the outcomes of care-seeking when distressed, and instances of rejection, separation, and loss.

The interview places great importance on vivid detail. Participants are first asked for up to five adjectives to describe their primary caregivers – e.g., 'loving', 'busy', 'normal Mum', 'away a lot'. They are then probed to flesh these out with specific illustrative incidents and anecdotes that bring them to life. By bringing to mind emotionally charged experiences of distress and threat, the adult's attachment system is activated.

When Main and her colleagues began their work, they thought that it would be the *content* of the parents' responses that were significant, e.g., experiences of rejection in childhood might lead a mother to reject her own child. But they were struck instead by differences in the ways adults *talked about* their childhood attachment experiences. Because the interview itself activated the attachment system, the *way* parents spoke about the past – their discourse style – revealed patterns of defence and adaptation comparable to the behavioural patterns of defence and adaptation seen with children in the SSP.

The AAI was famously described by Main as a 'move to the level of representation', focusing on how attachment is 'represented' in the mind, rather than, as in the pre-verbal SSP, manifest in observed behaviours. As described in relation to earned security, it was how parents *spoke about and remembered* their attachments – rather than adversity as such – that differentiated one group from another. And it was these differences in the *organisation of attachment narratives*, rather than their content, that predicted the child's attachment classification. As Main put it, the interview 'surprises the unconscious' into revealing an individual's 'state of mind in relation to attachment' (Main et al., 1985).

Main observed that some parents were able to speak coherently and openly about their childhood experiences, with access to both positive and negative affect. Their narratives were free from either defensive efforts to suppress affects or memories or being overwhelmed and flooded by them. These parents were classified 'secure', and their children were highly likely to be secure in the SSP. By contrast, some parents remembered little, stifled their responses or denied difficulty, even when reporting dire experiences. This was the 'dismissing' (avoidant) pattern: affect and memory were suppressed, resulting in constricted, barren narratives. In the third group, parents' narratives were incoherent and vague, with memories and raw affect flooding the story, efforts to contain and regulate them unsuccessful. This was the 'preoccupied' (anxious/resistant) pattern. Both were strongly correlated with organised attachment insecurity in the child.[3] These defensive patterns, as revealed in adult attachment narratives, compromised the parent's capacity to respond to the attachment needs of her child.

Main's efforts to make sense of interview transcripts were helped by another serendipitous discovery, post-dating the initial drafts of the AAI. This was the linguistic philosopher Grice's analysis of efficient and effective conversational styles. 'Grice's Maxims' (Grice, 1975) maintain that rational, cooperative, and coherent conversations are implicitly shaped by four precepts:

a. 'Be truthful and have evidence for what you say' (maxim of *quality*)

b. 'Be succinct yet complete' (*quantity* maxim)

c. 'Be relevant' (*relational* maxim)

d. 'Be clear and orderly' (maxim of *manner*).

The coding of AAI transcripts runs along Gricean lines. Features of 'secure/free-autonomous' discourse include: coherence; freshness (vivid imagery rather than stale or clichéd discourse); appropriate amounts of detail (the 'Goldilocks' mid-range criterion of neither too little nor too much, but 'just right', cf. Beebe et al. (2012)); correspondence between affect and content.

Insecure stories, by contrast, violate Grice's Maxims. They lack spontaneity, rely on hackneyed and tired language; are self-contradictory; are short on vivid detail; teem with trivia;[4] are confused about tenses so it is unclear whether discourse refers to the present or the past; have breaks in logical sequence; lurch incoherently from one seemingly unrelated topic to another.

Therapeutic Conversations

The principles implicit in the AAI have a number of implications for therapeutic conversations.

The use of the AAI in psychotherapy

We begin with the question as to whether the AAI is *itself* a useful tool for psychotherapists. Today, many psychotherapists administer all or part of the AAI at the start of therapy (see Steele & Steele, 2008) so as to observe the attachment dynamic and discover some of its historical roots. Whether or not this is part of a formal assessment procedure, we believe that psychotherapy assessment interviews can in most cases usefully incorporate the AAI 'five adjectives and illustrative episodes' rubric.

Asking potential psychotherapy patients to think of appropriate words to describe the relationship with their parents, backed up with episodes that bring these descriptors to life, has a number of immediately beneficial effects. It denotes the therapist's keen interest in the 'minute particulars' (Hobson, 1985) of a person's life. It encourages patients to begin to look back on themselves and their experiences with a detached yet sympathetic eye. Where this is problematic, as it often is, this points to the trauma and pain triggered by 'freshness' and detail in recollection, which are therefore avoided. Attention to detail and accurate recall gives the important message that therapy's project is to contextualise present difficulties in the light of past experience.

The listening stance

Perhaps the most important implication of Main's work on the AAI is that attachment-informed therapists attend not just to the *content* of the patients' narratives, but to the *style and manner* of their speech. Main (1995) describes a 'fluid attentional style' and its concomitant verbal manifestations as hallmarks of secure attachment. The secure child can move from playing alone to noticing his mother's presence, exchanging words with her, bringing a sibling into a game, etc. Secure-making therapists too need to cultivate the capacity to 'zoom' seamlessly from 'close-up' detail (e.g., the patient's fidgeting hands) to the wider picture (empathy for the feeling all alone and unsupported in the therapy room).

Therapists' job-description entails listening at many levels, both to themselves and to their patients. First are the clients' presenting stories themselves, the symptoms they bring for alleviation, together with a childhood history, episodes of neglect or trauma, all of which need to be described, brought to life, fleshed out, and acknowledged. Meanwhile, the therapist will note, AAI-fashion, *how* the subject tells her story. She will especially be on the look-out for the freshness and coherence of fluid-autonomous discourse, and may intervene to try to move the conversation towards the speech rhythms and patterns of secure attachment:

'Hang on a minute, you're going a bit too fast for me.'

'Can you say all that again? I can't quite visualise what you are describing there.'

'I've got the outline of the story, but can't quite grasp what it was like for you and how you felt when your father came home drunk every night...'

Therapists will also be noting their own reactions to the story – sympathy, detachment, anger, tearfulness, etc. This countertransference can also be seen as an 'internal' self-to-self conversation drawing on therapists' capacity to regulate and find appropriate words for their affect-experience. This can then be put to therapeutic use:

'You described the sudden death of your father in a very factual way, and I could picture it all pretty clearly, yet I found myself welling up with sadness at the shock and horror of it all, and I wonder if similar feelings have lain dormant in you ever since.'

Inner speech

The focus on narrative quality that is at the heart of AAI analysis also alerts therapists to the nature and quality of inner speech, and particularly the *self's relationship to itself*. In the example above, the therapist describes *his own* inner dialogue to the client. The therapist is standing back and reflecting on his own self-experience, using this as a potential means to understand the client's feeling. Mentalising, so central to psychotherapeutic work, offers the patient a window into the realm of inner speech. In the attachment model, the inner or subjective self is structured on the basis of primary relational experiences. If accurate and compassionate affect co-regulation has been the rule, the subject is likely to be able to *be* a subjective self: to experience, tolerate, name, and process their own feelings, however painful or scary, and to give voice to them when necessary. When affect-expression has been punished or discouraged, or felt to be chaotically overwhelming, the subjective self is correspondingly diminished and constricted. There will be a shying away from experiencing and naming feelings, or a tendency to project them outwards, or feel them as emanating from a repudiated 'alien' part of the self.

In psychotherapy with adults, the subjective self, or self-in-relation-to-self, is a central theme. The therapist here is not so much a 'real' 'external' attachment figure as a transferential representation of the sub-optimal caregiver. But in the context of emerging secure attachment, the therapist begins to represent a hitherto missing *interlocutor in the inner world*. Mears (2005) notes that children aged 3–5 have externalised inner conversations as they play 'alone in the presence of the mother'. Therapeutic 'dialogue' too can be thought of as an externalised inner conversation, i.e., an inner monologue hitherto excluded or avoided. The self is beginning to talk to itself. That avoided but longed-for conversation emerges as part of rebuilding primary attachment experience. The therapist represents the part of the self that knows itself better than it is consciously aware of, just as mothers 'know' their children before they have developed the self-awareness and language to articulate their feelings.

Patients often express surprise that their therapists are able to remember seemingly minor details of their life-story. But it is not that therapists are endowed with superior memorising abilities; rather that they are in the observing, parent-with-playing-child *role*. In the re-awakened sensitive period set in train by therapy, the 'borrowed brain' of the therapist modulates unstable PFC/amygdala cortisol-mediated fight/flight/fright tendencies, so that a playful inner dialogue becomes possible, sometimes for the first time. Let's illustrate this with an example, not from the clinic but from Wagner's opera-drama the Ring cycle.

Wotan and Brunnhilde: Finding the self in conversation

In *Die Walküre*, Wotan, ruler of the Gods, is confronted by his jealous wife Fricka's rage at his profligate infidelity. She is particularly affronted at his having fathered a child, Siegmund, by Erda, the earth Goddess.

Siegmund has fallen in love with a married woman, Sieglinde, wife of Hunding, the hunter, a violent and abusive man. Fricka insists that Wotan ensure that Siegmund dies in the ensuing husband–lover fight, as the law of the Gods requires. Depressed, bound by his 'superego' (an external constraint of conditional security, i.e., Fricka's message that she will only love him if he does her bidding), forced to choose between his child and his wife (the 'wicked stepmother, a prevalent theme in folk literature and family therapy) Wotan reluctantly agrees to his wife's demand bound by his superego's insecure attachment message that love is conditional.

But now Wotan's beloved daughter, Brunnhilde, another illegitimate child, and leader of the women-warriors the Valkyrie, appears at Wotan's side. Brunnhilde sees that her father is deeply unhappy and in his heart of hearts wants to save his son Siegmund. She asks:

> 'Father, father, tell me what is troubling you? How your worries upset your child! Confide in me, I am loyal to you.'

He now confesses – in terms instantly transposable to psychotherapy – that she has indeed seen into his heart:

> 'I only talk to myself when I talk to you.'

Finally, Wotan obeys Fricka and destroys Siegmund's power, thereby allowing Hunding to kill him. But he has also listened, with Brunnhilde's help, to the dictates of his heart, and saves the life of pregnant Sieglinde. The child she and Siegmund have created, his grandson, is destined to become the future hero, Siegfried.

Wagner's 'outcome' is far from a happy-ever-after fairy story; rather, it is a tragic compromise where difficult feelings are acknowledged, a balance between desire and reality is struck, and where pain can be managed and life go on. Fricka is satisfied – Siegmund must die; but so too is Wotan – Siegfried lives on to fight another day.

'*I only talk to myself when I talk to you*' could be a motto for the inner world-space of adult psychotherapy. In his moment of crisis, Brunnhilde *knows her guilt-driven father better than he knows himself*, as does the caregiver of a securely attached infant, and, at times, therapists their patients.

Speech acts

The AAI–SSP link and the role of inner speech just described show how inextricable are the links between thought, speech, inner and outer, and action, and how all three arise in a relational context, secure or insecure, mediated and motivated by language. We move now to thinking about the *performative* – as opposed to informative – role of language (Austin, 1962), and particularly the ways that *speech acts,* as they are known, shed light upon underlying attachment dynamics.

As Freud's compatriot Wittgenstein (1969) pointed out, as well as conveying information, speech is also an *action*. Language is one of the ways in which participants in a conversation structure their relationship, no less palpable than an 'actual' action,[5] such as a kiss or a punch. Thus in the concluding 'speech act' of a meeting, the Chair will pronounce that 'this meeting is now closed'; similarly an analyst after 50 minutes will say 'time's up'. These statements do not merely convey information, they also enact a change of scene and trigger reciprocal reactions in their recipients – moving from introspective free association to more informal off-the-couch 'chat', assembling papers into folders, rising from the couch, commenting on the weather, etc.

Alessandro Talia, Sarah Daniel, and their colleagues (Talia et al., 2014) have studied the relationship between speech acts in therapy sessions and attachment. They analysed transcripts of psychotherapy sessions where client's AAI status had been previously established. They found striking correlations between the *patterns of therapeutic conversations and patients' attachment status*. AAI-rated secure clients demonstrate relatively unconstrained dialogue with their therapists. The conversation moves in creative ways towards mutual influence and provisional agreement – reaching out from disparate viewpoints towards a 'fusion of horizons' (cf. D. Stern, 2010).

Contrastingly, insecure subjects manifest rigid, non-interactive discourse patterns. Dismissive subjects tend to downplay distress and ward off therapists' attempts to acknowledge and regulate their feelings.

A patient might be talking about an argument with his girlfriend.

Th: It sounds as though you felt really upset by her inability to see your point of view.

P: Well, no not really, it doesn't matter; all couples have rows don't they? [back-tracking and minimising the problem]

The effect of the patient's speech act is to distance and push the therapist away, so maintaining the internal status quo. The client remains 'safely' – but constrainedly – within the confines of his own assumption-determined world (i.e., *when you really need help there's no one there for you*). Change is dialogically blocked.

The therapist at this point might venture:

'Perhaps there is a parallel with what's going on here between us – I reach out to you, but you push me away. Sometimes I feel I'm pretty useless to you. Maybe the same sort of thing goes on with your girlfriend. Your seeming self-sufficiency provokes her to create a row; then at least she has your emotional attention, albeit in a negative way.'

If the patient then seems more able to respond to this comment by offering an elaboration and providing more detail or association, the therapist might go on to suggest:

'This reminds me of what you've said about your relationship with your mother. You've said she wasn't very much 'there' for you when you were in distress as a child. 'Home base' for you is 'splendid isolation', excluding others, even when they are making efforts to get close to you.'

Were the therapist to offer all of these comments in one gulp, we might suspect that *her* non-dialogic speech act was driven by the very problem she was trying to surmount – a 'self-representing event' (Hobson, 2015), or countertransference enactment. Such 'little lectures' are a typical therapeutic response to patient distancing. But, however clumsily, the therapist is drawing on 'meaning-making' links between therapist/client linguistic patterns and putative caregiver/care-seeker interaction in the patient's past. She is working on the hypothesis that should she see his rage and vulnerability, rather than distress being alleviated through affect co-regulation, further neglect, shame, or exploitation would result. Distancing speech acts are used to keep the therapist at bay. Self-sufficiency is clung to as the safest strategy, however lonely it may feel.

At the other end of the insecure attachment spectrum, subjects classified as 'preoccupied' on the AAI tend to express inchoate feelings, embedded in time-elusive, un-distanced, un-contextualised narratives. Attempts by therapists to introduce structure or change perspectives are resisted, often by 'not hearing' what the therapist has said or by active disagreement. This can be compared with the 'resistant' child in the SSP whose distress seems un-soothable, ensuring forced attention from an inconsistent parent, but with inhibition of exploratory play. The patient might say:

> 'I'm having an awful time at work; my boss is never around and I have to make decisions all by myself, and on the rare occasions he is there, he tears me off a strip for telephoning clients without first checking with him.'

The therapist tries to pin down the time sequence as well as moving in a problem-solving direction, e.g. by saying:

> 'Is this still going on now, or is there a particular incident you are describing?'

Or:

> 'Can we think together about how you might have handled the situation differently?'

The preoccupied client might simply ignore this overture and continue in the same vein:

> 'He really is horrible and insensitive, but what am I to do? There are no jobs going in our area at the moment and I know if I breathe the slightest criticism I'll be out on my ear.'

The client's 'speech act' discounts the therapist's interventions as though they haven't been heard, just as attempts at soothing by the mother of the resistant child fuel further crying and back-arching. Interactive discourse is inhibited, leaving the therapist forced either to agree/collude with the client or remain silent or unheard. An attachment-minded therapist might then venture:

> 'Let's think about what's going on right now. I get the feeling – *my* "ear" [picking up on the client's "out on my ear" metaphor] tells me – that you mistrust attempts on my part to think in detail about all this, or fear I will minimise your distress. Maybe you worry that if you were to become calm I might immediately lose interest.'

And then later, perhaps:

> 'That reminds me of how you described your father when you were young. For him no news was good news; however much you tried to gain his attention, he seemed not to want to know, especially when you got pregnant in your teens and then were dumped by your boyfriend.'

This conversation might be described as the 'battle of the speech acts'. The client tries to secure a modicum of attention via ignoring or overriding the therapist, while the therapist attempts to overcome this defence by inviting the client to join her in a meta-perspective on their conversation. The outcome of this struggle will depend ultimately on the attachment ambiance of the therapy and the extent to which the client feels sufficiently 'held' to be able to risk giving up entrenched patterns of maladaptive security-seeking. Crucial here is the therapist's capacity to create conversational engagement and mutual influence, in which, to use Malan's (1979) metaphor, the participants 'leapfrog' one another dialogically, turn and turn about.

Subject positions

In 'positioning theory', sociolinguists Davies & Harré (1990) describe the ways that individuals in dialogue use language to negotiate 'subject positions' or identities for themselves (Avdie, 2008, 2012). From this perspective, the self is viewed as a polyphonic assemblage of differing voices, representations, and points of view. Psychological health entails two contrasting yet related capacities: the ability to move comfortably from one position or inner voice to another, and the sense of a central ego able to orchestrate these varying voices into a coherent whole.

The idea of multiple selves resonates with Main's idea of fluid attentional style as a mark of secure attachment, transposed into the self-to-self realm of the inner world. The need for an executive ego points to the importance of 'exploration' or agency, discussed in the previous chapter, since effective action necessarily flows from a central motivational core. In insecure attachment, subjects are often confined to one or other rigid subject position, resulting in stereotypical narrative patterns in which the 'same old story' is repeated irrespective of circumstances.

Sandy's outrage

Sandy arrived for her session late, complaining that she had had to reverse her car 'miles' down a narrow lane because the oncoming vehicle refused to go back, even though it was much nearer to a passing-place than she. There was a tone of outrage in her voice. She then described a dream in which she was humiliated by having to crawl across the floor to beg for some food. Next, she complained that even though she had to go on a work trip, and so would be missing the next session, she was still expected to pay the fee.

Sandy here appeared to be stuck in a 'subject position' in which she was the victim of *force majeure*. She was out of touch with her own agency: her capacity to wave the oncoming driver back; the possibility of negotiating with the therapist about waiving the fee for planned non-attendance (a wave/waive pun lurks here; perhaps a tsunami of rage underlies both). Such subject positions are inherently relational: for every victim there is an oppressor – or back-down refuser! Ryle (1990) calls this relational aspect 'reciprocal role procedures'. People trapped in 'subject positions' may occupy either 'end', or pole, of a 'procedure'. This patient, while complaining about her victimhood, actually made the therapist feel slightly victimised, cast in the role of an inflexible money-grubber.

Moving from habitual organised insecure patterns to the openness and fluidity of security does not come easily. As with the speech acts, attempts to shift patients away from stereotyped subject positions and to view situations from an alternative point of view are often strenuously resisted.

Sandy, continued

Th: Some analysts see the 'characters' in dreams as different manifes-tations of the dreamer's self. Maybe there's a hidden coercive part of you, wanting to inflict the humiliation on others that you yourself have undergone. Then at least they'll know what it feels like to be made to 'crawl'. I notice that you haven't explored whether I might be a bit flexible about the fee; you never know, I might be more amenable to negotiation than you imagine. By perpetuating humilia-tion on yourself at least you are at some level in control of the pain, rather than exposing yourself to the uncertainty of my response.

P: Oh come on, that's rubbish, I know perfectly well you won't budge an inch!

An attachment-informed approach sees these rigid subject positions as arising out of what Bowlby (1979) called 'defensive exclusion'. The patient described above needed to block out, or 'exclude', her sense of agency, her anger, and her exploratory capacities for fear that, were they in evidence, she would be even further rejected and left to fend for herself. The need for crumbs of attachment security, however seemingly threadbare or self-defeating, tops all. Transposed backwards in time, this is true: infants must grasp at even a bare modicum of protection and nurturance if they are not to die, physically and emotionally. That dynamic can carry over into adult life. For Sandy, her transferential expectations were that if she asked for a fee reduction, she would be summar-ily dismissed, or seen, Oliver Twist-like, despite her love-starvation, as greedily 'asking for more'.

If therapy goes well, the patient comes to feel that a more secure attachment dynamic can be relied upon, and that distress or anger or neediness will, as with the 'horizontally-oriented', mind-minded secure parent and her child, be sympathetically and safely responded to. This opens the way to self-exploration. Disavowed parts of the self, jettisoned for the sake of minimal security, can be reclaimed. Guided by the therapist, and sometimes backed up by meditation/ mindfulness practice, patients acquire the skills to think about their thoughts and feelings as they arise in body and mind. No longer trapped in rigid subject positions, a broader scope of self and sense of agency gradually come to the fore. Just as novice pianists learn to notice and control their hands and fingers separately yet concertedly, so patients gradually gain self-awareness and control of their multifaceted self.

Language and the body

Attachment in infants is a psychosomatic phenomenon, mediated by mother– child biobehavioural synchrony. The distressed infant cries; sound waves impinge on the mother's auditory system. The child raises her arms; mother moves to maximise proximity. She picks the child up; her warmth, synchro- nous heartbeat, protective arms, soothing voice, and proffered breast or bottle together serve in an integrated way to soothe the child's distress. Once alleviated, the child returns to scaffolded self-sufficiency and her own goal- directed explorations.

These somatic aspects of attachment are never fully relinquished. Adults – romantic partners, grown-up children and their parents, comrades in sport or arms – are impelled by seemingly unseen forces to hug one another at times of great distress and jubilation. Mobile/cell-phone and Skype links facilitate attachment electronically across distances, but remain ultimately mediated through the speech systems and visual/aural interaction.

The neuroscientist Wolpert (Wolpert & Ghahramani, 2000) provocatively asks: why do animals need a nervous system? Our fellow life-forms – plants, fungi, and bacteria – manage without; among life on earth, why are animals alone equipped with brains? The answer is that nervous systems are neces- sary for *movement*, the mechanism by which muscles are coordinated and directed. Speech and language depend on muscle movements – tongue, vocal cords, and mouth – set in train by messages from the brain. Language and thought itself – internal language – are biobehavioural phenomena.

In their exposition of *embodied cognition* Fonagy and Target (2007) criti- cise Bowlby's phrase 'internal working models' for its reliance on an outdated neo-Cartesian computer metaphor of mind/body, in which thinking equates to software, and the physical properties of the brain to hardware. They argue instead that *all* thinking, however seemingly abstract, is 'embodied'. We think as much with our hearts and hormones, guts and muscles, as with our brains (Damasio, 1999), operating in concert. There are robust links between vagal tone and security of attachment (Porges, 2011), while an over- or under- reacting HPA axis (a mark of hormonal responses to stress) is an enduring residue of childhood trauma (Stovall-McClough & Dozier, 2016). Freud's aphorism remains valid: 'the ego is first and foremost a bodily ego' (Freud, 1923: 25–26).

Seen this way, speech and meaning are not arbitrary semiotic systems, equivalent to computer 'languages', but have their roots in specific bodily experience. Psycho-linguists Lakoff and Johnson (2003) argue that metaphors we use to describe the world, and our place in it, arise mainly in the body (see too Werner & Kaplan, 1963). A classic therapy-relevant example is the use of the vertical metaphor of 'up'/'down' to describe emotional states. When we are cheerful, our head is in the air (or sometimes 'in the clouds', 'on cloud nine'), we can 'eyeball' our problems, we are 'upright' and have a 'straight back', and are 'in good standing'. Depressed, we are 'laid low', 'under the weather', carrying the 'weight of the world on our shoulders'.

Back-translating these metaphors to the psychosomatic unity of youth, the child who is 'up and running' can seek help when needed, whereas the one who is 'stuck' and 'rooted to the ground' is vulnerable and in need of immediate succor. In the consulting room, a therapist might express his difficulty in understanding what the client is saying: '*I don't seem to have anything to hold onto here.*' Following Lakoff and Johnson, this could be summarised as '*understanding is grasping*'; a child needs a physically available parent whose hand they can hold if they are to develop 'epistemic trust'.

A depressed person might say '*I don't seem to be able to find a way forward*'; here '*learning is a journey*', a movement from A to B, best performed with the help of a trusted companion. Another attachment-related example might be a therapist saying to a client '*I think I can* nearly *see what you are driving at*', i.e., '*attention is proximity*'. Attentiveness implies a secure-making and proximate – approxi*mate* – caregiver (whose understanding is trying to 'mate' with the care-seeker's utterances).

Hiding Peter

The direction of travel from talk to body can be two-way: a bearded patient, who typically evaded his emotional pain by convoluted talk, arrived for his session clean-shaven. '*Ah*', said the analyst. '*I see you've decided to come clean at last!*' (Note the word 'decided' – the analyst emphasising agency as a mark of secure attachment.) On further exploration it emerged that his new girlfriend, later to become wife, had plucked up the courage to express her objections to his hirsute visage.

Here is an example from child psychotherapy where the coordinates of family 'longitude and latitude', literal and metaphorical, were tragically confused.

Winston topsy-turvy

Winston had already been excluded several times from school by the age of 8 for disruptive behaviour. He was 'accident prone', frequently falling over and hurting himself (these injuries were not thought to be parent-inflicted). During weekdays he lived with his mother, her new partner and several step- and half-siblings. His father had remarried but had had an 'ex-tra'-marital affair with his ex-wife, resulting in Winston's conception. At weekends Winston was parceled out from one family to the other.

During a psychotherapy session he suddenly and inexplicably fell off his chair, banging his head. The therapist had a flash of insight: in his chaotic and shapeless family, this little boy didn't know which way was up or down, left or right, coming or going. She suggested he make a drawing or 'map' of all the people in his family, and who 'belonged' to whom. She gradually tried to help him see where the lines of authority and security might lie in this complex family constellation, suggesting how important his role was as a tie between his two families, and a reminder of the once-strong love that brought him into being.

Here is another example of the use of a Lakoff and Johnson-type metaphor in therapy and its relationship to somatic experience.

Bryan's gate

Bryan was a farmer. He was 10 minutes late for his session. He apologised, saying that someone had forgotten to shut the gate into a field and, as a result, his horse had escaped into the lane; he couldn't leave for his session until the adventurous equine had been corralled back into its rightful place.

All this is very straightforward and clear – and a seemingly good reason for being late. And yet ... there was something else. In the previous session he had uncharacteristically abandoned his habitual stiff-upper-lip and cried copiously when describing a painful bereavement. Was the horse story, the therapist mused aloud, perhaps also the patient's way of referring back to the dangers of 'opening emotional flood-gates', and his wish to bottle up his feelings, to be 'left alone' with them in the 'missing' 10 minutes of the session?

As in every therapeutic conversation, there are two stories: one, in Langer's (1951) terms, 'discursive', factual, sequential, everyday; the other 'non-discursive': affect-related, tangential, symbolic, 'left-field' – and also given to puns – since it appears that here we have a story about a horse that had left its field!

The Lakoff and Johnson argument can be taken further. The depiction of affect through language does not just hark back to childhood states in which body and mind are not yet clearly differentiated. Conversational style betrays its bodily referents and origins through its shape and form. The sound-wave properties of words themselves, and especially the tone and timbre with which they are expressed, are the channel through which feelings are communicated. Some words, even if in languages unknown to the listener, are onomatopoetically experienced as 'jagged' and 'sharp' and reverberating, others 'smooth' and 'soft' and undulating. How words are 'delivered' bring these qualities out further. A study based on relating vocal utterances of therapists to their content divided interventions into *'validating/mirroring'* and *'challenging'* ones (Weiste & Peräkylä, 2014). The former showed a continuity between therapist's and patient's vocal pitch, whereas in 'challenging' interventions the therapist tended to adopt a higher tonal range,[6] as though to say, overriding responses limited to empathic resonance, 'now let's look at this *differently'*.

Contradiction and ambivalence – humour and irony – become expressible in the interplay between lexical meaning and non-verbal musicality. The classic Batesonian 'double bind' (Bateson et al., 1956) identified conflicting messages from parents of psychotic adolescents, who verbally express invitation and love, yet non-verbally indicate rejection. Contrariwise, contradictions can encompass tender amusement and love: a mother might soothe and transcend her own irritation towards the night cries of our familiar distressed child by saying in a loving and calming voice, *'Oh you are a horrible child aren't you, waking your poor mummy up when she was in the middle of such a lovely dream?'* Good therapists tend to be sensitive to, and skilled in the deployment of, these contradictions and dissonances, and their resolution.

Practice Implications

The meanings that psychotherapists establish with their clients go beyond and behind dictionary definitions, to a lexicon of personal resonances and idiographic references unique to that individual. The word 'mother' can be universally defined as a specific biological relationship between an offspring and its progenitor, but for each person the overtones and images and instances conjured up by the word will vary. This person-specific 'idiolect' (Lear, 2011) builds up a picture of a particular mother, in relation to a unique child, in distinct familial circumstances and social context. Therapy entails creating for each individual a bespoke developmental 'diagnosis', brought to life by examples from memory, by the therapist's imaginings of the patient's childhood experiences, and often enacted in transferential analogues. Together these provide an explanatory framework for thinking about current difficulties, with possible pointers – 'exits' (Ryle, 1990) – to their alleviation.

Life's journey[7] is constrained by certain bio-social universals: the helplessness of infancy; the need for enveloping family support; parental 'scaffolding';

'epistemic trust' and pedagogic encouragement; protection and security; sex and reproduction; status anxiety; competition for resources, with concomitant aggression; illness, decline, and death. Attachment-informed approaches highlight some (but not necessarily all) of these, especially the search for security, the relationship imperative, and the need for affect co-regulation. Based on awareness of early-established developmental pathways, the skilful therapist helps clients towards 'self-diagnosis', an objectification of a lived life. This is a first step away from immersion in misery, doubt, and despair, and towards the freedom which stepping back, however momentarily, from oneself brings.

The journey of this chapter has been from participant listening or mentalised participation, to the dance of the therapeutic speech acts, subject positions, and the metaphors that arise as the conversation unfolds. For Lacan (1977), humans are *parle-êtres*, 'speaking beings'. Therapists' observations of tone of voice, discourse style, unconsciously invoked metaphors, and interactive verbal patterns enable them to generate hypotheses about the patients' early attachment experiences, and how these form a template for subsequent relationships. But therapy is always a two-way street, a con-versation (a *'together turning-around'*), even if it is ultimately a 'dialogue for one' in which the subjects begin to listen to and learn from themselves.

We have suggested that secure parent–infant interactions tend to be 'mid-range', along a number of dimensions:

- *arousal* (over-stimulus vs. disengagement)

- *proximity* ('looming' vs. inaccessibility)

- *toleration of silence* (creating a space – *'time is space'* – for spontaneous thought, but not so long that it becomes persecutory)

- *contingent lead-taking* (control vs. laissez-faire)

- *play* (arising out of 'partially contingent or inexact mirroring', artistic rather than autistic).

It is likely that effective therapists – mainly procedurally and non-consciously – bring these principles into their therapeutic conversations. As one patient succinctly put it: '*My therapist brings me up when I'm down, and down when I'm up.*' Since mood impacts on speed and volume of discourse, therapists tend to 'pull' the tone, volume, and rate of their depressed patients' speech towards the mid-range, themselves modelling slightly louder, faster, less slurred talk. Conversely, over-active speech may need to be slowed down, moved from staccato to legato, and appropriately modulated, so that the sadness underlying manic pseudo-happiness becomes evident and accessible.[8]

But perhaps our exposition has moved ahead of itself (*stories are journeys*), from 'explanatory framework' to 'change-promotion'. The therapeutic interventions thus far described encompass two interrelated projects: developing an individualised explanatory framework for sufferers' difficulties; and using the therapeutic conversation to instigate care-seeker/caregiver affect regulation, typically absent currently and historically for the patient.

The affect-regulatory vector of therapy depends largely on the therapist's capacity for empathic resonance. This has a mimetic aspect, in which the therapist non-consciously reproduces in miniature the subject's facial musculature and body posture. This, via internal self-monitoring feedback, yields information for the therapist about how the subject 'might be feeling', which can then be put into words. This provides the 'holding' needed for effective affect regulation. A verbal – or sometimes pictorial or musical – story moves pain and trauma from the right to the left brain, making it available for mentalising and objectification.

Both are precursors to affect *self*-regulation on the part of the patient, but not at the expense (as happens in avoidant attachment) of the capacity to ask for help and comfort when needed, the hallmarks of independent/autonomous living. But there is more to therapy than empathy. The manner and timing of interventions (cf. Lemma, Roth, & Pilling, 2014) are crucial components of therapeutic skill. For therapists, there is a time and a place for mirroring, for describing, for empathising, for silence, for voicing one's inner thoughts, for challenge, and for interpretations. All this may be relatively straightforward when working with the organised forms of insecurity; even when, as is inevitable, one sometimes gets things wrong, it is unlikely to have disastrous consequences. But when faced with more complex cases of 'disorganised insecurity', effective therapy needs more specific tools, both theoretical and practical. It is to these we now turn.

Summary

- The Adult Attachment Interview links linguistic patterns with underlying attachment dispositions.

- Therapists listen for attachment dynamics in therapeutic conversations.

- Psychotherapy helps clients to generate and listen to their inner self-to-self speech.

- As participant observers, therapists need to be alert to the speech acts and subject positions they and their clients adopt, and the attachment information these reveal.

- Language is metaphorical, and metaphors ultimately derive from the body; attachment relationships are bodily in their origins.

- Therapists are sensitive to the ways in which language both reveals and conceals attachment orientations.

Notes

1. This applies even to 'non-verbal' therapies such as art, music, or dance therapies, which counterpoint with periods of reflection and discussion.
2. Freud's 'nothing' is enigmatic: the unconscious is a 'no thing' that contains 'every thing'. Attachment attempts to understand the physiology and evolutionary pressures behind the 'airy nothings' that shape our loves. But their final manifestation, we agree, is words.
3. Disorganised infant attachment has its adult analogue in 'unresolved' discourse patterns, to be explored in the next chapter.
4. Note, however, that from a psychodynamic perspective, 'trivial' aspects of speech are no less significant than apparent relevance and clarity – everything, however peripheral-seeming, is grist to the mill. Hence the psychodynamic maxim: 'nothing never happens'.
5. Literally, of course, speech, which involves movement of the muscles of lungs, throat and mouth, *is* an action
6. In musical terms, this could be seen, as in 'classical' form, as the introduction of the 'second subject'.
7. Another Lakoff and Johnson trope – *'life is a journey'*. Movement – with its neurological underpinnings – action, and agency are intrinsic to being alive; depression and misery betoken *stasis*; therapy's job is to remobilise and inspire hope-filled *progress* towards goals, achievable or otherwise.
8. And, as is sometimes necessary with hypomanic clients, the use of mobile phones for investment deals in the midst of sessions discouraged!

10

'Disorganised Insecurity'

Attachment Approaches to Complex Disorders

It is a sad fact that the course of true therapy never does run smooth, especially when its subjects suffer from complex and severe disorders, e.g., borderline and other personality disorders, life-threatening eating disorders, and the different forms of psychosis. We have considered the role of synchrony, affect regulation, mirroring, play, listening, and language in therapy. But sometimes these bare essentials are insufficient. There are clients who fail to turn up for sessions, are unremittingly depressed or deluded, disparage or unrealistically idealise therapy, are unreasonably demanding, become chronically dependent without signs of progress or change, break boundaries, harm themselves, come to sessions drunk or 'high', have to be admitted to hospital, starve or binge, drop out, or even – tragically and every therapist's worst nightmare – commit suicide.

To pause this litany, these tend to be people suffering from psychiatric disorders desperately in need of effective therapies to help them recover, or at least live with and survive the devastations of psychological illness. For their part, their therapists, despite best intentions, may at times feel unheard, angry, frightened, erotically stimulated, overridden, side-lined, squeezed out, overvalued, seduced, colluded with, in despair, or hopelessly confused. Such disparaging epithets represent therapists' attempts to deal with their own feelings of failure by subtle forms of blame. But, as the outdoor sports brochures say, there is no such thing as bad weather, only walkers without appropriate protective clothing.

In this chapter we show how the discovery of disorganised attachment helps develop a framework for understanding and working with 'difficultness' in therapy. Specifically, we look at how attachment approaches provide the necessary protection for therapists, as well as generating relevant formulations and suggesting effective interventions.

The Disorganised and Unresolved (D/U) Categories of Attachment

Main and Solomon's (1990) identification of the third insecure attachment type, disorganised/disoriented (D), marked a major advance in the evolution of attachment theory. To recap, this discovery followed the observation that certain children could not be reliably classified in the SSP's tripartite system. Upon separation and reunion in the SSP, this group showed some or all of the following: odd postures or contradictory behaviours (such as collapsing upon reunion), apprehension, stereotypies, trance-like expressions, freezing, disorientation, and/or repetitive hand and head movements. The D pattern is relatively infrequent in non-clinical groups (Bakermans-Kranenburg & van IJzendoorn, 2009). By contrast, maltreatment and high levels of accumulated socioeconomic risk (low maternal education, young maternal age at childbirth, single parenthood, minority group status, and substance use) predict high rates of disorganised attachment (Cyr et al., 2010). Longitudinal studies have consistently linked D classification in infancy with psychopathology or psychiatric disturbance in adolescence and early adulthood (Carlson, 1998; Lyons-Ruth & Jacobvitz, 2016; van IJzendoorn & Bakermans-Kranenburg, 2009).

Coincident with the development and validation of the D classification system, Main and her colleagues noted that just as there were SSPs that could not be coded using the tripartite system, there were AAIs that could not be coded with the AAI system (Main & Hesse, 1990). There were a number of interviews in which subjects became disoriented while describing experiences of loss. Such 'lapses in the monitoring of reasoning or discourse' (Hesse, 2016) revealed themselves in a number ways: e.g., the speaker might refer to a dead person in the present, 'alive' tense; or shift into a different vocal register; or speak in a eulogistic or funereal manner. Main and Hesse designated this the 'unresolved' or U pattern. Although first noted in relation to unresolved mourning and loss, it was later found in descriptions of other traumatic experiences, such as neglect and abuse (Lyons-Ruth et al., 2005). In such cases, 'raw experience' (aversive imagery, unprovoked panic, etc.) intrudes into and disrupts memory, consciousness, and the sense of time and reality. Note that unlike dismissing and preoccupied AAI classifications, which are identified from discourse style rather than content, U is a content *and* process-based measure. Also, lapses in monitoring may occur in a small number of passages dealing specifically with loss or trauma, or pervade the whole interview.

D and U are of relevance to clinicians because they highlight the developmental origins, discourse styles, and relational patterns of the pathological states found in the more severely disturbed patients who seek therapy.

As empirical categories they have been shown to be valid and reliable (Hesse, 2016). We shall use the composite designation D/U to characterise the states of mind and relational dispositions typical of 'difficult' clients, especially those diagnosed as suffering from personality disorder. While this begs a number of unresolved research and nosological issues (Rutter, Kreppner, & Sonuga-Barke, 2009), the portmanteau term 'D/U' is a useful approximation for clinicians.

It is likely that neither D nor U have specific aetiological origins, but reflect a spectrum of severe developmental difficulties. A number of conceptualisations have been proposed:

1. *Approach/avoidance model.* Main and Hesse's (1990) original idea, subsequently expanded by Liotti (2004), focused on the 'disorientation' observed in D infants, which these authors see as a form of dissociation arising from an insoluble 'approach–avoidance dilemma'. The attachment dynamic is activated in these children when facing threat or loss, and they are thereby impelled to seek out a secure base. But if the secure base (i.e., parent) is her- or himself the very source of the loss or threat, this presents an insoluble or unresolvable dilemma. The source of potential comfort is also the source of danger. With the only base a dangerous one, the child resorts to dissociation of unregulated feelings, or ineffective self-soothing measures such as stilling or rocking. U is similarly viewed as a form of dissociation, in which pain and fear are 'split off' into a fragmented, fractured self rather than, as in secure attachment, integrated into a coherent sense of self. In the Main–Hesse model, U and D are seen as manifestations of trauma, loss, abuse, or neglect. This operates as an AAI dimension separate from 'organised insecurity', i.e., the avoidance/dismissing and resistance/preoccupation vectors. Thus it is possible to be 'secure' with a generally fluid/autonomous discourse style, but also 'U' if there are islands of split-off, unprocessed trauma in subjects' narratives.

2. *Intergenerational transmission model.* Expanding on the approach/avoidance model, Main and Hesse (1990) suggest that one of the roots of D attachment in infants is parental *'frightened'* or *'frightening'* behaviour. We have described how some mothers, rather than responding to their children's distress, 'freeze' with fear and are unable to offer comfort. The child's pain triggers unprocessed memories of parents' *own* neglect and lack of childhood care, which paralyses their capacity to provide care themselves. This leaves the infant vulnerable, alone, and frightened.

   In the 'frightening' group, the parent responds to the child's distress in a self-referential way, with attack rather than comfort. For example, they might shout at a screaming child *'Shut up! You are just doing this to wind me up'*, thereby exacerbating the child's escalating terror, and pushing them towards dissociation.

   Main and Hesse (1990) linked these behaviours to mothers' own early unresolved traumatic experiences. Meta-analyses (Madigan et al., 2006;

Schuengel et al., 1999) support the link between frightening maternal be-haviour, unresolved maternal loss (U), and infant D status. All these pre-dispose mothers to frightening interactions with the child, unless mitigated by mentalising and 'earned security'.

3. *Hostile/helpless: the chronic relational trauma model.* The observation that only 50% of disorganised infants have parents with a U classification (van IJzendoorn, 1995) led Lyons-Ruth to ask whether other aspects of maternal representations of attachment might predict the intergenerational transmission of disorganized attachment. Her group focused on 'chronic impairment in caregiver responsiveness' (Lyons-Ruth et al., 2005: 5), and on the impact of 'chronic relational trauma, including but not limited to sexual, physical, or emotional abuse' (Lyons-Ruth et al., 2005: 7).

    This led to the description the Hostile/Helpless (H/H) coding system. Adults classified as H/H on the AAI display 'explicit contradictory but unintegrated emotional evaluations of a central caregiver', often including evidence of an 'unexamined identification with that caregiver' (Lyons-Ruth et al., 2005: 7). Individuals who have been traumatised internalise both a representation of the frightening caregiver as well as themselves as the terrified child. This can be reflected in devaluation of caregivers, identification with those caregivers, and laughter at pain. In other instances, it is reflected in fearful affect and a sense of helplessness in the face of threat. In Lyons-Ruth's study, the H/H system accounted for more of the variance in infant disorganisation than the U or preoccupied categories of attachment

4. *Severity model.* For Maunder and Hunter (2012), U is an extreme version of organised insecurity, but where organisation has broken down. What matters here is the *severity* of insecure attachment. Minor degrees of avoid-ance and dissociation are common, and can be defensively healthy, enabling people to function despite past difficulties or current problems. D and U represent the ultimate end of these processes, where such defences create or augment the very problems they attempt to solve. Self-defeatingly, border-line patients crave security, but are simultaneously terrified that, were this possible, it would be immediately snatched away. They therefore 'get their retaliation in first', often by systematically rejecting help when it is offered.[1]

5. *Positive connotation model.* Crittenden's (2006) circumplex 'Dynamic-Systems model' similarly sees U as part of a spectrum of attempts to adapt to sub-optimal or frankly abusive environments. She counteracts the nega-tive ambiance of professional discourse by showing how 'pathology' can represent a child's attempts at survival in unpropitious circumstances. The 'narcissistic', self-soothing aspects of D/U are positively connoted as attempts to do one's best in the absence of an 'older, wiser' secure base to whom one can turn for comfort and protection.

6. *Meta-analysis: multiple pathways model.* Van IJzendoorn and Bakermans-Kranenburg (2009) suggest that there are several developmental pathways leading to a diagnosis of D at 1–2 yrs. These include: *maltreatment* (as per the Main–Hesse model above); *family chaos*, which is likely to be associated with neglect, a potent precursor of psychopathology in adolescence and early adulthood; and *witnessing parental violence*, typically father towards mother, which destroys the child's sense of parents as safe havens and instigates ineffective attempts at self-soothing and self-reliance. A more recent meta-analysis (Cyr et al., 2010) reveals a link between D and severe socioeconomic risk, which is associated with all three of these pathways.

7. *Gene by environment interaction model (GxE).* The study of genetics and attachment is hugely complex, and we are currently nowhere near a clear picture of the relationship between specific genetic profiles and attachment patterns. To date, findings have been mixed (Bakermans-Kranenburg & van IJzendoorn, 2016). However, a number of studies hint at a GxE interaction, adding support to the 'differential susceptibility' hypothesis that infants vary in their sensitivity to environments, and that some are surprisingly resilient in the face of adversity (Belsky et al., 2007). In one study, van IJzendoorn and Bakermans-Kranenburg (2006) found that infants with the DRD4-7 repeat allele with U mothers were more likely to be found to be D in the SSP than those infants without this allele.

In a study of institutionally raised infants, Bakermans-Kranenburg, Dobrova-Krol, and van IJzendoorn (2011) found that the gene polymorphism 5-HTTLPR moderated the link between the caregiving environment and infant disorganisation. It seems that certain infants may be more genetically predisposed to disorganisation than others. From a clinical standpoint, these studies confirm what many clinicians know intuitively: that individuals vary in their responses to hardship and trauma. Individuals with the complex disorders we are describing here may well have been, from infancy onwards, more vulnerable to the world around them.

Each of these aetiological models has a relevant message for clinicians working with complex disorders. Before turning to these, however, we first consider 'radical acceptance'.

Attachment and 'Radical Acceptance'

In Chapter 3, we listed 'radical acceptance' as one of the guiding principles of an attachment-informed psychotherapist. This is a term first developed in the psychological literature by Linehan (1993) in her work on borderline personality disorder. By this she meant that such patients, to thrive, must strive to accept that '*what is, is*'. We extend this deceptively simple precept to therapists, whose first responsibility when faced with their patients' suffering must likewise accept that 'what is is' (cf. Levinas, 1961). While we believe this stance is essential to any therapeutic work, it is especially so with complex, difficult patients whose attachment relationships have likely been highly disorganised and traumatic.

The 'pathological' behaviours typical of personality disorders and complex cases are often seen as 'perverse', in that their end-result is even greater misery and isolation, destructiveness, and, at worst, self-slaughter. Envy, destructiveness, and the 'death instinct' are frequently deployed to 'explain' the forces motivating such perversity. From an attachment perspective, however self-defeating, these behaviours are viewed as meaningful manifestations of the attachment dramas from which they arise. People do what they do in order to survive. Radical acceptance implies that therapists are totally and non-judgementally open to the experience and meaning of patients' misery and seeming foolishness. This is not to say that an attachment-informed psychotherapist does not appreciate the difference between 'secure' and more problematic developmental pathways. Rather, they are receptive to whatever the patient brings, existentially accepting the patient's fundamental biology and the particulars of their caregiving dynamic, as these appear both in and out of session.

Radical acceptance thus represents unconditional security provision, and is the essential starting point for promoting the agency and understanding needed to release the sufferer from ineffective security-seeking. Rogers' (1985) triad of non-possessive warmth, authenticity, and accurate empathy remain at the core of the therapeutic project. The radical acceptance ethic is an antidote to the judgementalism inherent in so many therapies, the moralising and disapproval that can undermine the safe-space provision that is the precursor to self-examination. Radical acceptance allows the therapist to serve as a desperately needed secure base: providing safety via sensitivity, warmth, and the setting of boundaries, while supporting autonomy via reassurance, encouragement, instilling hope, and fostering agency. Radical acceptance keeps the therapist's mind and humanity alive, in contrast to patients' projections and attachment expectations. Doing so without threatening, exploiting, or violating boundaries is vital but also particularly difficult with D/U patients.

There is undoubtedly an angry/aggressive aspect to the self-injurious behaviours seen in severe depression and personality disorder. For Bowlby (1973), this was explicable as the protest of a suffering individual desperately trying to activate a caregiver. The child who cries when her mother leaves the room in the SSP is both communicating her pain by transmitting it directly to the caregiver (what could be more painful than the cries of one's suffering infant?), and activating the caregiver to return and alleviate separation anxiety. In deliberate self-harm cases this dynamic is often effective: the absent or erring partner appears at the abandoned sufferer's bedside, or, at the very least, professional carers tend the self-inflicted wounds, although, sadly, often in a brusque or frankly hostile way that perpetuates the sense of rejection, thereby sowing the seeds for further self-harm.

In D/U or H/H the attachment dynamic turns in on itself. Sufferers split themselves into a rejected care-seeker and failed caregiver self. The latter is then attacked as though it were a separate **alien being** (Fonagy et al., 2002), despite inhabiting the self-same body. The hand that holds the knife and the victim's wrist are symbolically split asunder. The knife-wielder might represent the alien abuser; the wrist is that of a desperate care-seeker wishing to awaken the caregiver from absence or self-preoccupation.

The **addictiveness** of self-injury also needs to be acknowledged, physiologically in the case of alcohol or illicit drug use. Symbolic or 'psychological' addiction – e.g., the manic oblivion associated with promiscuous sex seen in hypomanic states – can also assume a repetitive, self-reinforcing quality. When the sufferer comes 'down' and contemplates the loneliness and exploitative nature of his actions, this initiates a cascade aiming to eliminate those horrible feelings, eventually repeating the very behaviours that triggered them in the first place.

In thinking about 'perversity', the balance between activity and passivity, helplessness and control, is important. The majority of D/U or H/H cases have as children been passive victims of trauma, neglect, or abuse. The pathological manifestations of self-destructiveness – identification with hostile caregivers – turn this round and so bring the trauma within the subject's control. This is Anna Freud's 'identification with the aggressor'. While this can temporarily alleviate helplessness, with each cycle of self-harm the addiction takes a deeper hold on the psyche. In Lyons-Ruth's terms (Lyons-Ruth et al., 2005), the traumatised child internalises both the experience of his own helplessness and his caregiver's hostility, or the converse, his rage and her helplessness. These representations are triggered by threat, including the threat implicit in aspects of psychotherapy. Casement (1982), building on Winnicott (1971), argues that the pain and terror of trauma, if re-enacted in the 'playspace' of therapy, comes within the patient's control and choice, thereby helping redress the sense of victimhood. 'Battles' between patient and therapist, however difficult and painful, can be seen in terms of the patient's attempts to gain a measure of agency and control.

Clinical Implications

Some of the major themes that attachment approaches bring to working with D/U, H/H cases will now be outlined.

Boundaries

Attachment is a spatial theory. In the African savannah, the 'environment of evolutionary adaptedness' (Bowlby, 1969) in which *homo sapiens* emerged, physical separation of infants and children from parents spelt danger from predators. According to this hypothesis, the attachment behavioural system evolved to maintain child–parent spatial proximity. But, à la Lakoff and

Johnson (2003), 'space is time' and 'time is space'. At the start of a therapy session, patient and therapist are in physical proximity, but also share a 'space of time'. At the session's end, the space–time gap gapes once more.

The attachment dynamic is especially salient at the beginning and end of sessions, and around holiday and inadvertent breaks such as illness. Space–time boundary phenomena for people suffering from complex disorders include: missing sessions, arriving late, getting the time and day wrong, finding it difficult or even refusing to leave sessions when they are over, breaking off and storming out. Therapists' counterparts of boundary turbulence include 'forgetting' sessions, 'double booking', ending early or inappropriately, and letting them drag on past the appointed end-time.

Given the approach–avoidance dilemma with which D/U people struggle, and unintegrated H/H states of mind, these disturbances are understandable. Intimate relationships are simultaneously craved and feared. At the boundary, fight/flight dynamics and 'equivalence mode' thinking come to the fore; mentalising is in abeyance. If the therapist ends a session a couple of minutes early, or engages in more egregious errors such as double booking, for the D/U client this may only mean one thing: her therapist doesn't care a damn, and therapy is to be treated with suspicion, or forever shunned.

Fears of the potentially exploitative aspects of intimacy may be activated by therapy in people who have been abused. Therapists may be accused of money-grubbing, vicariously 'getting off' on their patient's miseries and sexual misfortunes, or unfeelingly 'just doing their job'. For the D/U client, trust cannot be assumed. The 'other' at the boundary is best viewed as foe, not friend, until proved – and proved again – otherwise.

Frida's aloneness confirmed

Frida, a young teacher, sought treatment for paralysing anxiety and other sequelae of an abusive, traumatic childhood. She had had two previous therapies, in one of which she became sexually involved with her male therapist. She was distrustful of her current therapist, who she repeatedly excoriated as inept, insufficiently clever, and technically limited. The straw that broke the treatment's back was the therapist's question about whether the patient's father would be attending a family event. Frida flew into a rage: did the therapist not understand that her father was toxic and deeply disturbed and would *never* be welcome at such an event? In this lapse (countertransferential enactment) on the therapist's part, Frida found evidence both of the therapist's incompetence and her strong belief that no one would or could ever listen to her or care for her. She discontinued treatment shortly thereafter.

Living with such disappointments and failures, learning from them, and taking responsibility while not berating themselves, is part of the therapist's task. The hyper-vigilance of the D/U or H/H client means that any hints of affective distancing or failure to empathise become intensely threatening. Under the aegis of the H/H dynamic, patients may become enraged and attacking, or switch to abject helplessness, incapable of managing on their own even for brief periods. Separation may arouse suicidal feelings, since, to repeat, to be alone and unprotected as an infant or small child is equivalent to emotional or even literal death. These 'primitive' fears remain unregulated and unmodulated at the core of the D/U, H/H psyche.

These themes are familiar in the psychoanalytic literature, although they are theoretically conceptualised rather than empirically validated. Balint (1968) talks of 'philobats' (who only feel safe in open spaces and shun proximity) and 'onchnophils' (for whom open space spells terror and whose only perceived route to emotional survival is adherence). Similarly, Rey (see Mizen, 2014) described the 'claustro-agoraphobic dilemma', in which people suffering with borderline disorders oscillate between clinging or flight, and cannot find a stable middle position from which to interact, negotiate (in the attachment model, co-regulate), or move freely between interdependence and autonomy.

Attachment-informed principles can guide therapists' responses to these polarities. First, boundary difficulties are to be expected, and, to an extent, tolerated, when working with complex cases. In the early stages of therapy, the mere fact that patients come at all is more important than that they come and leave on time. Second, it is important to bear in mind Dozier et al.'s (1994) work contrasting secure therapists, who counteract or redress their clients' insecure attachment styles, and insecure therapists, who tend to reinforce them. Secure therapists will make efforts to contact recalcitrant avoidant patients who miss all or part of sessions, rather than let such people slip away as 'drop-outs'. Insecure therapists, complacently telling themselves they have been 'sacked' or that a patient is 'unsuitable for treatment' are letting their own defensiveness get the better of them. Announcements of premature ending need to be challenged, without making the client feel controlled or coerced. Thus:

> 'You're telling me that you feel that therapy is a waste of time, that nothing is going to change and that you've decided to stop coming.' [straightforward mirroring response]

> 'I respect these feelings, and, given your experiences of having been trapped and abused, it is vital that you feel that it's your life, and up to you what you do with it. But, that said, can we just think this through a bit more?' [interpretation plus appeal to collaborative mentalising]

> 'I unexpectedly cancelled last week's session because of the 'flu'. I can see that interrupted our work together, and I'm really sorry. I wonder if that made you feel that I'm just not to be relied upon, any more than your mother was when she had to be admitted to hospital when her drinking got out of control. It wouldn't be surprising if you felt that the only person you can really turn to is yourself, and it's better to drop than be dropped. But maybe we could carry on thinking about this for a bit longer…' [therapist admits and apologises for his part and appeals to the client's mentalising capacity]

Conversely, preoccupied clients may evoke over-protectiveness in their insecurely attached therapists. This can lead to extended sessions (a common
problem for beginner therapists: '*I just couldn't break off after 50 minutes,
we'd just got to a really important topic*'), long inter-session phone calls, pro-
liferation of texting, etc. The difficulty of separation from what is unconsciously experienced as an inconstant or neglectful secure base needs to be
acknowledged. The client cannot reliably trust that the therapist will be there
for him or her when needed. At the same time, therapists need gently to hold
firm to boundaries, and find ways to negotiate agreed amounts of contact, e.g.,
allowing for a regular updating text/email between sessions.

Penny's credit

Penny regularly appeared in the accident and emergency department,
which would often lead to unproductive and prolonged hospital admissions. Eventually it was negotiated that, alongside her therapy sessions,
she was entitled to three unscheduled nights per month in hospital, to be
offered without question by the admitting staff. These were her 'credit', to
be 'cashed in' whenever she chose. Perhaps the most helpful aspect of this
was handing over choice to the client, who in so much of her life had felt,
and continued to feel, massively disempowered.

This '*would you rather be shot or hung?*' strategy may be a last resort when
therapists are confronted in complex cases with helping clients to make 'least
worst' choices. It can be justified on the grounds that giving the client a limited
degree of choice counteracts their eroded sense of agency.

Sometimes therapists have to impose unwelcome limits on clients. For
example, with a client who is habitually half an hour late, the dialogue might
run as follows:

Therapist: 'Look, I'm not sure we can go on like this. Therapy doesn't
work in half doses, any more than physical medicines do. How about we
give ourselves a month of you arriving no more than 10 minutes late, and
then see where we've got to?'

The client might then say: 'What about 15 minutes?', to which the therapist might proffer: 'Well, let's not get too obsessional about this. The
important thing is for us to try to work out what it is that makes it so
hard for you to get your full money's worth.'

Despite best efforts, things will go wrong when, under the sway of projective
identification, therapists find themselves enacting aspects of the client's world,
especially if this chimes with their own attachment history. This is the prob-
able explanation of Dozier et al.'s (1994) findings, where insecure therapists

reinforce rather than correct their clients' insecurities. Clinical supervision and personal therapy are the essential antidotes to this.

Touch

From an attachment perspective, sexuality and security represent different bio-behavioural systems, coming on-stream in the developmental process at different times. In principle, this would legitimise non-sexual touch and bodily contact as useful therapeutic tools. For body-oriented therapists who use various forms of massage, acupressure, and gentle healing contact, this is no doubt self-evident. For psychodynamically minded therapists, however, especially those working with complex cases, patient–therapist touch is inherently problematic (see Pedder, 2010). Cultural aspects also need to be taken into consideration. In some cultures, greeting and parting handshakes are conventional signifiers of trust and can be readily incorporated into the psychotherapy setting. In others, for a man, say, to touch a woman's hand in this way would be seriously taboo-violating.

On a lecture tour in South America, JH was conducting 'live supervision' in front of an audience. The supervisee, who was quite experienced, presented the case of a teenage girl with an eating disorder. She mentioned *en passant* that the patient had hugged her at the end of the session. JH picked up on this. Was the patient wanting to send signals about her sexuality? Was she feeling angry with her therapist? Wanting to make reparation, etc.? It emerged, however, that in this culture, including in therapy, a kiss on the cheek was a routine greeting and parting ritual. JH's surprise and implicit disapproval of this was met with universal audience amusement – 'Oh another typical up-tight Englishman'!

When working with complex cases, 'less is more'; half a loaf is often worse than no loaf at all; erring on the side of reticence is usually the best council. The 'slippery slope' (Gabbard & Horowitz, 2009) of sexual exploitation in therapy begins with well-intentioned attempts on the part of naïve, albeit often psychologically troubled, therapists to redress their clients' childhood neglect or exploitation, and can end up in disaster, for both parties. While attachment is a real and necessary part of therapy, a secure base is always a bounded as well as a loving one.

The Lakoff and Johnson approach suggests two-way traffic between the literal and the metaphorical. It is possible to 'touch' and be touched emotionally without physical contact. Therapy aims to help clients move in this metaphorical, mentalising direction away from enactments of unprocessed, unregulated feelings. Ironically, those most craving physical contact may well be those least likely to benefit from, and most in danger from, its provision. Conversely, those for whom the danger is slight are those who least require it.

Sight

Intense mother–infant gaze in the early months of life plays an important role in establishing secure attachments, stable self-representations, and reliable affect co-regulation. Assuming that people with D/U, H/H representations of attachment have had difficulties in this area, standard psychoanalytic technique – the therapist sitting invisibly behind a prone patient on a couch – might be problematic. But, like touch, 'gaze' too can be metaphorical. The lying-down patient can still, in his mind's eye, 'see' the therapist's physical being, reconstructed 'cross-modally' (Stern, 1985) from the sounds, shadows, and air turbulence created by body movements. As well as moving the couch/chair dilemma from the concrete to the metaphorical, the two contrasting examples which follow illustrate how 'radical acceptance' entails acute sensitivity to clients' sense of threat, and the importance of 'softening' rather rigid responsiveness.

Betty: From chair to couch

Betty suffered from overwhelming anxiety and panic attacks, for which she had been hospitalised several times. She had had several courses of short-term CBT therapy to little avail and was referred for psychoanalytic work. She spent a lot of time researching anxiety on the internet, seeking the ideal therapy for her problems. Sitting up, she engaged the therapist with gimlet eyes and written lists of questions. In response to her imploring facial look, despite best psychodynamic intentions, he found it hard to evade slipping into problem-solving suggestions.

After five sessions he spontaneously exclaimed: 'You are far more expert than I will ever be on methods of dealing with anxiety. My expertise, such as it is, lies in analytic therapy. I suggest that from now on you use the couch. But as we go along I hope to learn from you more about the latest anxiety-reduction techniques.'

She cautiously agreed. Thereafter the culture of the sessions changed. Betty became more reflective and better able to explore her feelings of anger towards those whom she felt did not really hear her cries for help, including therapists, and who, as she put it, merely 'fobbed her off' with 'banal solutions to pseudo-problems'. She began to explore the origins of these feelings in her relationship with her parents. The youngest of five girls, she felt they were bitterly disappointed by her gender, and even more so when her fifth sibling, the longed-for boy, 'came along' when she was only 11 months old.

Here, the interruption of the sight-lines brought much needed 'play' into the patient–therapist relationship, in contrast to the 'looming' (Beebe & Lachmann, 2013) quality of face-to-face therapy. The patient feared that she would immediately be 'out of sight, out of mind' – the therapist's attention, like her mother's, would be driven away by a 'new arrival'. Lying down challenged this presumption and introduced a more mid-range, multi-channel (aural, postural, verbal as opposed to purely visual) sensitivities.

Mary: From couch to chair

Mary, a talented artist, who was suffering from alcoholism and borderline personality disorder, had been in weekly lying-down therapy for two years. There had been some progress: her episodes of self-harm had reduced and she was living a more independent life than at the outset of therapy. However, after a drinking binge episode where she missed two sessions, the therapist, proud of his formulations but disappointed by their negligible impact, found himself quoting Marx's (1888/1998) famous eleventh *Thesis on Feuerbach*: 'philosophers have hitherto only interpreted the world, the point is to change it'.

He suggested that they move from couch to chair and focused more specifically on Mary's drinking and the minutiae of her lonely life. The introduction of face-to-face contact seemed to symbolise greater warmth and engagement. Mary commented that she now felt the therapist really cared about her suffering and whether or not she killed herself with drink, rather than merely 'doing his job' and making vague comments, while lazily reclining behind her befuddled head.

Encouragement and the instillation of hope

Several recent authors (Akhtar, 2009) have noted how positive emotions, such as hope, joy, love, and pride, are conspicuous by their absence in the psychoanalytic literature. When they do surface, they tend to be viewed with suspicion, as defences concealing predatory envy, guilt, rage, and fear. An attachment perspective takes a different view. We have mentioned the 'Circle of Security' (Powell et al., 2013), in which the role of parents is not just as a 'safe haven' and secure base, but as an essential source of 'narcissistic supplies': pride, reinforcement, and delight – *'well done!'*, *'clever girl!'*, *'you are brave!'*, *'gosh, you can run fast!'*. This shared pleasure underpins successful forays out into the world of excitement and one-year-old wonder. In an ingenious experiment (Stupica, 2016), the subjects were parents watching their children running a baseball circuit on a school sports day. First, they were instructed to appear distracted, checking their mobile phones while their offspring ran their races; in a second 'run' of the study they were asked to attend intensely and to encourage. Unsurprisingly, the children's speeds were significantly faster under the latter conditions.

Secure parental love, ultimately, is unconditional. As functional Magnetic Resonance Imaging (fMRI) studies show (Strathearn et al., 2008), good parents are even-handed, able to 'meet those two imposters, Triumph and Disaster, just the same' (Kipling, 1897/2014).[2] Therapists no doubt enjoy their patients' progress and achievements, but typically keep these feelings well concealed lest they be experienced as seductive or controlling. Attachment-informed therapists will feel relaxed about offering encouragement and praise when appropriate, even if tempered with transferential reservations.

Limit-setting

Security is not all about sweetness and love. The parent who loudly and firmly says 'No!' to her toddler approaching a hot fire or an electric socket is no less secure-making than when she is soothing the child's subsequent distress at being shouted at. Both encouragement and limit-setting take on a different complexion in the complex cases we are considering in this chapter. Encouragement may be interpreted as 'grooming' in people who have been abused as children, and therefore treated with terror and suspicion. The therapist's capacity for 'unconditional positive regard' (Rogers, 1985) will indeed be tested to the limit. Boundaries may have to be set: e.g. working out how to respond when patients arrive for sessions 'high', or having self-harmed.

The therapist may be pushed into trying to influence these self-injurious behaviours directly, seguing into the role of case-manager or life-coach. But a cobbler must stick to his last. The primary therapeutic task is to understand the *meanings* that underlie and propel acts of self-injury in the patient's life.

Marjorie's missed sessions

Although theoretically Marjorie was in thrice-weekly psychoanalytic therapy, in practice she missed at least one session per week, usually sending a text on the day pleading physical illness, exhaustion, or work pressure as her excuse. She was a heavy cannabis user, which she described as her primary 'medicine'. The therapist was tempted to confront her with the ways in which she was attacking therapy or even to issue an ultimatum saying that if she couldn't attend as agreed, and curb her pot habit, the therapy would be in jeopardy.

Thinking about her history from an attachment and D/U perspective helped generate a less punitive strategy. Marjorie's parents had divorced when she was 6 years old. Her mother became chaotic and self-preoccupied, while her father, whom she saw weekly, was, as she put it, 'everything' to her. He was then tragically killed in a car crash when Marjorie was 9. She had had little contact with her father's family since. There was no grave or memorial for her to visit, because his ashes had been 'kicked into the sea' by Marjorie's furious and grief-stricken paternal grandfather.

Marjorie's non-attendance for her sessions was understood in terms of:

a. Her need for a secure base to 'be there' for her *even in her absence*, hence the missing sessions.

b. Terror that were she to attend she would be forced to confront her *unbearable feelings of emptiness and grief*.

c. A wish to communicate to the therapist her experiences of the chaos and unpredictability of sudden loss by *evoking the same feelings in him.*

d. Anger at her dependence on others and her wish to '*kick her feelings*' and those that gave rise to them '*into the sea*'.

These themes gradually came into play as Marjorie's therapy talk became more reflective and less crisis-driven. This enabled the therapist to suggest that psychotherapy, no less than 'pot', was also a 'medicine', and possibly a more effective one in the long term, and that currently she was taking only half the correct dose, or less!

The therapist here could also have used a mentalising approach and asked Marjorie what she imagined might be going through the therapist's heart and mind when she cancelled her sessions at the last moment. The patient might have responded by saying, '*Oh, I imagine you are delighted, I'm sure I'm an awful nuisance to you.*' This thought could then be explored and challenged, and the therapist might 'confess' that her patient's non-appearance *did* make her worry and feel that she wasn't really helping. In general it can be useful for such patients to know that therapists are human, frail, and have their limits. This can mobilise a more mature and self-regulating aspect in the patient, hitherto obscured by the necessarily regressive ambiance of therapy.[3] Here is another example.

Edward's failure to turn up

Edward had had a bleak and neglected childhood, left by his single-parent mother to cope with his misery and fear on his own, and to look after his younger siblings while she worked to try to make ends meet. As a young adult he moved from place to place, job to job, and relationship to relationship, always moving on when the going got tough. The depression which laid him low, and for which he eventually sought help, produced a sense of isolation and lack of feeling. After a few months of therapy with a female therapist, there was an atmosphere of escalating contentiousness. Every attempt on the therapist's part to understand and interpret this was met with resistance: '*You don't understand; you have no idea what it's like to be me; everything you say is obvious, banal; I've thought of all your so-called interpretations myself a million times already, thank you very much.*' Then, without any warning, he missed three sessions in a row. The therapist was extremely anxious, thinking that he might have harmed himself. Eventually he turned up. The therapist asked him how he thought she might have felt about his non-appearance. In a sarcastic voice: '*Weren't you delighted – I'm sure you've got lots other things you need to get on with.*'

With much difficulty, the therapist tried to get across just how worried and concerned she had felt about his non-appearance. Edward seemed genuinely amazed that he could be missed, let alone thought about in his absence. Together he and his therapist began to reconstruct his feelings of being left as a child, and how he habitually turned the tables, not just on his therapist, but on his employers and girlfriends. He began to see that his 'done-to' self had became the 'doer'. It was *he* who had 'chosen' not to turn up for sessions, and this had meaning and consequences. Gradually, and with many set-backs, he began to translate this insight into his relationships at work and with his partner.

Another limit-relevant aspect is that the more loving, accepting, and encouraging the therapist appears, the more this throws into relief the inadequacies of the patient's real-life situation and developmental history. This in turn can stimulate attempts to denigrate or even destroy what is being offered.[4] Nevertheless, the therapist needs to stand firm to 'radical acceptance', seeing apparent self-destructiveness (including 'attacks' on therapy) as defensive means of survival and self-soothing in a hostile internal and external environment.

Jackie's illness

Jackie had suffered from major depressive disorder since her late teens. In the early years of a 20-year therapy, her therapist painfully discovered that his therapeutic opacity and efforts to 'interpret' her depression in terms of unexpressed anger and childhood trauma (for which there was much evidence) merely reinforced Jackie's feelings of failure, and her conviction that she, the victim, was to blame for her illness. He gradually came to acknowledge that what she needed above all was validation and confirmation that the world does really stigmatise the mentally ill, and a shared understanding that to be depressed is at best to live only partly.

It was only when he decided to move into this radically accepting mode that he felt that Jackie began tentatively to trust him. At times she continued to resist and resent him and everything he stood for, which in her eyes was a heartless, authoritarian, self-satisfied professional, inhabiting a horror-insulated world. He gradually learned to validate that resentment and its legitimacy, despite believing that such strong feelings were coloured by a depressive world-view. Painfully, Jackie taught him how corrosive the 'division of suffering' between patient and doctor can be. By acknowledging – mainly to themselves – their own vulnerability, therapists can lessen the need to project and sequester their own disturbances in their patients.

Psychopathological self-soothing

Based on the 'radical affirmation/acceptance' perspective, the attachment-informed approach conceives self-destructive and 'perverse' aspects as 'least/worst' options, attempted solutions to the insoluble, survival modes in lose–lose situations. In the AAI, U subjects' painful memories of trauma and loss may be side-stepped by sudden shifts of discourse and theme. In the same vein (itself a pun or 'switch word', Litowitz, 2014), seemingly self-injurious acts such as self-cutting, overdosing, starving/bingeing, outbursts of rage, etc., have a soothing aspect, subsuming their apparent harmfulness.

In the absence of a functioning caregiver, the oblivion of a suicide attempt, drug- or alcohol-induced sleep, is a 'perverse' version of the safety and relaxation that an effective secure base, were one at hand, would provide. Even in determined suicide attempts (as opposed to the much more common phenomenon of para-suicide), once the decision to die has been taken there is usually a period when the sufferer may feel a sense of preternatural calm (Holmes, 2010). The prospect of oblivion has become the balm, the all-accepting soothing other, so notably absent in their life. In this quasi-delusional zone, 'half in love with easeful Death' (Keats, 1819/2007), death itself becomes the secure base, a 'heaven-haven' (Hopkins, 1918/2008) where pain and suffering are finally assuaged. Suicide beckons when all attachments feel to have failed, turning out-of-control helplessness into action, providing a kind of mastery, both horrific and compelling. Acknowledging all this is part of any attachment-informed 'risk assessment'.

Exploration and activity

This leads us to the sense of *agency*, implicit in the AAI hybrid term 'secure-autonomous'. Children's capacity for exploration is a robust predictor of later attachment security (Sroufe et al., 2005). A secure base is a springboard for understanding and eventual mastery of the environment. But 'the environment' is a vague term, encompassing not just the physical environment – the toddler's climbing frame, the mountaineer's summit – but also the interpersonal milieu within which people find themselves.

'Agency' can be thought of as an interactive, two-way process. 'Proto-conversations' between infant and mother set the agency clock ticking. The infant's 'gesture' (e.g., extended arms 'saying' *'pick me up'*) is responded to with the caregiver's 'answer' (*'here I am, up you come'*), leading to further action and exploration, and so on. In secure attachments, the interpersonal dimension to agency and exploration are evident from the start. The caregiver waits for the child to make the first move, triggering contingent reactions on his or her part: Mum acceptingly allows her face to be squished or, to her offspring's delight, tolerates endless games of peek-a-boo. These are children who feel that they *matter*, that they can *make a difference*, and that, grit or pearl, the world is their oyster.

How different it is for D children and U or H/H adults. Victimhood and passivity prevail. Rather than doers, they are endlessly done-to. The sense that they can influence what happens to them, or even to assert their very existence, is precarious. And yet such people often appear to be instruments of their own failed agency, their own worst enemies, creating the very disempowerment of which they complain. As discussed earlier, the technical problem for therapy is that efforts to encourage this sense of agency are often felt as controlling, criticising, or 'blaming the victim'. Thus:

Abi and Mark

P (Abi):   Mark [her boyfriend] walked out on me last night. I'd done nothing; I just told him he could make his own tea for once, and off he went. I phoned my Mum, but she wasn't answering. I ended up cutting myself and spent half the night in the hospital Emergency Room. The apartment was so cold and empty when I got back.

Th: Do you think it could have been something you'd said that drove him away?

P: Oh, you're saying it's all my fault are you, that's just like my Mum... she's always taking Mark's side...

A better approach might have been marked mirroring:

Th: Cold and empty... that sounds very bleak and frightening, and when you turned to your Mum all you got was blame. We must make sure that you let me know if I sound like I too am turning into a Mark/Mum!

The 'masochistic' satisfactions of being hurt, victimised, and exploited represent extreme versions of the 'vertical' relationships found in insecure attachment. Low self-esteem, insecure attachment, and low 'ranking' overlap. A strong, albeit controlling or even exploiting secure base is the best hope for a degree of safety. A modicum of interpersonal connection is preferable to the dangers of isolation and disconnection. Abi at least linked up with her mother, even if it meant having to endure her criticism and disappointment. In Abi's attachment world, the 'horizontal' patterns of listening and being listened to, power-sharing, responsiveness, collaboration, and cooperation seem impossibly distant and unattainable. These are on offer in therapy, but may well be experienced as covert forms of control, especially in the early stages, and so rejected because they threaten well-established assumptions and pathways.

Viewed from a non-mentalising perspective, D/U or H/H clients appear far from passive. They 'act out', cut, drink, overdose, endanger themselves and others. But agency is absent; things 'just happen'. The existential sense of being self-directed is lacking: '*I found myself in bed with a stranger*', '*I landed up in hospital*', '*the drinks they gave me were "spiked"*'. 'Teleological thinking' (Fonagy et al., 2002) dominates: actions respond to events but without any apparent intervening mind.

There are a number of ways in which therapists can help foster a sense of agency in such situations. But they need to be highly self-aware, self-mentalising, in touch with their countertransference. This will counteract the temptation to push their exasperatingly passive clients in what seem like obviously favourable directions – giving up drinking, seeking help rather than cutting, not jeopardising therapy, etc. The problem with the 'life-coach' stance is that the client's active self becomes lodged in the therapist, while they themselves continue in the passive, victimised position. This has the 'advantage' perhaps of avoiding guilt and blame, and the risks implicit in action, but the disadvantage is that it leaves clients permanently prey to exploitation. Clients need to feel they have choices, and that if – with the help of the co-regulation of therapy – they become less affect-phobic, they will intuitively know what is right for them, and what they can cope with.

It is often helpful to make frequent use of the word 'choice' and its derivatives in the therapeutic discourse – '*I've noticed that you often choose to come a bit late to your sessions; can we think about what that might be telling us?*' (The 'we' word also aims to foster collaborative culture of 'borrowed brain' social neurobiology.) Therapists will persistently encourage the client to move from a 'teleological' to a more mentalising stance. This means finding that there *are* intervening minds between stimulus and response – their own and those of their intimates, including that of the therapist. This can often be teased out from a blow-by-blow 'action replay' of events.

> Th: If you can bear it, I'd like to try to go over again the sequence leading up to you choosing to take that overdose last Saturday. Your boyfriend didn't turn up; you phoned your Mum, but there was no response and then your phone ran out of charge. You thought of going to hospital, but decided it would be a waste of time. You imagined me happily 'off duty' and didn't want to 'bother' me with a text. It all sounds horribly bleak. Let's try to reconstruct what was going through your mind when you started swallowing those pills...

Lack of agency often links with another D/U plague: crippling indecisiveness. Unable to 'trust the universe', and to accept that the outcomes of actions are inherently unpredictable, the D/U client is existentially paralysed. Too much rests on any particular course of action. A putative inner monologue might run like this:

> If I take this job/get romantically involved with this person/commit myself to this therapy, then my life will go well; but if not, everything will fall apart... but then maybe it's other way round, and making the wrong decision will be fatal.

What is missing here is a confident sense of self-as-subject, an ability to steer a safe course through one's destiny, to enjoy success if it comes, or to survive fortune's slings and arrows if not. Seeing oneself as a passive victim can produce a number of 'secondary gain' pay-offs. It reinforces a position of chronic blame – one's own contribution to one's misery, and with it painful guilt and remorse, is discounted; helplessness usually elicits a degree of help and security from others, albeit of the 'vertical' variety. Therapy with such clients needs to tease out the low self-esteem that lurks beneath the sense that one's life chances rest on the spin of a coin.

Therapist countertransference

In several of the examples above, therapists draw on their *own* feelings – e.g. 'sounds horribly bleak' – to speculate about what might have been going through the client's body-mind. Therapist countertransference highlights clients' disowned, unformulated (Stern, 2010) feelings – now located, experienced, named, processed, and co-regulated in the therapist.

Bion (1970) saw this as 'normal projective identification', in which the mother 'metabolises' the child's 'undigested' thought-fragments, names them, and returns them to the child as a springboard for emotional development. Attachment-informed therapy conceptualises projective identification in terms of caregiver/care-seeker affect co-regulation. The Schores (Schore & Schore, 2008) hypothesise that for D/U clients, this process has been disrupted, leading to splitting, alexythymia, disssociation, and self-estrangement. Strong therapist countertransference reactions represent early stages of infant/caregiver development, in which affect *co*-regulation rather than '*self*-regulation' prevails. Although in 'real life' relying on others to process one's feelings is problematic, in therapy it denotes a sensitive period in which the client is existentially and neurophysiologically open to influence and change. Therapists' capacity to draw on their countertransference to identify and help 'name and tame' their clients' affective states forms a starting point towards more mature, self-regulatory mentalising pathways. Sadly – as in the case of Frida, above – failure to do so can precipitate abrupt termination.

Control and controllingness

Follow-up studies of D infants depict how, at age 6, some exhibit *role-reversal* with their caregivers: the child appears to be looking after the mother, rather than vice versa (Main & Cassidy, 1988), while others take a controlling/imperious stance towards their caregiver. An adult analogue of early role reversal might be the 'compulsive caregiving' often seen in members of the helping professions – not excluding psychotherapists! Such people seem inexorably drawn to those whose lives are miserable or chaotic. This 'division of suffering', already mentioned, where one party feels all the mental pain, while the other does all the 'looking after' may reproduce itself in therapy, as may the stance in which patients become subtly controlling or even domineering towards their therapists.

Sylvia's watch

Sylvia, a family physician, came for help with what she described as 'work difficulties' in which she felt that her partners loaded all the 'impossible' cases onto her. She toiled all hours, while they blithely headed for the golf course having bundled off their last patients. Towards the end of her 50-minute sessions she would invariably consult her watch and insist on calling a halt. The therapist challenged this, arguing that it was his job, not hers, to bring sessions to a close. '*But I know what it's like*', she would say, '*some people just drag on and on.*' The therapist responded: '*Ah... you are looking after me, rather than the other way round. That's very sweet of you, but maybe we need to try to get behind that generosity a bit...*'

More then emerged about Sylvia's mother's badly controlled diabetes, and how Sylvia's job from an early age was to make sure she checked her blood sugars, took glucose when needed, etc. Sylvia's terror that her mother might die and her fear about her own loneliness didn't get a look-in. She began to see how that pattern reproduced itself with her colleagues, whom she was resentfully 'looking after', and now with her therapist.

She decided to remove her watch at the start of sessions and gradually became more relaxed and expansive. Disturbed and disturbing feelings of vulnerability and isolation surfaced. Very tentatively she began to express some anger and disappointment towards her therapist, without fearing that he would immediately drop dead or have a diabetic crisis if she did so.

Mentalising

We return, finally, to the all-important theme of mentalising. For people suffering from borderline personality disorder and other complex conditions, there is robust evidence (e.g., Bateman & Fonagy, 2009; Fonagy & Bateman, 2006; Choi-Kain & Gunderson, 2008) that Mentalisation-Based Therapy (MBT) reduces time spent in hospital, numbers of suicide attempts, and psychotropic drug usage, with consequent significant savings in costs to medical and social services. A consistent explanatory principle in working with D/U or H/H clients is that they will have compromised mentalising, and will be highly likely to operate in 'pre-mentalising modes'. The therapeutic aim, therefore, must be to deploy and foster mentalising skills whenever possible. While this anticipates the theme of the next chapter, we will enumerate some of these.

- *Perspectivism*: helping the client to step back from their actions and find a vantage point from which to think about the thoughts and feelings that drive them. This 'vantage point' has the characteristics of a secure base – calm, safe, even-handed acceptance of negativity and positivity.

- *Mind-mindedness*: always reaching out to identify the mental states that might have been operating in any given situation. Several examples of unanticipated non-attendance at sessions have already been given. Here are some of the kinds of things therapists might say in their attempts to promote mentalising, but also (in brackets) the possible hazards of such statements. Effective co-mentalising is easier said than done.

The focus could be on the client:

> 'You didn't come last week. That was just after I'd taken a holiday break. I wonder if there could be any connection between the two? Can we try to recall what might have been going through your mind around the time of last week's session?' (Patient may feel criticised.)

Or on the therapist:

> 'I know this is difficult, and maybe you feel it is inappropriate – I know it's my problem not yours – but can you put yourself in my shoes for a minute. I wonder what you imagine I might have felt when you didn't turn up last week. I was really worried about you.' (Therapist's anxiety means he doesn't wait for a response and then inappropriately intrudes himself into the conversation.)

Or on their interactive 'dance':

> 'I've been thinking about what might be going on here between us. When I was away, I sort of 'dropped' you last week – rather as your father did when he walked out on the family. You then perhaps felt abandoned, frightened, and pretty angry, and maybe there was even a part of you that felt 'I'll jolly well show him what it's like to be let down.' Maybe something like that was going on in your unheralded non-appearance?' (Again, the patient may feel criticised, and the 'little speech' is over-long.)

- *Self-revelation:* in the above examples, the therapist is using her own thought processes to model discourse in which thoughts and their conse-quences can be discussed. The therapist here provides a window into his or her own thoughts:

> 'As you were talking about the times your mother had to go into hos-pital as a child, I found myself feeling vicariously frightened. What came to mind when you were telling that story was a sense of what it might be like to be completely alone in the world.' (Possibly inappropri-ate shift in focus away from client and onto the therapist.)

These mentalising efforts have a number of beneficial effects. They demon-strate the humanity and vulnerability of the therapist, which may lessen the client's sense of isolation. They emphasise the role of thoughts and feelings in driving actions and interactions, counteracting 'teleological', if-this-then-that, states of mind. They model the importance of free-associative access to one's inner world, taking seriously what one finds there, and being able to differentiate fact from feeling.

We have repeatedly emphasised how, alongside the mentalising benefits, there are dangers in too much therapist self-revelation. The 'Oedipal' barrier needs to be kept in mind at all times. It would be totally inappropriate for the therapist to say, '*when you came in that short skirt I found myself having, however unbidden, sexual fantasies*', but he might venture, if other material in the session justified it:

> 'I found myself wondering if you sometimes get confused between security and sexuality. While you might be in search of the first, your partners might be looking for the second. Do you think this might lie at the root of some of the difficulties you run into in your relationships?'

Another danger might be that the therapist appears at ease with his or her thoughts in ways that make the client feel inadequate:

> P: 'It's all very well for you Mr. healthy middle-class ever-so well-analysed types, but if I were to really let everything come into my mind as you tell me I should, I would be staring into an abyss of misery, chaos, and cruelty.'

While mentalising remains a key aim and technique in therapy, the 'privacy of the self' (cf. Winnicott, 1971) needs also to be respected and protected. The focus for therapists' efforts is the educational psychologist Vygotsky's (1978) 'zone of proximal development'. This concept refers to the way caregivers (parents, teachers) 'scaffold' children's developing capacities, helping them to progress from one step to the next on whose threshold they're teetering. Teachers don't introduce differential calculus to children who have only just learnt to count. Similarly, clients need a gentle leg-up or nudge towards what is just – but only just – beyond their current developmental stage. With attachment help, man's reach can truly exceed his grasp (cf. Browning 1855/2000).

Summary

- The attachment model of disorganised attachment provides a framework for thinking about severe psychological disturbance.

- Radical acceptance is a crucial stance for therapists working with such clients.

- The 'Unresolved' category in the AAI produces a concept of D/U, which helps us to think about the difficulties which such people generate in therapy.

- The Helpless/Hostile (H/H) dynamic likewise helps us to understand patients' unintegrated states of mind.

- A number of other attachment-derived strategies are relevant for work with 'difficult' clients. These include: marked mirroring, empathy within firm boundaries, fostering agency, and mentalising.

Notes

1. Encapsulated in Groucho Marx's famous aphorism: 'I wouldn't join any club that would have me as its member.'
2. Written 20 years before his beloved son John was killed in the First World War.
3. Parents are often similarly surprised when their teenage children 'rise to the occasion' if they become ill and, temporarily at least, demonstrate unprecedented maturity, considerateness, and organisation.
4. In parent–child therapy, likewise, it is very important that parents not be made to feel that the therapist would be a better parent than they.

11

From Stasis to Movement

An Attachment Model of Psychotherapeutic Change

We started by looking at how attachment theory informs our understanding of the therapeutic relationship and moved on to the attachment-informed explanatory framework for thinking about psychological health and disorder. We come now to catalysing change.

The literature on change in psychotherapy is vast and complex (Lambert, 2015); this and the succeeding chapter approach the theme with due humility and trepidation. We shall be returning to the central questions raised at the start of this book: what are the underlying 'mechanisms' of psychotherapeutic change and how can attachment principles and research findings help clinicians put these to good therapeutic use?

Change: The Groundwork

As a preliminary to developing our attachment perspective, we examine some general themes and issues relevant to change in psychotherapy.

Psychotherapy and the 'drug metaphor'

Much of the current methodology of psychotherapy research is based on 'the drug metaphor' (Stiles & Shapiro, 1989), in which a specific psychotherapeutic procedure is identified and tested for its capacity to alleviate target symptoms of psychological disturbance. The current ascendancy of CBT as a psychotherapeutic modality is largely due to its success in using and promoting itself as the psychotherapeutic 'drug' of choice. CBT is promoted as a 'treatment' for a wide variety of psychological and physical illnesses, including depression, post-traumatic stress disorder (PTSD), anxiety disorders, delusional disorders, etc. It is however debatable whether the principles of drug evaluation can be transposed wholesale from pharmacological to psychotherapeutic therapies (Wampold, 2015). It seems improbable that a multifaceted phenomenon such as the therapeutic relationship can be reduced to a unique 'active ingredient' alone responsible for producing change. We shall argue that sophisticated models based on complexity theory are needed in order to encompass the multiple elements – biological, contextual, relational, linguistic, sociological, and even 'spiritual' – which underlie psychological change.

Structure and flux

In thinking about 'change' in therapy, two poles, and the interplay between them, need to be borne in mind. At one end lies Heraclitus's (1846/2008: iiv) aphorism that *'no man ever steps in the same river twice, for it is not the same river and he is not the same man'*. It is an empirical fact that, once we step outside (mentalise) the short-term perspective of our species' psychology, continuous change is inherent in the material world, inanimate as much as animate. The universe is in a continuous state of flux.

It is also true that continuity and stability are important features of the psychological and physical world: *'plus ça change, plus c'est la même chose'*.[1] Systems, especially biological systems, have self-maintaining tendencies. The seeming solidity of things is not entirely illusory: like breeds like, one thing leads on to another, often of very much the same ilk. All that is solid does *not* invariably melt into air (cf. Berman, 1983).

In human biology and psychology, between these two polar principles lies the developmental process itself, carrying us from cradle to grave, via Shakespeare's 'seven' – or, for Erikson (1950), eight – (st)'ages of man' [*sic*]. Each represents a phase of temporary stability, while movement from one to the next reflects the essential transience, forward movement, and irreversibility of life.

All three aspects – flux, stability, and development – are relevant to psychotherapists. The fact that suicidal depression and delusional states remit with time is the primary justification for the compulsory detainment of suicidal people. How one feels today does not necessarily mean one will feel the same tomorrow. Saving a suicidal person from self-injury is predicated on the principle that 'this too will pass'.

Outcome research in psychotherapy needs to take account of this tendency to remission, posing tricky methodological problems. Improvements claimed as the consequence of an intervention may represent no more than the 'natural history' of the condition. There is a myriad of contextual factors influencing a person's well-being, few of which are easily controlled for in the way that drug trials use dummy pills. 'No treatment' is unethical; 'treatment as usual' (TAU), if well carried out, may contain the elusive active ingredients, especially the relational aspects which attachment emphasises.[2] Unlike drug trials, psychotherapeutic 'placebo' can never be identical in all other respects to active treatment (Rutherford & Roose, 2014); the 'gold standard' of double blind controlled trials is inherently unattainable in psychotherapy.

Symptomatic versus structural change

The philosophy of continual change is to some extent counterintuitive. We may comfort ourselves with the thought that 'tomorrow is another day', but on waking we would be surprised not to see, in a seemingly stable mirror,[3] the same face as the one that went to bed the night before.

A distinction is frequently made in the psychodynamic literature between symptomatic and 'structural' change – 'first-order' and 'second-order' change, as systemic therapists put it. A repainted house is 'symptomatically' improved, but structurally unaltered. Dismantling and remodelling it into a new configuration would represent structural change. The well-worn metaphor for structural psychotherapeutic change is insect metamorphosis, where, after a period of pupation, a butterfly emerges from a radically transformed grub.

But while 'structural' change might be the acme of therapists' work, symptomatic change is, for the sufferer at least, far from trivial. The distinction is in any case not clear-cut, in that symptomatic relief may trigger deeper developments. The act of giving up smoking might give ex-addicts a sense of mastery extending to other aspects of their life: improved pulmonary health means they become more active, which in turn counteracts depression, etc. Conversely, the value of apparent structural change in the consulting room but not translated into symptomatic improvement in the patient's 'outer' life must be questionable.

Models of change

A number of models or metaphors are available for thinking about change in psychotherapy. Staying with the butterfly metaphor, the first move is the need to find a vantage point on one's troubled existence, and so begin to 'see oneself from the outside'. Therapy offers a period of 'pupation' in a safe relational space where new forms of living can be gestated. There may need to be a period of sensitive period 'regression' where, with the help of therapist co-regulation, pre-existing structures are reabsorbed and remodelled. Finally, if all goes well, new approaches and projects can emerge.

Another model is that of human development itself, where preparation, practice, and play are followed by rapid growth spurts or turning points. In ongoing therapy there are often periods of seeming stasis or doldrums, where 'nothing much' seems to be happening, followed by 'great leaps forward', where the patient might find a new good relationship, finally put an addiction behind him, and/or start moving out into the world from behind his or her defensive neurotic shield.

The next chapter develops the idea of psychotherapy as a 'complex system', comparable to that of climatic or economic systems. The Nobel Laureate chemist Prigogine (1980) argued that order arises out of chaos, but only under specific conditions. The basic requirements are a *closed system plus energy*. Psychotherapy can be thought of as a closed system in which the 'psychic energies' of the participants – typically therapist and patient, but in systemic therapy, family members – are brought into close proximity. This leads to initial de-stabilisation or chaos; we shall argue that the very purpose of therapy is to disrupt habitual maladaptive relational pathways and patterns. If things go well, this is followed by the emergence of new structures built from elements in the system hitherto unlinked or actively kept apart.

From the perspective of this book, therapy gains purchase when – and only when – the therapist becomes a significant attachment figure/secure base in the patient's life. The re-establishment of a 'sensitive period' in which the individual is in close affective and cognitive communication with another is vital. The therapist is now no longer a 'stranger' but is incorporated into the patient's inner world. This process may happen almost instantaneously, or take months, occasionally years, to come about. The conditions for novelty emerging from chaos are now met: a 'closed' caregiver/care-seeker system, plus the exploratory dynamic released by a degree of attachment security, representing Prigogine's necessary injection of energy.

Neuroplasticity

Let's return to the theme of 'neuroplasticity'. The serotonin transporter gene site (5-HTT) is polymorphic, with 'short' and 'long' alleles, and is present in macaque monkeys as well as humans (Bakermans-Kranenburg & van IJzendoorn, 2016). Suomi and colleagues' (Suomi, 2016) peer-reared monkeys with short alleles were more likely to indulge in self-injurious alcohol consumption than those with the long-allele versions. But when these 'vulnerable' capuchins were mother-reared, they consumed *less* alcohol than their long-allele counterparts.

Belsky and colleagues (2007) conclude that individuals vary in their susceptibility to environmental influence, whether adverse *or* favourable. Short-allele individuals do worse when conditions are bad, better when they are good; the long-allele group is more impervious to influence for good as well as ill. At a group or species level, the evolutionary success of a species benefits from phenotypic variation of this sort: specific environments 'select' those most adapted to it for differential survival. This is a reminder of the attachment normative misnomer, in that 'insecure' attachment may be advantageous in adverse environmental conditions, where 'security' may well be a handicap.

The life history of the existential analyst Victor Frankl illustrates both the disadvantages and advantages of secure attachment. When the Nazis arrived in Vienna in the 1938 'Anschluss', his fame meant he could have escaped to the USA. But his secure attachment pattern meant that he chose to stay with his beloved parents. All three were interred in a concentration camp, where his parents died. Frankl's secure attachment also saved his life, however. On the march to a lethal work detail he would listen to an unhappy guard's troubles, who repaid him with lighter duties and more food (Frankl, 1946/2006).

These findings are relevant to change in psychotherapy. Those most likely to benefit most from psychological therapies will have high levels of neuroplasticity, possibly mediated via 5-HTT. Compared with their 'long-allelle' counterparts, patients coming for psychotherapeutic help are likely to have been traumatised by adverse developmental experiences, but are also more able to respond to the favourable environment of therapy.

Change in the less neuroplastic group will be slower and less dramatic. For them, supportive therapy (Holmes, 1996) – open-ended, non-intensive, positively connoting, where maintenance or partial improvement is the aim – may be the approach of choice. This is particularly the case for borderline personality disorder sufferers, where diminution of chaotic life circumstances and relationships is a worthwhile goal, even if overall quality of life remains poor (Bateman & Fonagy, 2009). As advocated in the previous chapter, here 'radical acceptance' is often the best psychotherapeutic strategy as it avoids the implied criticisms associated with a more 'interpretive' approach, which can merely lower already rock-bottom self-esteem.

Developmental pathways

Bowlby (1969) was influenced by the theoretical biologist Conrad Waddington's notion of developmental pathways. Vicious and virtuous circles abound in nature, including in human psychology: nothing succeeds like success, and, often, nothing fails like failure. Secure and insecure attachment relational patterns tend to be self-perpetuating. A secure child has a sense that help is reliable and at hand when needed; the resultant 'scaffolded autonomy' facilitates playful learning and exploration, enhancing self-reliance, self-esteem, and an understanding of how the world works. This picture encompasses Main's (2000) 'fluidity of attentional gaze' of the secure child, in contrast to the rigidity of insecure infants, ever wary that their secure base may reject or neglect them, and closed to other possibilities and potentialities.

While secure and insecure attachment can both be conceptualised in terms of self-perpetuating developmental pathways, they differ in kind. Crittenden (1990) describes secure IWMs as 'open' and 'working' and insecure ones as 'closed' and 'non-working'. The insecure track has a built-in rigidity or inflexibility, making such children less open to the positive experiences that might move them on to a more favourable life course. Much of the 'resistance' seen in psychotherapy can be thought of in terms of wariness and mistrust that keeps the insecurely attached firmly stuck in their avoidant or anxious/dependent ways.

'The university of life'

Therapists sometimes struggle with the fact that most people, most of the time, get along fine without resorting to therapy. How can this be, we might ask ourselves? Few are immune to fortune's slings and arrows. Loss, disappointment, emotional pain, rejection, broken relationships, unemployment, trauma and displacement, bereavement, illness, and the ravages of time are ubiquitous and often inescapable. Therapy can certainly help with all of these, and should undoubtedly be more widely and affordably available. But for most people the passage of time, the support of family and friends, and – 'perish the thought' – healthy repression and narcissistic bounce-back, spell recovery and good-enough psychological functioning. The 'university of life' – the need to make a living, find a partner, a place to live, friends and hobbies, bring up children – stimulates developmental progress, and gets people over their difficulties, or at least helps them to get by.

Viewed epidemiologically, however, insecure attachment represents a large sub-group of the population, possibly as many 40% (Maunder & Hunter, 2015). Insecure attachments are risk factors for poor health, physical and mental. Although the risks in individual cases are not high, the widespread nature of insecure attachment means that in the population as a whole it has a highly significant impact. Confined by rigid and sequestered patterns of living and relating, it is difficult for this substantial minority to access the healing potential of everyday life. Avoidant people shy away from close emotional engagement, and have to work hard at keeping their stress responses under control. The anxiously insecure relinquish autonomy and agency in favour of helplessness and excessive dependency. In both groups, learning from experience is compromised and 'closed'. Worse, in disorganised attachment there is 'stable instability', with cyclic recurrences of approach/avoidance, crisis piled on crisis, and the lack of a still point or fulcrum from which to grow. This substantial minority probably forms the bulk of psychotherapy patients – and perhaps even a proportion of psychotherapists!

When therapy gains traction, there is a synergy between the changes that therapy brings about, and the client's relational environment. As 'epistemic trust' builds, clients relinquish rigid and sequestered relational patterns, becoming open to the opportunities that the flux of secure living affords. IWMs become open, appraisal processes freed up. Therapy helps clients turn towards the winds of change, and resume stalled developmental maturational processes.

Suffering

Underlying therapy there is an implicit – sometimes explicit – ethical stance, whether this is a valuation of autonomy, of enhanced self-awareness, the need for integration and wholeness, or of emotional freedom (Holmes & Lindley, 1997). The prime purpose of therapy is to alleviate mental pain and the processes that maintain it. In Buddhism, the 'solution' to suffering is the realisation that 'suffering' and change are synonymous. The paradox, intrinsic both to Buddhist philosophy and dynamic psychotherapy is that the way to overcome pain is to acknowledge and embrace it. This is not so far removed from Freud's (Freud & Breuer, 1895: 305) famous stoical assertion:[4]

> ...much will be gained if we succeed in transforming your hysterical misery into common unhappiness. With a mental life that has been restored to health, you will be better armed against that unhappiness.

Secure attachment is not distinguished from insecure attachment by the absence of pain, but, in the latter, by the inhibition of free interplay between bodily feelings, affects, and relational patterns. For the securely attached, able to draw on help when needed, emotional pain, however intense, is intrinsically bearable, transient, and transformable. By contrast, the insecure frequently find themselves stuck in emotional turmoil, caught between the twin poles of inflexibility (organised insecurity) or chaos ('D/U').

Therapists and their skills

Recent research has focused on skill acquisition in therapists (Miller, Hubble, & Duncan, 2007; Miller et al., 2013). We know that therapists vary greatly in their skilfulness and that skill, more than the specific modality practised, greatly affects psychotherapy outcomes (Shedler, 2010). Therapeutic skill varies, like most traits, according to a bell-shaped curve. A few 'supershrinks' get almost all of their clients better; some struggle to make an impact and are beset by client drop-out or deterioration; most of us are placed somewhere in between (Miller et al., 2007). Providing feedback on client progress to therapists improves outcomes (Miller et al., 2013), especially for those whose clients are failing to improve.

Psychotherapy can be compared with other skill-dependent activities, such as musical or sporting prowess. The key to success is 'deep domain-specific knowledge', acquired by the triad of *intensive practice, feedback,* and *non-punitive self-criticism.* Psychotherapy requires 'facilitative interpersonal skills' based on sensitivity, perceptiveness, and understanding (Miller et al., 2013). This echoes the attachment perspective, in that maternal sensitivity is intrinsic to secure mother–infant dyads, and that both perceptiveness and understanding can be subsumed under the rubric of mentalising.

Let's now look in more detail at how some of these themes apply in the consulting room.

How Attachment-informed Therapy Brings about Change

The theme of change-promotion in psychotherapy has been implicit in our discussion so far. Here, with some inevitable recapitulation, we carve the topic into three aspects: corrective experiences, skill acquisition, and the emergence of new psychological constellations. We shall develop the first two in this chapter; the latter is the theme of the next, where we attempt a neuroscience-informed synthesis.

Corrective emotional experiences

Alexander and French asserted that what gets patients better is not insight or interpretation, but *'actual experience in the patient's relationship to the therapist'* (1946: 46). From an attachment perspective, this makes perfect sense. Nevertheless, it remains controversial. First, the unique expertise of psychoanalysts is called into question if 'accurate interpretations' (see Eagle, 2011) are not the crucial mutative factor. Providing a 'corrective experience' is likely to be based on a more diffuse and less specialist skill-set than that claimed by psychoanalysts. Equally, CBT therapists are unenthusiastic about the concept of corrective experience, since they like to describe their relational role as that of 'collaboration', focusing primarily on the 'tool-sets' needed to counteract affect-driven cognitive faulty assumptions.

Perhaps too there is a deeper philosophical worry about the value judgement implicit in the term 'corrective': if a 'corrective' is needed, there must have been something needing to be put to rights. Also, there are the practical considerations of how *much* 'corrective experience' is needed, and how it can withstand the prevailing counter-therapeutic contextual forces – social and interpersonal – that perpetuate people's unhappiness.[5]

Let's remind ourselves of Bowlby's position on this topic. He implicitly agreed with Alexander and French. For him, therapists provide

> …the patient with a secure base from which he can explore the various unhappy and painful aspects of his life, past and present, many of which he finds it difficult or perhaps impossible to think about and reconsider, without a trusted companion to provide support, encouragement, sympathy, and, on occasion, guidance. (Bowlby, 1988: 138)

Two 'corrective' aspects of this formulation stand out, addressing the fundamentals of effective psychotherapy. The first is the need for trust. Without trust, no matter how clever, well-qualified, or knowledgeable the therapist, the patient will be unable to profit from the relationship. The second imperative is the need for help with 'exploring' pain and unhappiness. We have seen how insecure attachment is associated with both inhibition of exploration and lack of co-regulation of negative affect. If therapy is to be effective, both of these need to be turned around.

Trust

Consider an attachment analogue with the immune system. *In utero*, baby and mother share circulation across the placenta. But post-birth, the baby's immune system distinguishes 'self' from 'other', developing tolerance/acceptance to the former, but treating the latter as potentially harmful and to be repelled via antibodies, T-cell clumping, etc.

While not so sharply differentiated at the moment of birth, a comparable process occurs in psychological life. From around 7 months, infants develop 'stranger anxiety', triggering the attachment dynamic and seeking out a secure base for protection. This stranger anxiety is an early manifestation of a life-long 'friend or foe' appraisal capacity, which Porges (2011) sees as mediated through the vagal system. We become experts in deciding whether someone is or is not trustworthy. As with other species, alongside love, friendship, and trust, humans are equipped with the capacity for lying, mimicry, dissembling, exploitation, and abuse. But people with the D/U attachment constellation are particularly ill-equipped in this vital psychological friend/foe appraisal function.

In secure attachments the self–other gulf is bridged. Biobehavioural synchrony means that the mother–infant dyad operates as a psycho-physiological unit, in which the baby draws on or 'uses' the caregiver[6] as an extension of his or her self. This applies equally to adult romantic/marital relationships. In Coan's (2016) work on happy couples, whether conventional or same-sex, when one member was subjected to the threat of a mild electric shock, hypothalamic activation – the stress response – was markedly reduced when subjects were holding their partner's hand compared with facing threat alone.

Stress is lessened when one member of a couple is supported by their secure base partner. Coan's key finding, however, was not that the presence of the partner augmented the subject's defensive system, but rather that when holding a loved spouse's hand, the threat of shock had *little or no perceptible impact on the stress system*. The attachment figure – caregiver or spouse – becomes an extension of the self, vicariously undertaking the threat response *on behalf of the subject*. Perhaps because the threat is not directly experienced by the co-regulating partner, it becomes manageable. Neural energy is conserved for other tasks – feeding, planning, nurturing, mating, etc. Similar phenomena have been observed in avian species, where flocking birds (e.g., rooks) spend more time foraging and less nervously watching out for predators, compared with more solitary species, such as their close cousins crows (Wilson, 2012).

In secure attachment, the secure base becomes part of the extended self; the result is reduced stranger vigilance and enhanced trust and exploration. Secure attachment leads to the development of 'epistemic trust' in the child, defined as 'trust in the authenticity and personal relevance of interpersonally transmitted information' (Fonagy & Allison, 2014: 372). This allows for imitation and learning, and thus the transmission of cultural knowledge and values to the next generation. As development proceeds, this is generalised to a wider range of adults (grandparents, siblings, teachers, etc.) and later to social and political institutions. Societies run on trust; where trust breaks down, either from the top, as in grossly unequal societies,[7] or from the bottom in the case of family disruption and breakdown, the prevalence of psychological illness increases.

Let's return to the attachment model of *developmental pathways* and to our familiar story of the child waking up from a bad dream, crying for mother.

> She will take the child and cradle him with the timeless gesture... 'Don't be afraid, everything is in order, everything is alright'. Yet this common scene raises a far from ordinary question... **is the mother lying to the child?** (Berger, 1970: 54)

In the context of secure attachment, parental care is timely, sensitive, and mind-minded. Truthfulness is established when external and sensory input corresponds with enteroceptive experience. A baby waking in the night, perceived to be wet and cold by the mother, who changes the nappy and adds an extra cover, will, without cognitively 'knowing' what was wrong, feel better, snugger, able to fall asleep once more. The mother's response here is congruent with the child's experience. She has 'read' his body-mind, contingently and markedly ('*Oh, you poor thing, you're freezing, soaking wet*', etc.). Her communications are apposite and 'ostensive' in the sense that they point to appropriate actions – the nappy change and warm blanket.

From the child's point of view, this person, this caregiver, this attachment figure, this secure base, this parent, *is to be trusted*. Not only does the child trust the mother, the mother trusts the child: trust goes both ways. She relies on the baby to signal for help when needed – to call for a supplementary brain for co-regulation – and when to be left happily playing 'alone in the presence of the mother' (Winnicott, 1971). This is a mentalising, secure-making, trust-inducing parent, seeing the child with a life and mind of its own.

This caregiver/care-seeker trust dimension endorses children's autonomy and creativity, and respect for their inner privacy. Finessing trust remains a challenge throughout parenthood: when to trust a toddler's palate preferences and when to insist that broccoli be eaten; how much to give vent to 'tiger mother' tendencies and enforce a daily piano practice regime, versus conceding that guitar-strumming might be an OK route to musical stardom; when to sense that one's teenagers won't do anything stupid with drink, drugs, or sex, and when to 'ground' them; and even in adulthood, when to endorse offspring's life choices and when to express tactful reservations.

Contrast this no doubt somewhat idealised picture with that of insecure attachment. Here caregivers' capacity for contingency and marking may be compromised by depression, addiction, socioeconomic stress, marital discord, haunting past fears, and traumas. The child is faced with a conflict: her caregiver is essential both for physical survival and for acquisition of relational and cultural knowledge, yet to what extent is that caregiver be trusted? The two prototypes of organised insecurity represent 'defensive' solutions to this dilemma. Both entail suppression/repression: in avoidance, affect is damped down, in enmeshment, autonomy. Both strategies may have long-term consequences for mental and physical health (Maunder & Hunter, 2012). Without the capacity to recognise and regulate negative affect, people are liable to make bad choices of partner, unconsciously using them as dumping-grounds for their own bad feelings, and/or become overly self-reliant, unable to access help when needed. At the other extreme, jettisoning autonomy while remaining suffused with negative affect paves the way for over-dependency, low self-esteem (i.e., self-mis-trust), separation anxiety, and abnormal grief.

In organised forms of insecurity, the caregiver is at least *there*, a partially available resource, albeit one that cannot fully be trusted, especially with negative affect. With the help of a degree of repression or regression, vigilance is to an extent relaxed, and cultural transmission facilitated. But in D/U individuals, the caregiver is either absent (frightened) or the source of threat (frightening): the child is essentially alone and in a swirl of emotion. The more the world is not to be trusted, the greater the need for trust. The child is trapped in a state of *epistemic hypervigilance*, exquisitely sensitive to the merest hints of inattention, exploitation, or rejection, ready to retreat into an inner world of phantasy and self-sufficiency, primed for fight or flight, vulnerable to neglect and/or exploitation. The 'epistemic highway' providing access to vital cultural knowledge is blocked. Learning from experience is inhibited.

Anthony

Anthony, in his late 20s, presented with extreme withdrawal, cannabis addiction, and a possible psychotic disorder. He had grown up in a working-class family where his parents were in a constant, bitter battle and his father often turned his rage on his youngest son. What was striking about Anthony was his anachronistic 'hippie'-like hair in a long ponytail, his language full of 1960s jargon, his body language an extreme version of the languid, laid back, 'cool' guy. The mantle of 'hippieness' was not an integrated identification, more a rigid mask of rebellion against his father. It gave him something to *be*, a 'negative identity' in that it stated who and what he was *not*, but left him with no sense of be-*ing* in the world. His peers and friends peeled away; it was as if he was frozen in time. Living in an extremely insecure environment, he had rejected his parents' rigid cultural beliefs and replaced them with something equally empty and equally rigid. In therapy, he was at a loss for words, as he was for a self. After realising that talking, even in the most basic ways, was not helpful, his therapist introduced Winnicott's

(1965) 'Squiggle' game in an effort to bridge the gap between them. She drew squiggles on blank pieces of paper and invited him to make something of it, to extend, elaborate, and 'play' with it, and tell a story about it. With this child's game, the young man relaxed, smiled, loosened his arms, and allowed himself to imagine, ever so slightly.

What kinds of 'corrective emotional experiences' might help redress such pathologies of trust? Central to attachment-informed therapy are the parallels between the therapeutic relationship and secure caregiver/care-seeker relationships. We repeat our mantra: reliability, consistency, warmth, sensitivity, responsiveness, appropriate limit-setting, rupture/repair pathways, encouragement, and respect for autonomy.

Exploring pain and happiness with another

The second of Bowlby's precepts comes strongly into play here: therapy's role in providing patients with a secure base from which to explore the 'various unhappy and painful aspects of [their] life' (1988: 138). Without a secure base, exploration of mental pain is almost inevitably inhibited.[8] Negative affect-regulation is one of the prime functions of a secure base – helping to cope with fear, panic, misery, depression, confusion, low self-esteem, sense of failure, impotence, victimhood. Difficulties in processing and transcending these emotions are central to many psychological illnesses.

The classic ingredients of effective psychotherapy were enumerated by Rogers (1985): accurate empathy, non-possessive warmth, and congruence or authenticity. Accurate empathy entails being able to 'read' another's emotional states, consider them, and reflect them back. This is exactly what secure base parents do for their children. 'Warmth', literal and metaphorical, including the ability to challenge in a non-destructive way, is also a feature of secure-making therapists. Authenticity relates in a circular way to epistemic trust. Secure children are experts at knowing when caregivers are genuine or when they are just going through the motions of love and concern; equally, feeling that one's supposed caregiver authentically does care helps to build up a sense of security. Authenticity also means that caregivers themselves are able to detect when they are 'wrong', or being 'unfair', and to initiate a rupture/repair cycle to heal the breaches of trust – all of which adds up to 'good-enoughness' (Winnicott, 1965).

Sceptical therapists might object that all this is well and good in theory, but what about clients who seem impervious, however much 'corrective experience' is on offer, or actively spurn their therapists' best efforts. The 'inverse care law' (Tudor-Hart, 1971) of therapy applies: the more someone is in need of help, the less likely are they able to make use of it. We tried to address this issue in the previous chapter. Why do people immerse themselves in interpersonal disturbance, self-injurious behaviours, clashes, and discord rather than harmony and mutual respect? Why, when healthy and rewarding developmental pathways open up, do they seemingly choose to remain on problematic tracks to perdition?

Our explanations fall under the interrelated dyad of *defence* and *deficit* (Bateman & Holmes, 1995). We will expound a third 'D', *decompression*, in the next chapter. The defence viewpoint sees current difficulties as residues of outmoded childhood systems of self-protection; what was a necessary 'solution' has now become the problem. In childhood, the avoidant/deactivating attachment style enables a degree of security to be achieved in the context of an emotionally unavailable caregiver and adverse environments. In adult life, the same interpersonal suspicion and withdrawal is associated with emotional impoverishment and superficial, serial, and unsatisfying relationships.

We have already mentioned Fonagy et al. (2002), who postulate an 'alien self' that invades the mind of D/U clients, instigating seemingly perverse and negative responses to good things in the environment. Maltreated children's 'secure base' doubles as the source of threat or neglect. This contaminated internal secure/insecure base is then built into the structure of the self. The 'alien self' embodies the internalised abusive caregiver, bent on destroying the 'good' and indulging the 'bad'. While the end-results of this structure are deleterious, it has immediate benefits, summarised by Fairbairn's (1952: 189) famous aphorism: '*better to be a sinner in a world ruled by God, than to live in a world ruled by the Devil*'. Being a 'bad guy' in a good world at least provides a degree of control, avoidance of helplessness, and a degree of vitality. Self-destructiveness can represent defiance and revenge on the abuser ('*Look what you've made me do! Now you can see how it feels to maim and emotionally kill a child*'). Lyons-Ruth et al's (2005) work on identifications with hostile and/or helpless caregivers reflects a similar dynamic; identification with the aggressor is preferable to annihilation.

Luisa and her mother, Cynthia: Taking turns at helplessness and hostility

Cynthia came to treatment when the relationship with her 13-year-old daughter, Luisa, had broken down completely. Luisa, who had always been a reactive, challenging child, was diagnosed with ADHD at 3. Her parents' intensely conflictual marriage ended when her father was killed in a car accident when she was 8. At this point, she became provocative, disorganised, and lost. Her mother, Cynthia – also traumatised – had grown up in a privileged but devastating environment. Her father, severely mentally ill and an alcoholic, beat her and her siblings on a regular basis, and may have sexually abused at least two of them. Emotional, rather than physical, abuse was Cynthia's mother's stock in trade. Both Cynthia and Luisa were clearly disorganised in relation to attachment. In her own sessions,

Cynthia was consumed with the battles with her daughter. It became clear that she vacillated between being terrified and humiliated by Luisa on the one hand, and terrifying and threatening on the other. As time went on and the therapeutic relationship slowly deepened, Cynthia could begin to see both herself and her H/H dilemma. When she was with her daughter, however, this dynamic often took over and mentalisation failed, with the two of them alternating positions of attack and submission. Efforts to address this in dyadic sessions when Luisa was 16 were unsuccessful, and indeed it was not until many years later, after periods of complete estrangement, intensive attachment-informed treatment for both, and Luisa's near complete collapse, that Cynthia was finally able to provide a reasonably secure base for Luisa, and that Luisa could trust her mother enough to turn to her for real comfort.

Defences create deficits. D/U clients have difficulties with mentalising. They cannot read their own or others' minds; they are primed for a hair-trigger arousal; they are in states of 'epistemic hypervigilance' so they cannot trust or incorporate good things even when they are available.

How can attachment-informed therapy help find pathways from these insecurities to (l)earned security (Fear, 2016; Hesse, 2016)? We offer three ways of thinking about this. Implicit in Bowlby's corrective experience model is the gradual fading or 'extinction' of previous maladaptive patterns, and the instillation of new and more environment-appropriate ones. The secure base dynamic makes this possible: the persistent, gentle presence of the therapist, unfazed by setbacks, stasis, and defiance, and imbued with unwavering hope and confidence in the ultimately health-giving benefits of a loving relationship.

Time here is the key variable. Recovery from mistrust, and the birth of trust, can happen in a single session or (as in the case of Cynthia, above) may take many years. The mutative factor is the attachment *ambiance* of therapy, which research shows strongly impacts on feelings of security or their opposite (cf. Mikulincer & Shaver, 2016). Therapy fosters security both subliminally, via the therapist's warmth, consistency, regularity, commitment, tone of voice, and explicitly through affective sensitivity and verbally expressed mind-mindedness. These reduce the imperative for defensive insecure survival strategies. Exploration and self-regulation of feelings are instantiated, and later generalised to the clients' outside life-world.

Skill Acquisition

In sensitive periods in development, humans – and other mammals – become open to caregivers' collaborative affect co-regulation and rebalancing of the amygdala-PFC circuit; phobic avoidance and aversiveness is replaced with exploration and adventurousness. The establishment of a more secure therapist–patient relationship enables a reopening or 'regression' to this sensitive period phase. The client is once more open to the mood-management and mind-mindedness needed for more secure psychological functioning. This brings us *skill acquisition*, and specifically the interrelated skills of affect-regulation and mentalising. While both are part of normal good-enough family environments, therapy contains these functions in a 'pure' form, uncontaminated by the everyday constraints and struggles of life.[9]

We have suggested that many of the disturbed behaviours seen in public health settings – deliberate self-harm, alcohol and drug addiction, interpersonal turbulence – can be conceptualised as pathological attempts at self-soothing, i.e., attempts to manage negative affect in the absence of a co-regulatory secure base. Such sufferers have missed out on the sensitive period of affect co-regulation with a caregiver. This in turn compromises later self-regulatory skills and those entailed in mature dependency. Once empathic co-regulation is instated, therapy focuses on the antecedents and sequelae of affectively charged episodes, and attempts to mentalise them, especially those that arise in the therapy context itself.

Janet's absent father

70-year-old Janet suffered from recurrent depression and OCD. She was raised from infancy by a war-widowed mother. Janet felt her mother had never 'got' her, unlike the idealised father whom she had never met, and always favoured her older brother. She had been in weekly therapy for a couple of years without much change. The therapist, for whom the brother transference fitted glove-like, rather dreaded their sessions, often feeling trapped like a mouse with a cat, neither killed off nor allowed to run free. Here is an example of an attempted *in vivo* affective co-regulatory sequence.

Th: I noticed you looked pretty pissed off just now when I tried to talk about the way you brush off my comments...

J: Yeah, you treat me like shit, a waste of space, the lowest of the low.

[Therapist bites his tongue to stop himself saying: 'Here we go again, that's exactly what I mean.' However true that might be, he felt the timing would be wrong and serve merely to exacerbate the problem.]

Th: That sounds an absolutely horrible feeling. It's really upsetting to think that therapy, which is supposed to help, makes you feel so shitty.

J: Well, don't worry about it. I feel like that most of the time, so it's nothing new....

Th: Can we look at exactly what it was that I said that triggered the bad feeling this time?

J: I suppose its your tone of voice – you always sound so confident and pleased with yourself, as though you, and only you, know best.

Th: Again, I'm really sorry, and I need to guard against that pseudo-omniscience. I think you may have put your finger on one of my weaknesses. But could it be possible that I am also a replay of someone from the past who treated you like that?

J: Well of course my bloody brother, Mum's favourite, my mini- self-styled pseudo-Dad, the blue-eyed boy, damn the man....

A number of attachment-informed principles are illustrated here. First, as in the Talia et al. study (2014), therapeutic dialogue maintains the status quo rather than revealing new truths. But, second, 'the devil's in the details': the therapist puts his cards on the table, homing in on what is happening here and now between himself and the client. Third, the therapist tries to make affective-cognitive links: client and therapist are both aroused. Together they try to find a vantage point from which to think about those feelings. Fourth, the therapist is prepared honestly to acknowledge a rupture and honestly to apologise.

Once the specific case has been exhaustively looked at there might be an attempt to see to what extent this bitter self-abnegation stymies the client's life more generally. Eclectic therapists might try to help clients towards specific ways of managing overwhelming negative feelings: (a) identifying the early stages of the build-up to an affective 'episode'; (b) developing simple diversionary tactics such as 'counting to ten', going for a walk, putting on a favourite bit of music, watching a comedy video, etc.; (c) exploring mindfulness rituals such as meditation and 'watching the breath'.

Acquiring the skills of affect regulation also entails learning to mentalise, especially when moving from co-regulation to self-regulation. While mentalising, implicit or explicit, is a normal part of daily interpersonal life, it is almost never seen in its pure form. In the mutual mentalising of parent and child, or between spouses, both parties have their own 'agenda'. In therapy, however, the therapist's one and only aim is to help the client learn more about herself in the context of interpersonal life, and to be able to put this understanding to good use in everyday living.

How is this to be achieved? We can't see the back of our own head; the inner world of others – even if (or perhaps especially if!) we are passionately 'in love' – is essentially opaque. How do we learn to 'see ourselves from the outside and others from the inside'? An analogy can be drawn from teaching a child or a friend to play a new card game. The initiate is not handed the rule-book and told to get on with it. Instead, the tutor will play the first few rounds with the cards 'face up', until the beginner has grasped the rules and so begins to learn from the *experience* of playing itself. In Dennett's (2006) exploration of the psychology of religion, he argues that an all-seeing 'God', or the omniscient author in a novel, is granted unveiled access to the secret 'cards' in the human heart. Religion, literature – and, arguably, card games – play with and help foster understanding motives and feelings that in everyday life are never fully transparent. In attachment terms, these – and psychotherapy – are social institutions designed to develop and strengthen the skills of mentalising. Therapy is a third case of 'facing up' in the service of moral and psychological development.

In attachment-informed psychodynamic therapy, the 'rules of the game' require both therapist and patient to attend to and give voice to their inner thoughts and feelings, however irrelevant or embarrassing-seeming they might appear. This is no more and no less than Freud's (1913) 'fundamental rule'. In normal life, even with our nearest and dearest, a degree of reticence and tact prevail; in therapy, such constraints are actively discouraged. For therapists, Freud's precept is an invitation to self-reflection and judicious self-revelation, but of course only in so far as thoughts and feelings are relevant to the therapeutic relationship:

It is the last session of the day. The therapist suddenly remembers that she needs to buy some milk on the way home. She is not of course about to 'share' this seemingly irrelevant thought in its raw form with the client, but might say:

> 'I wonder if you worry that I fail to notice how deprived and under-nourished you often feel, especially with a long summer break soon to be upon us.'

The specific ways in which mentalising skills can be therapeutically fostered have been discussed in Chapter 7 and extensively expounded by those mentalising maestros, Allen, Fonagy, and Bateman (2008). To reiterate some key aspects:

1. Mentalising and arousal are mutually incompatible. Affect regulation comes first. We need to 'calm down' before we can 'think'.

2. Mentalising is an essentially 'slow' psychological process (cf. Kahneman, 2011). In therapy, mentalising is analogous to a sporting 'action replay', where therapist and patient together look back at an event, in or out of therapy, and try to reconstruct the thoughts and feelings driving the participants' actions.

3. Understanding 'transference' entails mentalising the anachronistic assumptions that patients bring into interpersonal life, learning how they 'belong' to the past rather than the present.

4. Pre-mentalising modes – teleology, equivalence, and pretend – are common and need to be identified as such, and often form the basis of transference assumptions.

5. The 'modern' concept of countertransference can be a useful aid to mentalising, especially when working with D/U clients (J. T. Holmes, 2014). The therapist listens to the feelings brought up in her in relation to the client. Giving voice to these provides the client with a window into the inner world of the other.

6. Mentalising is inherently subject to error. Therapists will acknowledge this by using phrases such as '*It seems to me that...*', or '*I've been thinking, but of course I could be wrong...*', or the 'perhaps...' preface.

7. Honest and unconditional apologies are called for when, as will invariably happen from time to time, they get or do things wrong.

8. Mentalising's first focus is the here-and-now. Scrutiny of current thoughts and feelings takes precedence over putative reconstructions from the past.

Summary

- The secure ambiance of therapy helps clients relax defences.

- This paves the way for affect co-regulation with the therapist, especially in experiencing and verbalising negative feelings, previously suppressed or repressed.

- Many of the psychologically troubled in search of therapy suffer from developmental deficits in affect regulation and mentalising skills.

- Therapeutic change re-awakens sensitive periods where the client is open to the influence of an intimate other.

- With the help of that influence they can acquire, or re-acquire, undeveloped mentalising and affect-regulatory skills.

Notes

1. First attributed to Jean-Baptiste Alphonse Karr in his journals.
2. See the recent study of depression in adolescence (Goodyear et al., 2017). At one year, no significant differences were found between CBT, psychodynamic psychotherapy, and 'skilled clinical management' (i.e., 'treatment as usual').
3. A longer time perspective would reveal change even in apparently immutable objects – mirrors tarnish and degrade no less than humans, merely at a slower pace.
4. There is a whiff of 'giving a little lecture' in this famous quotation. No doubt psychoanalysis's founding father could get away with it, but, as mentioned, lesser mortals are advised, when the lecture mode comes upon us, to keep our interventions brief and simple.
5. See Taylor (2014) for an autobiographical account of the author's transformation from borderline personality disordered in-patient to university professor, in which she asserts: 'after nine years of analysis suddenly something changed'.
6. Cf. Winnicott's (1971) 'Use of an Object': the term 'use' is deployed in the positive sense of 'useful', rather than exploitative 'using'.
7. There are strong correlations between income inequality and the incidence of mental illness, suicide, teenage pregnancy, murder, and other indices of social breakdown (Pickett & Wilkinson, 2009). This theme is developed further in Chapter 15.

8. A possible exception applies to creative artists who can use their medium – musical, visual, or verbal – as the 'other' with which to explore and transcend their pain (cf. Holmes, 2014b).
9. 'Purification' can be compared with the transition from 'herbal' to pharmacological remedies: foxglove becomes digoxin, willow-bark aspirin, etc.

12

The Improbable Profession

An Attachment-Bayesian Model of Psychodynamic Change

In the previous chapter we discussed the anachronistic *defences* associated with insecure attachment and the skills deficits, especially that of mentalising, which shape the self-defeatingness of neurosis and personality disorders. We come now to our third 'D' – '*decompression*'.

This term goes back to Freud's (1900) image of 'packed crystals' in both neurosis and dreams. He visualised unconscious themes as jumbled together, the therapist's task being to dissect them apart so that they can be thought into consciousness and so thought about – i.e. mentalised. Decompression in attachment-informed therapy is a metaphor for the mentalised 'space' – geographical and temporal – which opens up in therapy, enabling exploration, movement, and recombination; perhaps, too, deep-sea divers' need for slow-release 'decompression chambers', essential if potentially fatal 'bends' are to be avoided.

According to Freud (1937), psychoanalysis is an 'impossible profession' in that its outcomes are 'impossible to predict', a feature, he claimed, it shares with education and politics. Let's assume that the Master was not merely being disingenuous about the efficacy of his love/work-child and was on to something important. Psychology and neuroscience, on whose foundations the psychotherapies rest, start from the assumption that human relationships are amenable to scientific investigation. We shall argue that if they are to be fully – rather than simplistically and uncritically – understood, the perspectives of complexity and chaos theory are needed. Neither of these was available to Freud.[1] With their help, we hope to show that psychotherapy, far from being impossible, can be more usefully seen as an *improbable* profession.[2] But what exactly do we mean by that? For us psychotherapy is the 'art of the improbable' in the mathematical sense of creating conditions – unlikely under normal circumstances – which catalyse psychic change. Psychotherapy subverts 'normal circumstances'. The format of therapy and the skills of the therapist facilitate the uncoupling of entrenched sequences of expectations and actions which, in non-psychotherapeutic life, perpetuate patterns of unhappiness and self-defeatingness. 'Improbably' surprising revelations and new configurations thereby emerge.

Our exposition brings together three rather disparate intellectual roots: the Strachey model of transference, Bayesian probability, and chaos theory. All have strong connections to the fundamental principles of attachment.

Therapy as a 'Benign Bind'

The purpose of psychotherapy is to produce, accelerate, or facilitate psychological change. But what exactly is meant by 'change' in this context? Based on his medical background, Freud saw therapy as treatment for an illness, helping patients return from 'neurosis' to normality. His schema went roughly as follows. The 'talking cure' fosters self-knowledge; sufferers, no longer in thrall to unconscious drives of which they are unaware, can now direct their wishes in goal-satisfying directions, curbing their destructive and socially unacceptable impulses and/or directing them into channels of healthy 'sublimation', such as artistic or intellectual activity. The necessary 'insight' for all this is transmitted via the observations and interpretations of the analyst.

So far so good. To Freud's dismay, however, he found that however accurate or apposite his insights, he would come up against 'resistance' or 'negative therapeutic reactions'. Like Hamlet, it seems we'd 'rather bear those ills we have, / Than fly to others that we know not of'. Characteristically, Freud turned this to advantage, fighting paradox with paradox, as students of the ironies of the mind necessarily must. Welcoming, and then overcoming, 'resistance' became one of psychoanalysis's central tasks.

In his now classic paper, Strachey (1934) proposed that 'mutative interpretations' help circumvent this pesky problem. The patient, he argues, is faced with a *discrepancy* between his negative expectations and the actuality of the analyst, which is one of benign helpfulness, albeit muted by degrees of neutrality and reticence. The patient's negative feelings, carried over from adverse past experiences, are projected into what Klein later called the 'bad object'. Clients assume their analysts will, as happened in the past, neglect, reject, ignore, abuse, seduce, or exploit them.

The analyst's job is to mount a *benign interpretive challenge* to these assumptions, confronting patients with their transferential misperceptions, while neither blaming nor distancing them. This, in Strachey's model, triggers structural change in which the patient becomes more trusting and confident. We would add that this in turn opens up the 'epistemic superhighway' towards learning from experience, rather than the sequestered self-absorption of neurosis. Strachey noted how difficult it can be for analysts to stick to their last; remaining benign in the face of negative transference is a far from easy task. Let's illustrate with an example.

James's change of heart

The Robertsons' (1952) films of children before, during, and after admission to hospital poignantly illustrated how, under the prevailing regime, parents were discouraged from visiting their sick children. When eventually reunited, the children would appear emotionally withdrawn, turning away or even seemingly not recognising their parent. Bowlby saw this as representing the 'despair' stage of the bereavement reaction that children undergo when they feel abandoned by their secure base.

This turning-away stance characterised James, a 30-year-old divorced man, plagued with ambivalence in his relationships, both at work and in his love-life. As a child he had suffered from Perthe's disease, a dislocation of the hip, which required several long hospital admissions and confinement in a plaster-cast. A mathematics teacher, he would start new jobs with great enthusiasm, but soon run foul of his headmaster, and start looking for employment elsewhere; similarly, he would 'come on strong' with new sexual conquests, and then quickly withdraw, leaving his partners mystified and angry.

In thrice-weekly therapy, he was rather guarded and unforthcoming. The analyst commented on this, but, while James superficially acknowledged its validity, he seemed unable to overcome his old emotionally inhibited ways. The analyst, a smoker, then had to cancel a number of sessions because of pneumonia. On his recovery and return, James reported at the start of the session that, while waiting, he had noticed his analyst through the window, arriving slightly late. This triggered a memory – whether veridical or 'screen' – of James seeing his mother – visible but inaccessible – through the supposedly infection-protective window while he had been in hospital as a child.

James was suddenly flooded with feelings of sadness and loss, and revealed how much he'd missed his analyst and their sessions during the unplanned 'break'. The analyst wondered aloud if James's tendency to 'turn away' from close involvement in relationships – including from therapy – represented a residue of the despair he'd felt as a child when in hospital. Rather than risk further abandonment, he'd chosen the not-so-Jolly-Miller path: 'I care for nobody, no not I/ for nobody cares for me.'

Startled, James started to cry – and then, in a regressed way, blurted out *'I want my mummy... I was really worried about you when I heard you were ill.'*

(Continued)

(Continued)

On the same evening, a Friday, James phoned his therapist asking for an extra session on the Monday. The therapist said this was not possible, but reminded James that he would be there for him as ever on the Tuesday. James was later able to tell the analyst how rejected he'd felt at this rebuff, but also empowered, as though the analyst was giving the message that he had the strength to cope on his own, but without resorting to his habitual suppression of feelings.

This was one of those rare but precious pivotal moments in therapy. James thereafter became much more trusting of his analyst, more open, and made a commitment to his girlfriend, with whom he now started to live. It was as though he had moved from a habitual rejecting position of 'I don't want...', to a seeking, yearning one of 'I want...'.

An attachment view of the Strachey model would be that the analyst has first to connect with the patient as he is, validating the fabric of his experience and discourse, however insecure – in James's case, a markedly avoidant strategy. This then moves to a phase of challenge, which for James was serendipitously created by the analyst's illness. At last somewhat secure, if shakily so, James felt safe enough to give vent to his sadness and anger at abandonment. His negative affect was co-regulated at last, releasing him from his pattern of neglect-induced mistrust and suppressed rage.

The repair of this fundamental psychic rupture cleared an inner space in which he could experience need and positive loving feelings.

Therapy had thus placed James in a '*benign bind*'. If he was to stay in analysis, and justify the time and money entailed in doing so, he could not go on with the old ways. Continuing mistrust meant merely 'more of the same'. Trust was dangerous, but in the 'as-if', metaphorical culture of analysis – and so at one step removed from real life – there was less to lose. In the context of being 'held' by the therapy, the risks of emotional vulnerability were more virtual than real. He could at last chance it. Being in therapy meant that he couldn't *not* change.

An important feature of this model is the therapist's countertransference. Therapists' own unconscious themes play their part in shaping the therapeutic relationship, for good or ill. Strachey emphasises the difficulties therapists experience with their own anxieties when attempting to make 'mutative inter-pretations'. They may shy away either by collusive reinforcement of clients' insecure attachment patterns, or precipitate impasse or drop-out by labelling them as 'narcissistic', 'difficult', or unmotivated. In a mutative, therapeutic relationship, the client feels both held and challenged, as James did when his request for an extra session was refused. The phone call stimulated simultane-ous irritation and empathy in the therapist. It felt important to hold the frame if the treatment were to be truly 'mutative', and avoid either fostering depend-ency, or reinforcing the avoidance that had brought James into therapy.

Bayesian Probability and Transference

The future's not ours to see. Yet to operate successfully in the physical and social world we need to be able to predict what lies ahead. The only reliable guide to the future is the past; we cannot be absolutely certain that the sun will rise tomorrow, but, on the balance of probabilities, it is highly likely that it will! The Reverend Bayes, an eighteenth-century mathematical clergyman (McGrayne, 2011), described how, faced with uncertainty, we automatically assign 'prior' probabilities to future events, and then 'posterior' probabilities in which these predictions are updated in the light of experience.

Staying alive is hard work. Peacocks' tails notwithstanding, evolution ensures that living organisms are energy-efficient, seeking maximum benefit from the minimum effort. Friston (2010) applies this principle to the brain, whose aim, he argues, is to convert 'free energy' into the less energy-demanding 'bound' form. If every trivial sensory event had to be considered on its merits and from first principles, the energy required would make action impossible (the brain consumes up to one-third of the body's energy requirements). By sticking to prior assumptions and pathways, the brain reduces the 'free energy' associated with uncertainty. But here's the rub: updating predictions, or 'posteriority', is also essential, however energy-consuming. Without this updating we would be forever stuck in the past: i.e., shaped by transference-dominated anachronistic assumptions.

Neuroscientists like Friston see the brain as a 'predictavore' (Clark, 2016). Sensory input is neutral – its 'meaning' is generated by converting incoming *sensations* into prediction-coloured *perceptions*. The painful tingling associated with a serrated, green-leafed garden weed equals, on the basis of prior experience and language, a grasped 'nettle'. Sensory input is matched with pre-existing mental structures, which then guide behaviour, and trigger reflection, expression, and action ('*Ouch! I must wear gloves next time*').

The brain shapes sensory input into experience/perception according to Bayesian probabilistic calculus. In healthy functioning, discrepancies between prediction and input are: (a) identified, via 'tolerating uncertainty', (b) explored, by *action* aimed at reducing uncertainty, (c) leading, finally, to cognitive restructuring and updating of 'prior' probabilities.

One fine spring morning, in the course of JH's daily run across agricultural land, he noted that the farmer had recently sprayed weed-killer, and, as he ran, he experienced an unpleasant sickly smell and slight feeling of nausea. Worried that he might be adversely affected, as he had been in previous years, he returned via a detour. The next day, following the same course, the smell had gone, but he noted in his peripheral vision a *dark flapping object*. His first thought was that this was a bird, perhaps a crow, affected by the previous day's poison. He approached to investigate further and, if necessary, to rescue the creature. The closer he got to the 'object', however, the more the putative stricken bird revealed itself to be no more than a fragment – no longer imagination's figment – of wind-blown black plastic.

This minor incident illustrates a number of Bayesian principles.

- The *meaning* attributed to sensations (in this case visual/aural flapping) is guided by enteroception and higher-order concepts. JH's own slight feeling of nausea on the previous day and knowledge of the hazards of weed-spraying raised the possibility in his mind of a sick bird.

- JH's (temporary) 'somatising' mind-set led him to interpret the 'external' world in terms of his inner dispositions.

- The 'free energy' generated by an ambiguous stimulus led to a motor response. JH turned his head and moved towards the flapping object in order to align sensation with concept-derived perception and minimise unbound energy.

- JH's freedom of (a) movement ('let's go and investigate and rescue that poor bird') and (b) cognitive hypothesis-testing ('the poison will have dispelled by today so it would be odd if the bird were still affected') led to a stable, energy-minimised, representation of external ('it's flapping plastic') and internal ('it was an optical illusion') conclusion.

If we accept the 'transference hypothesis' of the previous section, clients enter therapy in thrall to their 'prior probabilities'.[3] In the earlier example, James assumed no one would care about his fears of abandonment. He protected himself with an avoidant wall of self-sufficiency, dating back to childhood hospitalisation and maternal separation. Bayesian revision in the light of posterior probabilities was inhibited: the analyst's comments and interpretations were brushed aside. Prior assumptions have the appeal of free energy/surprise minimisation: 'Always keep a-hold of nurse / For fear of finding something worse' (Belloc, 2007). The uncertainty needed for James to expose himself to new sensations, and revise perceptions, meanings, and assumptions in the light of them felt too dangerous. The attachment figure is assumed to be rejecting, unreliable, or absent. But then, *improbability* was allowed into the equation. The contingency of the therapist's illness-enforced absence re-awakened memories of childhood abandonment, and the accompanying affects: fear, sadness, anger. But now, instead of denying or turning away from them, James approached them, knowing the analyst, restored to health, would be there if needed. Feelings finally could be co-regulated: thought about, validated, moved on from.

Secure attachment allows for improbability: uncertainties are tolerable, because they can be resolved through action, either on one's own or with the help of an attachment figure. In insecure attachment, rigid prior probabilities are clung to, either by isolationism or dependency. Some, or all, of this may be neurochemically potentiated. In secure attachment, the therapists' and clients' oxytocin systems become entrained. This in turn cross-talks to the dopamine system: 'reward' – the therapist's approval and love – enables the 'settings' of prior predictions to be altered, allowing the free energy of health to overcome the bindings of neurosis. Revised assumptions become possible; inhibitions of feeling, thought, and action lifted.

As suggested in the previous chapter, all this depends on the re-establishment of a developmentally sensitive period in which the client becomes open to synchrony and entrainment with a caring other. By drawing on the therapist's brain, as in Coan, Schaefer, and Davidson's (2006) hand-holding experiments, clients' need to minimise free energy is alleviated. The neutrality and reticence of the psychodynamic therapist generates an *ambiguous stimulus* or '*enigmatic signifier*' (Laplanche, 1999), analogous to the vague flapping sensation in JH's peripheral vision. Prior probabilities, aka transference assumptions that the therapist will be critical, indifferent, all-embracing, abandoning, etc., rush in to fill this cognitive vacuum. *But in the laboratory of the consulting room, these become visible, discussable, and available for mutual mentalising.*

Discovering a discrepancy, as in the Strachey model, between assumptions and reality creates 'surprise'. This is Friston's 'unbound energy'. The therapist's skill lies in putting this surprise to good use and, via revised assumptions, converting it into bound energy, but now at a 'higher', more environmentally sensitive and flexible level. The security of the therapeutic relationship means that it is safe to be 'surprised' and become less passive. 'Posterior' probabilities can be revised and updated, learning from experience restarted, not just in the consulting room but via the 'epistemic superhighway' in the outside world. Therapists help clients to tolerate temporary states of uncertainty and 'not knowing', and to 'explore', both behaviourally, as in 'testing hypotheses' (e.g., discussing contentious issues with loved ones), and psychologically, in allowing new thoughts, feelings, and structures to emerge.

Chaos Theory

Freud's impossibilism had a point. Although at a population level the statistical evidence strongly supports the effectiveness of psychodynamic therapy (Fonagy et al., 2015; Shedler, 2010), in any given case the outcome cannot be guaranteed. Not only that. Although there are pivotal 'ah-ha' moments, turning points, sudden breakthroughs, and great leaps forward in therapy, there are also setbacks, snags, relapses, and one-step-forward-two-steps-back. There is rarely a linear causal relationship between 'intervention' (e.g., a dream interpretation, cognitive homework assignment, etc.) and outcome. A balance needs always to be struck between bound-energy conservatism and innovative surprise; where the equilibrium comes to rest can never fully be predicted.

This built-in uncertainty is the bane of psychotherapy researchers, and even more so for service managers and clinical administrators. A frequent error is to conclude that the explanation lies in the paucity of research findings and funding. Much as both are in need of augmentation, the problem lies in the nature of psychotherapy itself. Human relationships, like the weather and economies, are inherently complex and chaotic systems. Fluid, not Newtonian, mechanics is needed to capture their mathematics (cf. Rose & Shulman, 2016). Two features of these complex systems are particularly relevant to psychotherapy. The first, discussed in the previous chapter, is the Prigogine principle that new structures emerge from the combination of a closed system and the injection of energy. The intensity of the therapeutic relationship, within the confined system of bounded sessions, fulfils these criteria.

The second relevant chaos theory concept is the observation that minute differences in initial conditions in systems can lead to very different outcomes – the famous flap of a butterfly wing in Brazil triggering a tornado in Texas. A tiny difference in barometric pressure or air temperature in a particular location may spell mild drizzle or a torrential downpour. For weather forecasters, especially in temperate climates, the solution to this problem is the 'numerical modelling method', in which the computer generates a large number of possible future weather patterns based on small differences in prior assumptions. When these collectively predict essentially similar outcomes, forecasts can be confident; where they vary, forecasters warn of uncertainty. Occasionally, despite an overall consensus of equability, a small number of scenarios may predict catastrophic events; these also need to be taken into account and due warnings issued.

The reader may feel that the discussion has strayed far from therapy. But we contend that therapists similarly need to hold in mind all possible outcomes of the therapeutic relationship.[4] The skill of the therapist lies in being aware of the small but vital adjustments to 'initial conditions' more or less likely to either perpetuate problems (as in 'impasse'), eradicate them (as in 'easy' cases), or (the norm) help generate sufficient uncertainty for change to emerge, but not so much as to scare the client away. These 'adjustments' concern subtleties of the therapeutic ambiance matched to the specific needs and style of the patient. Therapists intuitively – or guided by explicit supervisor experience – adjust for each client their tone, volume, and timbre of voice, body posture, forms of words, timing of 'interventions', flexibility versus firmness in relation to boundaries, maintaining hope in the face of seeming despair, etc.

Case Example

Our final example in this chapter illustrates some aspects of this intuitive 'numerical modelling' in a case of time-limited therapy. It illustrates the movement in successful therapy from 'bound energy' avoidance, through therapist–client biobehavioural synchrony, to 'surprise', the release of action in the place of closed passivity, and the establishment of new and less restricted 'prior probabilities' and openness to experience.

Mrs Brown gets a car

Mrs Brown, a 62-year-old retired teacher and housewife was referred by her GP after her globe-trotting engineer husband of 40 years had threatened to end the marriage unless she 'did something' about her depression and heavy drinking. He 'chauffeured' her to the assessment appointment and sat in the car while Mrs Brown was interviewed. She made it clear from the start that she had come on sufferance, to satisfy her husband, and that she had no hopes or expectations of therapy.

She was dressed in a rather 'unfeminine' way, made poor eye contact, with a typically avoidant narrative style. She gave a dismissive, unelaborated account of her life, minimising her alcohol intake and describing how she had followed her husband from post to post while bringing up her two children in often hostile and unpropitious circumstances.

Mrs Brown's older brother was her 'malicious mother's' (i.e., daughter down-putting) favourite. Mrs Brown was close to her father but he was mostly working and 'never there'. She'd met her husband, three years her senior, while she was still at school. She described how he was in control of 'everything', imposing his routines and rituals on her.

At first sight there seemed obvious marital difficulties. The husband was in the car outside; why not, thought the therapist, invite him in and work with them as a couple? Against this, however, was the therapist's countertransferential sense of fatherly protectiveness. He sensed a suppressed neediness in Mrs Brown. Might including the husband not reproduce the problem of his controllingness and replay the scenario of the favoured older brother? Maybe Mrs Brown needed exclusive attention from an attentive therapeutic 'father'.

This 'initial conditions' thinking therefore led to the offer of a series of time-limited sessions – which was all she said they could afford. This was perhaps a manifestation of her sense of deprivation, but at this stage it was left unchallenged.

In the first session, the therapist suggested that her drinking was a way of coping with feelings of trapped-ness and anger towards a husband whom she both desperately needed and deeply resented. She then 'confessed' that she often went alone into an empty room after he'd upset her, muttering out loud, 'hate, hate, hate…', and that this was usually a precursor to a bout of drinking.

At this stage she made it clear that from her point of view her problems were insoluble, and that her only options were more of the same, or disastrous divorce and family break-up. Therapy would either do no good at all or blow 40 years of marriage apart. When the therapist tried to reflect this stark picture back, she immediately defensively backtracked, excusing her husband, saying he was a good man doing his best, etc. As per Talia et al. (2014), the therapeutic dialogue neatly reflected her attachment avoidance and 'bound energy' clinging to the status quo.

Next came a break, where she and her husband went on holiday. On her return she reported that she had managed to control her drinking, but had

(Continued)

(Continued)

been 'surprised' when her husband complained that 'she wasn't much fun to be with'. The therapist explored her feelings of hurt and anger about this critical remark, which she reluctantly acknowledged. In the next couple of sessions low self-esteem was the theme: she compared herself unfavourably, and resentfully, with her brother, husband, and now the therapist. But somehow there was a sense of a working alliance beginning to emerge – she was beginning to 'open up' and allow at least a modicum of affect co-regulation.

Mindful of 'initial conditions' – Mrs Brown's ingrained low self-esteem but low-level satisfaction that she had stayed the course of marriage with this difficult husband – the therapist ventured some positive comments. Praising her articulacy, he ventured: *'and when did you discover you had a brain?'* She revealed, to their mutual surprise, that she had excelled both academically and in sport at school, and went on to talk about her work as a teacher and how she was currently helping a particularly disturbed girl. The therapist was tempted to make a 'transference interpretation' at this point, picking up on the parallels with her situation in therapy. On balance, and again surveying the range of possible interventions, he felt this might distract from tentative steps towards co-regulation of new-found self-esteem, and so held back. In the next session she revealed that she had confronted her husband with her hurt feelings when he had, as usual, 'put her down'. In response, he initially 'forgot' that he had done anything untoward, but then, to her amazement, acknowledged that he had indeed been hurtful.

She arrived at the next session in a state of elation: 'My mind's been buzzing all week. I couldn't sleep. I have been thinking of all things I've achieved over the past 30 years, of all the strange places I've lived in and survived...' She then revealed that, to her utter surprise, her husband had said she needed a car and that she deserved to be able to go to wherever she wanted and whenever she wanted.

In the penultimate and final sessions she duly arrived alone, having driven herself for the first time. The atmosphere was flirtatious. In the very last scheduled session, she described how on her return her husband had welcomed her back, kissed her and asked *'How did it go?'* A two-month follow-up was arranged, at which she revealed that, although she hadn't drunk, she had at times been sorely tempted.

P:　How did you get me, who never talks, to talk?

Th:　I wish I knew the secret. What do you think?

P:　It was something about having something finally for myself, and not feeling guilty about it. Plus writing things down in preparation for my sessions. Plus getting that car.

Black swans notwithstanding (cf. Hinshelwood, 2013), this isolated example of brief therapy by itself proves nothing. The account is doubtless shaped by the therapist's own 'prior predictions', and our wish to leave readers near the end of our joint journey with a success story. But it serves to illustrate some salient points from this and the previous chapter.

1. The therapist's sense that *'initial conditions'* (individual or marital therapy) might make a big difference to outcome guided his choice of therapy mode. He intuitively ran a number of different possible scenarios in his mind and, based on experience, opted for individual therapy.

2. His initial strategy was one of *acceptance, contingency,* and *'marking'*: acknowledging Mrs Brown's 'no-win' sense that therapy would be either useless or dangerous, and how drink helped her to live with that dilemma.

3. Once his *countertransference* told him that the client was in a more open and trusting state, he moved the 'conditions' towards *challenge*.

4. Her 'hate, hate...' mantra epitomised *unregulated negative affect*. Co-regulation was what was needed – her feelings of unacknowledged hurt when her husband upset her with his controllingness and denial.

5. Given her low self-esteem, the therapist sensed that confronting her with her failure to tackle her husband might simply reinforce feelings of inadequacy. *Building up her self-esteem* via enumerating her strengths and achievements seemed a better way forward.

6. *'Unbound energy'* was released as manifest in her excited sleeplessness, freeing her, temporarily at least, from low-self-esteem and resentment.

7. This led to *mentalising*, in that Mrs Brown was able to begin to think about herself and her life in a more objective way, rather than perpetuating denial and guilt-inducing self-denigration as the necessary price for a degree of security.

8. Now she began to move towards the *actions* that would lead to changed perception and cognitive structures. The concrete symbol of independence, autonomy, and value – the car – reinforced her new-found sense of worth.

9. Under the umbrella of therapy, she could allow herself to be *'surprised'* by her husband's enthusiasm and generosity, rather than resorting to the perverse security represented by her secret drinking.

Conclusion

In this chapter we have put forward an attachment-informed model of change in therapy, drawing on three sets of ideas: the *'benign bind'*, *Bayesian probability*, and *chaos/complexity theory*. All three are consistent with the idea of the therapist and her setting as a *secure base*. Half a century of research has anatomised this portmanteau term to encompass: sensitive periods, sensitivity, mirroring, marking, tact, affect co-regulation, challenge, and developmental 'stretching'. Together and separately these create the possibility of change.

Research suggests that the key to therapeutic success lies in 'deep, domain-specific' understanding (Miller et al., 2013), rather than in theoretical knowledge *per se*. The *therapist's own sense of security* plays a crucial role in this. Over-anxious therapists engage well with their clients, but then hold back from the friendly challenge inherent in a 'benign bind'. At the opposite extreme, therapists with a tendency to avoidance may be discouraged by clients' imperviousness to democratic discourse. They may impatiently and insensitively be drawn to challenge, precipitating 'impasse' and/or premature drop-out.

Secure therapists welcome feedback, or 'posterior probabilities', and use them to deepen the skills of their craft. On this rests the case for continued supervision throughout the working lives of therapists. Based on feedback, whether through self-supervision or the help of others, they are better able to visualise, and tolerate the uncertainty associated with, a range of different possible outcomes. This enables them to adapt their stance to the needs and style of the client, maximising the likelihood of change and/or minimising the pull of stasis and resistance.

Summary

- Psychotherapy is a complex rather than a linear system.

- Inhibition of agency means that the psychologically troubled are trapped with Bayesian 'prior probabilities', not updated in the light of experience.

- The secure ambiance of therapy enables clients to begin to risk being 'surprised' and so revise their predictions about themselves in relation to others.

- This opens up the epistemic highway to learning from experience.

- Therapists' skill depends on holding a range of different possibilities in mind, and being able to learn from their mistakes.

Notes

1. Cf. Einstein (1901), 'make things as simple as possible, but not simpler'.
2. Suzanne Hicks (2016), in a very different context, suggested this felicitous gloss on Freud.
3. These ideas have, of course, much in common with Bowlby's IWMs, and Crittenden's notion of 'open' and 'closed' representations, as well as Stern's (1985) description of Representations of Interactions that have been Generalised (RIGs)s, abstractions of interactions that serve as the basis for predicting future interactions.
4. JH's 1970's neurology trainer, Dr Gerald Stern, would succinctly ask his patients: 'better, worse, or the same?' Numerical modelling demands those three possible outcomes be multiplied tenfold.

13

Attachment, Mentalising, and Child Psychotherapy

Working with Parents

We now turn to the relevance of attachment ideas for child psychotherapy. Our particular focus will be on using an attachment framework in assessment and clinical formulation, and in conceptualising and providing a rationale for child/parent triadic and dyadic work.

We will spend relatively little time in this chapter focusing on individual treatment with children. This is not because we do not value such work. On the contrary, much of what we have emphasised about adult work can be transposed to child and adolescent psychotherapy. The secure base, co-regulating, and mentalising functions of the child–therapist relationship help reorient derailed developmental processes arising out of disrupted parent–child relationships. Play, mirroring, synchrony, sensitivity, and affect regulation play key roles, as do playfulness, warmth, and full emotional engagement.

As with adults, we use the attachment experiences and orientation of the child to guide therapeutic interventions. The avoidant child must be approached cautiously, his defences challenged only when he has begun to trust the therapist, while the anxious dependent child's autonomy can be encouraged only once she feels safe enough to explore. *What differentiates child from adult work is that when we work with children we are inevitably, and desirably, also working with their caregivers.* Our focus here is on the ways attachment helps frame the opportunities and complexity afforded by their presence within the child psychotherapy context.

Despite the fact that most dynamically oriented child therapists regularly interact with the parents of the children they see, the literature on parent work is relatively thin (but see Hurry, 1998; Novick & Novick, 2005; Siskind, 1997; Slade, 1999, 2008b). And while behavioural therapies for children often include parent skills training (Centers for Disease Control, 2009), there has been little discussion of the importance and complexity of this work in the CBT literature. There is, however, currently a variety of different intervention models available for working with parents and very young children, all of them deeply informed by attachment theory and developmental science. These include: intensive home visiting to support high-risk young parents in the transition to parenthood (Olds, Sadler, & Kitzman, 2007; Sadler et al., 2013; Slade, Sadler et al., 2017); the Circle of Security intervention (Powell et al., 2013); and Child–Parent Psychotherapy, a manualised treatment for traumatised young children and families developed by Alicia Lieberman and Patricia Van Horn (Lieberman, Ghosh Ippen, & Van Horn, 2015; Lieberman & Van Horn, 2008). These approaches rest on several core assumptions, all relevant to the relationship between attachment-informed and more traditional child psychotherapy models.

The first is that – consistent with the central premises of this book – parental care and the parent–child relationship are integral to children's development. A second core assumption of these models is that in order to provide a secure base for their children, vulnerable parents need a range of supports to help them live with psychodynamic 'ghosts' (Fraiberg, 1980) and summon up 'angels' (Lieberman et al., 2005) in the nursery, to provide psycho-education about the attachment circle and its functions (Powell et al., 2013), and to offer material help. The third is that a *unique synergy* takes place when the care-seeking/caregiving system is activated and examined therapeutically. This synergy, arising out of the activation of attachment systems in both parent and child, has the potential to promote change within the mother, within the child, and their relationship. Recall that in Chapter 11 we described the basic requirements of a move from chaos to order as a *closed system plus energy* (Prigogine, 1980). Dyadic or triadic work can be thought of as a closed system in which the 'psychic energy' of the participants is activated in ways that can be used to promote change and the development of new ways of being in relation to one another.

These perspectives dovetail with what has been a key point throughout this book: parental care is essential to and inseparable from the development of the person. In child psychotherapy, we have an opportunity to influence this, directly or indirectly. When the relationship is precarious, and/or parents are having difficulties making sense of or connecting with the child, *we need not only help the children make meaning of their internal experience, but also* repair *this crucial and fundamental relationship*. In Winnicott's terms, we need to foster the mother or caregiver's capacity to provide a *holding environment* (Winnicott, 1965), or, in Bowlby's, to develop their capacity to provide a secure base (Bowlby, 1969). So, not only must we give meaning and shape to the child's inner life, *we must work to shape parental care*. Holding the parent in mind, and/or working with and in the parent–child relationship helps enliven the parent's connection to the child in ways that bring a sense of pleasure, meaning, and agency. This can lessen the child's fears, allowing him the safety to seek security and love on the one hand, and explore with creativity and passion on the other. As Winnicott (1965: 49) put it:

> The mental health of the individual, in the sense of freedom from psychosis or liability to psychosis ... is laid down by this maternal care, which when it goes well is scarcely noticed, and is a continuation of the physiological provision that characterises the prenatal state.

When parental care goes not so well, however, the dangers for the child are legion, and the challenges for therapists are correspondingly great.

This chapter focuses on three specific applications to child assessment and treatment. First, we recommend assessing the quality of the parent–child attachment relationship at intake, and integrating this understanding into dynamic formulations and treatment goals (Slade, 2004). Second, we emphasise the importance of engaging caregivers' capacities to reflect on the child's experience, along with activating their desire to protect and nurture their child. Our job is to hold and make meaning for them of their experience as caregivers, and the child's reciprocal experience of being looked after. Third, we encourage child therapists to remain open to working *with and in* the relationship with the parents, and to see where integrating parents into child sessions may be both appropriate and helpful. To reiterate: *none of these applications supplants a child's individual treatment; rather, they can greatly support it.*

Look at the Relationship: Attachment as Predictive and Prescriptive in Child Treatment

Mary Ainsworth's SSP reveals what children feel they can *expect* from their parents once the attachment system has been activated. In the moment of reunion we see the whole history of the caregiver–child relationship. The child is distressed, aroused, and biologically primed to seek safety. How do they get what they need in that moment? Can they approach mother freely and seek comfort? Does need have to be downplayed? If frightened of approaching the caregiver, does the child dissociate, collapse, or freeze? The SSP reveals *in vivo* how fear is regulated in the dyad, and how – successfully or unsuccessfully – child and caregiver cope with this quotidian yet developmentally crucial occurrence (Slade, 2014).

In secure parent–child relationships, the mother is sufficiently organised and regulated to be able to see, hear, protect, and nurture her child. When she is traumatised, stressed, or dysregulated, or when children have difficulties that make them particularly hard to parent, the child becomes a vehicle for her projections, remaining unknown and alien to her. Instead of activating empathic and mentalising networks, and triggering both attachment and pleasure centres in the parent's brain (Feldman, 2015b), the child – his mere presence, his proximity seeking, his needs, his emotions – can trigger destructive and malevolent processes. The child's approach elevates the parent's stress, and she cannot see or respond to him. All this helps therapists think about how best to approach their work with the child, and what areas of the parent–child relationship needs addressing.

Typically, when children are referred for treatment, the parents are seen first and then a session is scheduled with the child. The first session (or sessions) with parents not only provides an opportunity for history taking, etc., but also establishes the therapist as trustworthy, and as interested in working collaboratively to help the child. When it is time to see the child, we suggest that – for pre-adolescent children[1] – the primary caregiver and child be seen together, regardless of the presenting problem or clinical situation. If there are two parents in the child's life, both parents come in for (separate) initial dyadic sessions. We also suggest that a brief separation from the parent be introduced into this first session, a kind of mini-Strange Situation. All this enables the clinician to assess the tenor and quality of the parent–child relationship with each parent separately.[2]

During this 'attachment assessment' session, parent and child play together for about 20 minutes, with the therapist in the room, interacting with both. Next, the parent is asked (in front of the child) to leave the room and return in anywhere between 10 and 20 minutes. The length of the separation is determined by the clinician, based on the child's age and presenting problem.

While the parent is absent, the child and the therapist play, talk, and get to know each other a little. Care is taken not to frighten the child; flexibility is key. Occasionally the child cannot tolerate the parent's departure, in which case the parent remains. But if mum can leave, even for a short time, this reveals what happens when the child is mildly stressed and the attachment system is activated in a strange place with a complete stranger, however friendly and unthreatening we may feel ourselves to be. If the child becomes distressed, the parent will be retrieved. The parent is instructed to knock on the door when she returns, so that the child and therapist are both primed for the reunion. All this, of course, is a clinical version of the Strange Situation. While not a formal assessment, it provides an invaluable opportunity to observe what happens when the attachment system is activated in the child *and* in the parent. The therapist pays particular attention to the moments before and after separation, and before and after reunion.

Disorganised attachment: Louis

Louis, age 7, came with his mother for an evaluation at a community mental health centre at his school's request. Mother described a series of fights with the school administration about Louis's behaviour, particularly his academic difficulties and tendency to get into minor trouble with his peers. As had been the case with his prior three schools, she was locked in a battle with his teachers and the principal. During the initial sessions, she focused hardly at all on her son's difficulties and dwelt instead – in an almost paranoid way – on how unsupported and criticised she felt.

Louis was a fearful and disoriented-looking boy who seemed flat and disengaged before his mother left the room. He relaxed in her absence, and opened up, becoming mildly enlivened. When she returned, she greeted him with what was ostensibly a smile, but was clearly a threat gesture, teeth bared and lips snarled in a look that conveyed dominance and frightening power. If an animal were to 'greet' another animal in that fashion, the message would be unmistakable: I can kill you. Louis looked up fearfully and flattened again. His eyes combed her face.

The mother's grimace upon reunion was striking and chilling, a clear sign that the child might well be disorganised in relation to attachment. The moment vividly reflected his terror, and her rage.

Another sign came two sessions later, when Louis was alone with the therapist. He suddenly got up from the table where they were working and wordlessly collapsed in her arms, sobbing.

Given these signs, the treating therapist worried about the child's physical safety and the mother's potential for maltreating her child. She also wondered how to best engage this mother in a way that would meet her son's needs but also help her create the holding environment Louis so desperately needed. Unfortunately, the mother decided that the school was the problem, and declined treatment.

Avoidance: Nicolette

Judy brought her 3-year-old for a consultation. She described Nicolette, seemingly an adorable, energetic preschooler, as a tormentor, misbehaved, and uncontrollable, clinging and unable to separate. She presented herself as overwhelmed and at her wits' end, helpless in the face of her child's malevolence. Judy was certain she'd never be able to get out of the room when it was proposed that she leave Nicolette with the therapist for a short while. Meanwhile, Nicolette explored the room enthusiastically,

(Continued)

(Continued)

mostly ignoring her mother. When Judy left the room, she continued her explorations without any protest or apparent signs of distress. If anything, she seemed slightly less frantic. On mother's return, Nicolette ignored her and went on playing. Judy was surprised and slightly deflated. This classically avoidant response told the story of a child who likely felt she could not turn to her mother when distressed.

Sroufe and his colleagues (Sroufe et al., 2005) describe seeing children like this in their longitudinal research. Often viewed by their teachers and parents as clinging and dependent, they 'shut down' in the SSP, as though knowing that to seek a genuine, loving response from the caregiver upon reunion would be a sure path to disappointment and rejection. The message is clear: '*When my attachment system is activated, I down-regulate.*'

Following the next session, when mother and child had been seen together, the therapist happened to look out of the window as they left. Mum had strapped Nicolette into the front seat of their large SUV. They were on their way out of the driveway when mother stopped the car to get something out of the boot. In the time that it took her to go to the rear of the car and back, Nicolette had unstrapped herself, let herself out of the car and run in front of it, *apparently seeking her mother.* At that same moment, mother got back in the car and began to engage the motor when she saw Nicolette standing directly in front of the car. She jammed on the brakes and flew out of the car, yelling angrily, roughly picking up Nicolette and shoving her back in the car.

This brief encounter was telling. The avoidance, the imperviousness of Nicolette, the alternating helpless and hostile postures of her mother all indicated disrupted/disorganised attachment. The therapist was serendipitously given a window into danger-seeking and provocation as ways of seeking proximity, albeit of the most unsatisfying sort (Zeanah & Smyke, 2009). The therapist gently raised this encounter in the next individual session with the mother. The mother was never to return again.

Both of these cases demonstrate the fragility and vulnerability of parents coming for assessment when their children are experiencing major difficulties. They also demonstrate how observing parent and child together from the outset provides an invaluable picture of their mutual dynamic. Assessing the attachment system tells the therapist about children's response to threat, and their safety-seeking strategies. Even if this is the one and only time that parent and child are seen together, it can be a critical step in the assessment process.

Hold the Parent in Mind: Working with Parents

When parents bring their children to therapy, they often feel defeated and hopeless: shut down and disengaged ('*You fix him!*'), or agitated/worried/

dysregulated and over-protective (*'Is he OK?'*, *'Tell me what to DO!'*). They may vacillate between these places as they struggle with the intense feelings that the child's difficulties and their relationship arouse. Their capacity to care for, protect, and support their child's autonomy has been disrupted or disabled. They are too detached or dysregulated to provide the secure base the child so badly needs. The therapeutic aim is to help parents to become sufficiently 'present' to see and feel the child's needs and find ways to meet them. They need help to re-find the deep feelings of connection and reward that come from knowing one's child and caring for him or her. Those feelings will operate synergistically to transform their relationship, and thus the child himself (see too Slade, 2008b).

In attachment-informed terms, we help the parent mentalise – to imagine the child's subjective experience and make meaning of it. Reflective parents have secure children (Fonagy et al., 1995; Slade et al., 2005). Work with the parents alone, or in parallel with individual child psychotherapy, helps build these reflective capacities by activating the parents' attachment representations: of the child, of themselves, of their own parents. This is the 'energy' that will promote change. Parents typically bring children, wanting us to change their behaviour, but lack curiosity about its origins or meanings. Or they assume – taking a prementalising stance – that they know what the child is thinking and feeling, unable to look past their own projections to the child's actual experience. When they begin to see the child's behaviour as meaningful, and allow themselves to become curious about the child's intentions and feelings, everything shifts: they become softer, more open, less threatened and threatening. And so too do their children.

Many of the prescriptions for parent work in the psychodynamic literature are based on the developmental guidance model developed at the Anna Freud Centre in the 1950s (Hurry, 1998), or on an analytic model in which the parent's unconscious is a primary focus of parent work (Novick & Novick, 2005). While these approaches are important and valid, mentalisation theory helps clarify the aim of all parent work. The goal, ultimately, is to help them to *see* the child as a separate being in their own right, and crucially to *be moved* by them, and – as a result – *connected* to them. When the parent cannot see the child as a sentient person, violence – emotional or physical – is possible (Fonagy & Target, 1999).

Fonagy and colleagues (1995) suggest that in secure attachment the mother '*re*-presents' the child's mind to him in an organised, coherent fashion. As with Stern's attunement (Stern, 1985), Beebe's mutual influence (Beebe & Lachmann, 2013), and Winnicott's 'meeting the child's spontaneous gesture' (1965: 76), the mother's reflections and extensions help the child to begin to know himself. Parental care organises, gives meaning, and brings vitality to the child's internal experience. When the caregiver recognises only parts of a child, or distorts communications, fear, isolation, and rage result.

Child psychotherapists similarly strive to redress adverse developmental experience by organising, giving meaning, and bringing vitality to the child's internal experience (Tuber & Calflisch, 2011). But, and this is a big 'but', *unless children find similar mirroring, acceptance, and reflection at home*, it will be difficult, particularly if they are young, to hold on to a coherent, organised sense of themselves in the face of parents' projections and chaos. That means resorting to the defences that have made for survival, but which are also problematic. Change in the child can sometimes trigger change in the parents, but to assume this is to place too great a burden on the child and his therapy.

Let's return to the notion of '*re*-presentation' (Fonagy et al., 1995). Working with children individually, we come to know them, and they themselves, in new ways. With parents we first engage with and validate/'radically accept' *their* representations of the child, however distorted; eventually, as trust builds, we *re*-present a newer, less distorted version of the child, the one that we have come to know through our work. Even with the parents of autistic children, trying to mentalise the unmentalisable (Slade, 2009), we may be able to help them make sense of, and thus respond more sensitively to, the child. Here, as ever, 'the devil is in the details'; bringing to life specific events and minutiae gives parents a window into children's actual experience, activating the parents' attachment organisation. Thus, discussions frequently focus on often recurring episodes of conflict, affectively supercharged moments when Mum and child are activated, aroused, with neither able to 'see' the other's point of view.

Michael and the arousal curve

Michael, aged 4, was dysregulated from birth (Slade, 1999), and by the time the parents sought treatment for him, they were equally dysregulated. Mother found him overwhelming, and could not discern any triggers for his distress. She saw him as a '*zero to sixty*' child with nothing modulating his rapid and intense distress. The therapist began trying to think with the mother in a detailed way about episodes of dysregulation, using the 'arousal curve', which describes shifts from sleep to waking to focused attention, to excitement, to distress, to describe the trajectory of Michael's misery. Slowly mother began to recognise the shifts in his arousal before he got to '*total meltdown*', and began to be able to anticipate and de-escalate before things got out of hand. The therapist repeatedly drew the arousal curve in the air with her hand, making concrete the shifts from low arousal, to active focus and interest, to dysregulation and collapse. She tried to depict the situations that triggered dysregulation in language that the mother could understand, hoping it would help her make sense of and not be so overwhelmed by her son's affective states. By regulating mother, the therapist helped her to regulate her son. Eventually, mother was able to discuss her own mother's harsh parenting, and her loneliness as a child.

The mentalising paradox – repeated throughout this book – is that it's hardest to mentalise when you're upset, but that's when mentalising is most urgently needed. Children's distress is often as painful for the caregivers as for the children themselves. The presence of a 'third' can change this dynamic for the better – one of the many reasons why lone parents' job is so difficult. The therapist's mentalising, regulating presence helps ameliorate these destructive cycles in which neither parent or child can make sense of one another (Fearon et al., 2006).

Parent work is largely about 'containment' and holding. Parents need someone who can acknowledge and empathise with their unhappiness, guilt, hatred, and confusion, without judgement. They need us to listen to what a lousy kid, partner, and/or job they have. If we move to the child too quickly, we may lose them. On the other hand, if the child fades from therapeutic view, it is not 'parent work' but individual adult therapy. The constant aim is to engage the parent's mentalising function, to stimulate their understanding, curiosity, and pleasure in their child, however problematic.

It can be difficult working with the parent of a child we are also seeing in child psychotherapy. Beginner therapists often feel more comfortable with children than they are with parents, who may well be a generation older than they are. Nevertheless, this relationship is the key to success, because it protects the parent from the inherent threat in seeking therapy for one's child. Parents will feel frightened, exposed, and 'a failure'. They fear being judged and examined, particularly against the backdrop of a racial and class divide, and find it hard to imagine the value of their child coming and playing with an alien 'middle-class' stranger. They may imagine that the therapist will be 'better' at connecting with the child than they are. The potential for shame and humiliation is huge.

By connecting with parents in ways that diminish their sense of being judged or threatened, and by mentalising *their* pain and worry, thereby making meaning of their experience as parents, we make it possible for them to tolerate our becoming important to the child. If we don't work on our relationship with parents first, expecting to become important to the child without their support and sanction, the enterprise is doomed to fail. Unfortunate examples of this are the cases of Louis and Nicolette described above, where treatment was broken off by the parents before trust with the therapist was established.

Work 'with' and 'in' the Parent–Child Relationship

Let's turn to the synergy released when caregiver and child are seen together: working 'with' and 'in' the parent–child relationship. Fraiberg (1980) said that having the infant present when working with vulnerable mothers was akin to having 'God on your side'. The child's presence in the session enables the therapist to help the mother distinguish her fantasies and projections from the real needs and experiences of her actual child. But real-life activation of these representations is often the most direct route to this and is undertaken through dyadic work.

More Michael

Meltdown Michael (described above) came to therapy when he was 4 years old. He already showed clear signs of obsessive compulsive disorder (OCD) and could not be away from his mother for even short amounts of time. At first, he could not even look at the therapist in the joint sessions. He turned his whole body towards his mother and whenever the therapist spoke to him, he looked at his mother anxiously, waiting for her to speak for him.

Over the months he gradually allowed the therapist to get closer to him, and to participate in his play with his mother. Throughout, the therapist tried – in overt and covert ways – to reinforce the idea that mother was right there and he was safe. She explored what mother was feeling, both about her son's clinging, and his tentative steps towards independence. Eventually, Michael allowed mother to move outside the play zone, and even to move to the other side of the room. When something happened in the play, he called out: '*Hey, Mom, look at GI Joe! He's all dirty!*' Eventually, he could tolerate individual sessions. This opened up a long and fruitful therapy: twice weekly sessions with the child, and weekly or biweekly sessions with mother (and sometimes father) for the next five years.

Anna and the 'complete waste of time'

Anna, aged 5, was stealing, lying, and tormenting her younger sister. She could not tolerate her mother leaving the room, so the first six months' sessions were dyadic. She repetitively and rigidly played out a scene of a harsh, mean mother punishing her child on the slightest of grounds, and of playmates cruelly excluding her – presumably Anna's versions of her everyday experiences. Mum was horrified, repeatedly turning to the therapist, interjecting '*I'm not like that*'. The therapist reassured her that this was fantasy, but it was very difficult for the mother to witness this 'pretend' evocation of their relationship. Gradually, Anna's play became less rigid and aggressive, and her constriction and concreteness began to shift. She slowly allowed the therapist to join in her play, her mother to sit to the side and eventually to leave the sessions.

Once individual sessions began, mother (and sometimes father) continued parent work. Sessions with the mother explicitly focused on helping her make sense of Anna – who seemed to her so challenging and mysterious – and exploring some of her own historical barriers to connecting with her angry and disorganised daughter. But the mother, whose avoidance had helped her survive her brutal father, found it impossible to acknowledge that this work was helpful. After a year she said: *'You're a very nice person, and I know that you care. But I really think this has been a total waste of time.'* Nevertheless, she continued to send the therapist regular updates of Anna's progress and her many successes throughout adolescence and early adulthood. Perhaps, after all, parent work, however painful, had not been *such* a waste of time!

Sometimes such dyadic work may be seen by therapists unfamiliar with the attachment tradition as antithetical to the goals of dynamic treatment.

David and the tale of two supervisors

David, aged 3, had been brought to the clinic for evaluation by both his parents. They described him as completely unmanageable: aggressive (biting, hitting) and out of control (impulsive, running away), with dysregulated sleep, activity levels, etc. The modified Strange Situation with both parents suggested disorganised attachment. Of two very distressed parents, mother seemed somewhat more amenable to therapeutic engagement. She felt helpless *vis-à-vis* David, and unable to imagine what might be going on inside him. Nevertheless, there was – despite all – a tenderness towards him that could, hopefully, be built on. Father was consumed with rage towards the child. They had had a fight in a grocery store where the father became so enraged that his screams led the boy to cower on the floor behind a bin. Father was hostile, Mum helpless, both manifestations of the parents' own disrupted histories.

The intake supervisor recommended dyadic work with the mother and mentalisation-based parent work with both parents as a precursor to individual work. But the case was then assigned to a more analytic supervisor who felt that dyadic work would rob the child of the space to express his aggression, and that he should be seen individually. Perhaps as a function of this confusion – as it reflected the chaos and dysfunction in this young family – the parents, led by the father, turned down the offer of treatment.

There is no knowing who in this dispute was 'right'. No doubt both professionals were drawing on their 'deep domain-specific knowledge' and the ability to correct their mistakes in the light of experience. But here was a live 'enactment' of an old psychoanalytic vs. attachment battle: the relationship vs. the individual; fear vs. aggression; reality vs. fantasy. The intake supervisor believed that while the child was undoubtedly angry, he was primarily and fundamentally terrified because he had nowhere to turn but to his frightened mother and terrifying father. David's fear was having a major effect on his neurobiology and physiology; he could not find safety. The parents' arousal was so perilously high that they simply could not 'see' the child. She thought lessening his fear by working on the relationship was the first order of business.

By contrast, the therapy supervisor felt that the child needed above all a safe space within which to process all his intense feelings about his parents. Perhaps the best advice to the confused student therapist in the face of this stalemate would have been the following: do *both* dyadic work and individual work; use the unique synergy of the dyad to help the mother discover the boy, find pleasure in him and provide him safety, and the privacy of the individual work to find symbols for his fear and his anger.

Ryan's translocations

Ryan was 5 years old. He had been separated from his parents for most of his early childhood, living with two different sets of grandparents in his homeland while his parents emigrated and found work. Now reunited with them, he presented with a range of behavioural, social, and school problems, and had been diagnosed as autistic. The mother was traumatised by the repeated separations from her child; she herself had had long separations from her own mother in early childhood.

The therapist worked dyadically with the mother and child for a number of months, while at the same time seeing the mother on her own and occasionally the father for parent sessions. Under the guidance of a new supervisor, she decided to move to intensive psychoanalytic play therapy, and suspended dyadic sessions with the mother and child. The child blossomed in these sessions, and his fragmented communication began to take shape, his emotions becoming clearer. He also began to express aggression. In what was to be his last session, he acted out a fight with both parents. The parents pulled him out of treatment that night.

Clearly, the child benefited from individual sessions, but this was likely threatening for the parents, and represented yet one more sense of 'failure' where someone other than themselves engaged positively with their child. A crucial connection was lost when dyadic work was discontinued and replaced by individual therapy from which the mother was excluded, relegated to the waiting room, and reproducing both her and her child's mothering history. Musing on why she had moved to individual sessions, the therapist felt that there were things that the child needed to express away from his mother. But, from an attachment perspective, the relationship also needed protection and the many broken strands repaired. After all the separations, 'losing' her child to a second 'good mother', the therapist, must have been very difficult for the mother. As much as Ryan needed to find himself, his mother needed to find him. There was a need to work through the multiple traumas they had endured together. Individual sessions were needed *in parallel with, not as an alternative to*, working with the dyad. Ryan's emerging feelings of rage at his losses threatened both parents terribly, but without their having a frame for understanding them.

Occasionally, despite the prevailing thrust of this chapter, dyadic work is difficult, if not impossible:

Galen and Mum's newspaper

Galen, an isolated, avoidant, little 3-year-old began individual play therapy after a brief evaluation. In parent sessions, the therapist gradually came to appreciate how little his parents knew or were curious about him, and suggested to mother that they do some dyadic work. Mother agreed, but then lay on the floor passively observing the therapist and child together, despite the therapist's efforts to engage her in the play. In one instance, Galen was playing out a lonely game of soldiers shooting a lone soldier 'loser' over and over again. Mum slowly moved, without standing up, to the far side of the room, eventually managing to pull a newspaper out from under the therapist's chair. She lay on her stomach reading while Galen shot his soldiers. Over the next few sessions, the therapist came to appreciate that, despite her efforts, the mother was simply unable to engage successfully in this kind of work, and moved back to individual work with the boy, and conjoint parent work with both mother and father.

Conclusion

From an attachment perspective, therapists working with children of all ages need always to consider and feel confident about parent work. When there are signs of severely insecure or disorganised attachment, the relationship will need direct help if the child is to change. Dynamic child psychotherapy has a long and robust history. Adding relationship repair to the goals of treatment provides another vital dimension. It has the potential to restore proper functioning of the fear system, revive biobehavioural synchrony, activate oxytocin release and dopaminergic reward systems, and engage the developing prefrontal cortex of the child. In plainer language, it could help parents do what they want, and from an evolutionary standpoint need, to do: to take care of their children in the best way possible (Benedek, 1959). That too is just plain good for children, however 'messy' (Stern, 1995) – i.e., unpredictable and complicated – that may be.

Summary

- Attachment-informed child psychotherapy sees parent work as an essential accompaniment to individual therapy.

- The fundamentals of the attachment dynamic can be assessed by observing child and mother before, during, and after a brief separation.

- The aim of working with parents dyadically or individually is to provide a holding, accepting, secure environment where parents can – using the energy of their attachment to the child – disengage from their own projections and arousal-driven anxieties and see and accept their child in their strengths and lovability, as well as in their difficultness and vulnerability.

- When there are signs of disorganised or otherwise significantly disrupted attachment, it is especially important to work on the here-and-now parent–child dysregulation and non-mentalising environment before embarking on, or in parallel with, child psychotherapy.

Notes

1. Many adolescents cannot tolerate being seen with their parents; for them the suitability of a dyadic session needs to be approached carefully.
2. A separate family session may also be indicated.

14

Attachment in Couples and Families

The attachment paradigm is primarily based on the dyad. Our mission thus far has been to describe how one might understand and foster security in a two-person relationship. In this chapter, we look more closely at attachment-informed couple therapy, before extending the dyadic perspective to encompass the 'three plus' complexities of family therapy.

Attachment and Couple Therapy

Attachment concepts and research methods have been extensively used to analyse the formation, maintenance, and breakdown of romantic and marital[1] relationships, and help guide therapy (Brassard & Johnson, 2016). Here we address a number of salient themes.

Secure and insecure marital patterns

Unsurprisingly, couples whose members are securely attached tend to fare better than their insecure counterparts – they have fewer rows, less marital violence, and more enduring relationships (Noller & Feeney, 2002). This is understandable, given that shared pleasure, comfortable emotional self-disclosure, positive facial gaze, capacity for mutual attention, together with well-functioning rupture-repair systems – as opposed to fight, flight and/or neglect – are skills that secure individuals bring into their marriages. As the saying goes: 'if you want a happy marriage, marry a happy person'.

Contrastingly, insecure individuals, especially the dependent, anxiously attached, tend to form relationships when they are still psychologically immature

(Morgan & Shaver, 1999). Lacking a strong internal secure base, the haze of romantic love promises relief from feelings of insecurity. Sadly, such hopes are often short-lived. The insecure are mutually attracted, but two anxiously attached individuals tend to form unstable partnerships (Noller & Feeney, 2002).

Jane: who is the primary attachment figure?

Jane presented with depression, irritable bowel syndrome, and panic attacks not long after the death of her mother, who had lived next door, her constant companion, confidante, and 'best friend', the person she could turn to whenever things were difficult – especially when she developed bouts of abdominal pain. When Jane was 7, there had been a three-month separation when her mother had to go to a far-away town to look after Jane's grandmother when she became ill. On Jane's honeymoon she became temporarily deaf after the flight to an exotic destination. Her new husband was dismayed when she rang her mother for reassurance rather than turning, as he expected, to him. Jane's mother remained at the apex of her attachment hierarchy, with her husband, for all his good qualities, definitely at number two or below. This pattern continued and her mother's death left a vacuum of which Jane was painfully aware whenever she felt in need of succour.

Jane's vulnerability to separation, fear of abandonment, and difficulty in transferring her attachment feelings on to her husband (chosen perhaps as a complement to, rather than replacement for, her mother) can perhaps be traced to her early, anxious relationship with her mother. The anxiously attached, lacking a bridging *internal* secure base, find it difficult to transfer their attachment allegiance from parent to spouse.

When anxiously attached people find an avoidant spouse, the relationship tends to be more enduring, but the potential for conflict or violence is greater. Escalating 'seek and find', 'pursuit-withdrawal' (Bartholomew & Allison, 2006) cycles prevail. The anxiously attached member of the couple wants reassurance. But for avoidant people, bids for intimacy feel intrusive, stimulating greater avoidance. This prompts the anxious partner towards yet more desperate reassurance-seeking. Finally, a fight/flight crisis erupts – a row or a temporary separation – followed by a momentary period of calm. But it is only a matter of time before the cycle restarts, when a minor act of avoidance once again lights the hair-trigger abandonment fuse in the anxious partner. The combination of 'over-' and 'under'-accessibility of negative emotions, and their problematic modulation, fuels the combustible roundabout. When relationship stresses arise, as they invariably do, secure couples are able to recall their mutual commitment or 'vows'. For the insecure, trivial arguments end with 'throwing in the kitchen sink', as past betrayals and emotional unavailability come all-too-readily to mind.

Despite research suggesting stable attachment orientations, clinical experience often finds more fluidity and reversibility in attachment patterns, depending upon what IWMs are triggered in a particular pairing.

Margaret

A generally emotionally guarded woman, Margaret tended to pick anxious men as boyfriends. They would find her distant and somewhat closed, and the relationship would founder. She eventually married an even more avoidant partner than herself. To her surprise, she now found herself feeling anxious and needy, for the first time on the receiving end of affective rejection.

The 'benign bind' rubric suggested in Chapter 11 can also be applied to romantic relationships. Marriage is a species of 'therapy'. The couple bring their pre-existing attachment constellations into the marital mix, including traumatic expectations of rejection, betrayal, abandonment, etc. But the eternally springing hope is for 'new beginnings': for loving and accepting response to their attachment needs to be evoked. Where previous patterns are reinforced or colluded with, as is typically the case in couples coming for help, the relationship tends to be unstable or unexciting. Where there is freshness and vitality, previous attachment expectations can be confounded, but within a context of mutual ongoing commitment. Emotional progress and consolidation generally follow. The task of couple therapy is to set that train in motion.

Attachment injury

Susan Johnson used attachment theory as the basis for her model of Emotion Focused Therapy (EFT) for couples (Johnson & Whiffen, 2005). One of the most significant of her many contributions was her description of the role of 'attachment injuries' in stalling couples' ability to change (Johnson, Makinen, & Millikin, 2001). In those couples who found EFT relatively unhelpful, she discovered that there was often a recurring trauma in their history as a couple in which one member felt let down, betrayed, unheard, and/or un-held. These might be episodes of illness, a death, a physical injury, or an extra-marital affair. In marital conflicts, starting from minor present-day irritations, all roads lead back to the moment where, for one partner 'you just weren't there for me'. The 'injury' here is to the keystone of marriage, the attachment system itself. By definition, a crisis triggers the attachment dynamic. The frightened, threatened, ill, betrayed, or stressed partner seeks out comfort, security, and reassurance from their spouse – only to find a void where a secure base should be.

The vicissitudes of real life evoke an analogue of the SSP-like temporary ruptures. The securely attached rise to the occasion, while the insecure fail, in major or minor ways. In the less serious variants, the injured spouse will respond either avoidantly by emotional withdrawal, or anxiously by angry clinging. Both impair spousal emotional communication. In the more serious D/U-type pattern, the suffering spouse may resort to desperate forms of attempted self-soothing – drugs, alcohol, promiscuity, etc. Partners end up feeling mystified about how a toothpaste-tube squeezed in the wrong way can lead on to an exhausting battle to the death. But to be alone and without a secure base is tantamount to physical or emotional expiry. Such feelings, however much overlaid by maturation, remain latent within the psyche, reawakened in the life-or-death situations of attachment injury.

Sex and attachment

The attachment perspective has been criticised by the psychoanalytic community for underplaying the role of sex in psychological life (Widlocher, 2002).[2] There is some truth in this. Based on his ethological perspective, Bowlby felt that the search for security, rather than 'infantile sexuality', was the main dynamic of the parent–infant bond. For him, attachment, with its implicit altruism, is no less salient than sex as the 'glue' that holds couples, families, and ultimately societies together. Bowlby saw separation and loss and their impact on the attachment system as the principal sources of conflict in human relationships, rather than innate aggression played out in the Oedipal and Electra 'situations', however fertile those archetypal metaphors might be.

Bowlby (1969) noted, however, that there are significant overlaps between the attachment and sexual systems: neurochemical, hormonal, intrapsychic, and interpersonal. Subsequent research has confirmed the differences and connections between the dynamics underlying both attachment and sexuality. As we have seen, oxytocin, the attachment hormone, 'cross-talks' (Feldman 2015b) to the pleasure-mediating dopamine reward system. Attachment behaviours are pleasurable in themselves; sex strengthens the attachment bond. Monogamous male prairie voles' pair-bonding behaviour – spending time with their mate and showing aggression to other males – is blocked by oxytocin antagonists (Insel, 2000). No such effect is seen in their promiscuous Montana vole cousins, but if the latter are then injected with oxytocin, they too begin to show monogamous characteristics. These effects are transmitted epigenetically to the next generation (Wang et al., 2013). This 'conversation' between the attachment system, mediated by oxytocin, and the pleasure and sexual systems, mediated by dopamine and the sex hormones, forms the biochemical substrate of the quintessential human emotions of jealousy and possessiveness.

As maturation proceeds, the child comes to accept that his or her secure base/safe haven is perforce shared with others – father with mother and vice versa, and both with siblings. Both pleasure and security can be swept away, whether 'Oedipally' (i.e., as a universal developmental hurdle) or arbitrarily (i.e., as part of the inherent unpredictability of life). In secure attachment, this built-in vulnerability is balanced by the altruism of caregivers, and the capacity of care-seekers to cope with loss and mourning and to trust that the lost object will return.

In the varieties of insecure attachment there is much that can go awry. Contra-Freud, kin interbreeding – aka incest – is uncommon in mammals.[3] Among humans, older siblings are often attachment figures for their younger sibs, but rarely sexual partners. When it does occur, fraternal sexual abuse is usually a mark of highly disorganised families, where the attachment system is severely disrupted.

In adult life, sex and attachment are clearly distinct but related phenomena; most marriages contain a mixture of both, in varying proportions and varying times in the marital life-cycle. Unconsummated marriage represents attachment without sex; rape the ultimate example of 'sex' devoid of attachment. Given that sexuality depends on the excitement of difference and novelty, while attachment relies on familiarity and predictability, Eagle (2007) argues that marriage represents a happy – or sometimes less than happy – compromise between these two poles.

Holmes (2007), by contrast, argues that security, especially for females, is a pre-condition for the mutual exploration that is the basis of 'good sex'. Target (2007) retains an ingenious variant of the psychoanalytic model, differentiating infantile sensuality – the kissing, tickling, stroking, cuddling rewardingness of babies – from explicit sexuality. She argues that parental mirroring and physical reciprocity typically excludes genitality. Children's exhibitionistic and masturbatory proclivities are usually discouraged, punished, or ignored. This, she argues, leaves a residue of 'mirroring hunger' in relation to sexuality, eventually alleviated when adolescence is reached, partners are found, and mature sexual life begins. In her model, sexuality is inherently problematic in this sense of being an un-mirrored, un-reciprocated aspect of the self. Hence the potential subversiveness of sexuality, and the draconian measures which puritanical societies employ to limit and corral it.

The relevance of this to attachment-informed psychotherapy is that for some couples sexuality can be problematic, despite functioning well in other areas of their joint life, including security provision. For others, the absence of mutual security and affect co-regulation eventually undermines even well-functioning sexual relationships.

Many of the individual therapy principles outlined in previous chapters can be readily transposed into the couple setting. Married couples are self-evidently 'attached' to one another. From this it follows that a crucial feature of marriage is the availability – for undivided attention, empathic resonance, affect mirroring, protection, and soothing – of partners, one for the other, at times of threat, stress, or illness. But if it is accepted that the creativity of sexuality is potentially disruptive, the insecure, with compromised capacity for tolerating uncertainty and surprise, may be especially vulnerable to sexual dysphoria.

Marital conflict

Main and Hesse (1990) describe the 'approach–avoidance dilemma' when a child's secure base is the very source of threat and stress that triggers the attachment dynamic. Herein lies a common marital conflict theme, at least in western-type, love-based, democratic marriages. Conflict, with its attendant threat, triggers the attachment dynamic in both partners. Each member of the dyad will therefore be in search of comfort co-regulation and security. But the very person to whom they would turn for succour is felt to be the root of their unhappiness. The result is an escalating spiral of negative emotion – a '*row*'.

Where there is secure attachment and an underlying 'benign bind' dynamic, conflict can be productive and healing. One of the functions of anger is to help overcome attachment estrangement, pointing to problems needing solving. Bolstered by good rupture-repair histories, the securely attached are able to modulate and transcend their own and their partner's negative affect. Their capacity to listen and respond to one another's distress is well developed. They can stand back from their own and their spouse's emotions sufficiently to mentalise about 'what's going on between us' – to understand emotions and learn from experiences, rather than suppressing or being dictated to by them. They can comfortably alternate between the comfort-seeker and secure base, turn and turn about.

All of this becomes problematic when threat or stress is so great that it overwhelms normal attachment strategies and/or where one or both partners is insecurely attached. The extreme example is the death or serious disability of a child. This form of intolerable bereavement often has a major deleterious impact on the marriage and mental health of the parents (Rogers et al., 2008). Both partners are in states of anguish, unable to stand back sufficiently from their mental pain to provide the open-ended succour the other needs.

In more everyday forms of marital difficulties, insecure attachment can compromise normal repair mechanisms. This applies especially in anxious forms of attachment, where one partner teeters continually on the brink of attachment arousal. Since mentalising and affect arousal are mutually incompatible, finding a vantage point from which to think about their situation is inherently problematic for these couples. In addition, there may be clashing cultural discrepancies in the ways in which insecurity is handled. One partner may expect and resort to strategies in which threat is dealt with by a 'vertical' chain of command from above; this often entails suppression, distraction, moralising, and/or prohibition, all adaptive in their way, but highly discrepant with a 'horizontal', 'borrowed brain' method of sharing and overcoming difficulties. The other partner may want to look at and learn from conflict, rather than banishing or condemning it. Both will claim that they are 'right', which indeed both are, coming from their respective but discrepant set of expectations and history. This may set off further conflict about how problems might be solved in addition to the problem itself!

Attachment-informed Couple Therapy

Attachment perspectives suggest a number of guiding principles for couple therapy.

1 Lowering arousal

An overall aim of attachment-informed therapy is to foster the capacity for mentalising – for 'thinking about thinking'. Couples may arrive for therapy in a state of conflict. He (it is usually a 'he') may feel he is being 'dragged along' and respond with sulky withdrawal. Or a row – say about parking arrangements – may have escalated even before they enter the door.

The therapist's task here will be to calm the situation sufficiently for mentalising to be possible. Validation of the more aroused partner may help: '*It sounds as though you had severe doubts about coming here today*', or '*Oh, the horrors of parking! That's always a trigger point for me and my wife!*' (a 'joining' as well as validation move).

The 'push the pause button' metaphor (Bateman & Fonagy, 2004) can be helpful: '*Let's stop for a minute and see what's going on here.*' Sometimes an orchestrated moment of meditation of 'watching the breath' for both partners is useful.

2 Validation

A basic principle of attachment-informed couple therapy is that if someone feels an emotion it cannot be denied. Warring couples typically disqualify or express contempt for one another's reactions, e.g., '*You always make such a ridiculous fuss about parking – can't you see there are much more important things in life.*' Here the therapist might (a) pick up on the word 'always' (and henceforth ban it from therapy!), (b) focus on the feelings: '*Let's try to get behind the word "fuss"; I wonder if you could ask your wife what is going on for her when she criticises your parking strategies.*'

3 Empathic listening

Helping couples to listen to each other, without interruption, criticism, self-justification, invalidation, or withdrawal is a crucial couple-therapy skill. Here the therapist acts as an orchestrator, holding the listening partners to their task, forestalling interruptions and invalidations, helping them to sit silently and authentically absorb and consider what their other is saying and feeling. This is especially important where there has been an 'attachment injury', where acceptance and acknowledgement of former hurt is an essential precursor to forgiveness and 'moving on'.

4 Turn taking

In their proto-conversations with caregivers, babies learn from an early age the art of turn-taking. This capacity is often lost when couples are at loggerheads: speaking over one another, blocking, angrily interrupting, ear-occluding, or storming out. Organised empathic listening needs to be built into between-session homework. Friday might be designated as the day when the husband talks about what has been upsetting him; the wife is instructed to listen calmly and carefully and take seriously what is being said; *his* task will then be to listen with no less sensitivity on a Tuesday, 'How they got on' (expectably not well!) will then be examined in the subsequent session.

5 Defences

We are all survivors. Insecure attachment patterns represent necessary protection for the vulnerable self from hostile interpersonal forces. Encased in our defences, we fear to cast off these Lear-like 'lendings'; at the same time, we long for our vulnerable selves to be held, nurtured, and valued. Couples need to be helped to reveal themselves emotionally, to be tender to and value one another's emotional as well as physical nakedness. All this has to be done at a pace that slowly rebuilds trust rather than rushing on in ways that once more trigger flight.

6 The relationship itself as a 'third'

It can be helpful for couples to think of 'the relationship' as an entity, distinct from both members of the dyad, a metaphorical 'child' that is in trouble and in need of help. The attachment dynamic then applies. Like a baby, their 'relationship' is stressed, threatened, ill, and needs comfort and soothing before it is ready to face the world and explore. This might lead to planning a weekend 'away' from quotidian cares – work, parenthood, money worries, etc. – where 'the relationship' can begin to feel safe again and resume its role as a place where emotional, sexual, and developmental needs can be met.

7 Mentalising

Parents of secure children are able to mentalise about their offspring – to understand their needs and motivations, while putting their own pressing emotions to one side. Comparably, couples in therapy begin to think of their relationship as a child in need of safety and nurture, rather than further fueling its ills with their own difficulties. '*What's going on between us right now? How did we get to this point? What do we need to do to restore balance and love?*' are all questions that flow from this mentalising perspective.

8 Refinding the positive

Attachment is a source of essential 'narcissistic supplies'. Parents delight and take pride in their children's very existence, their achievements and pleasures, and the overcoming of setbacks. This applies, too, to a couple's enjoyment of one another, and their relationship, but can easily be lost sight of when things go wrong. Wedding photographs on the mantelpiece remind couples of past passions and commitment. Therapists will prompt couples to re-discover, value, and weigh these against the negatives, and to rekindle mutual attraction, shared interests and goals, finding hope in trials and tribulations overcome.

9 Attachment and the body

Attachment is ultimately mediated through the body: hugging, holding, hearing, touching, seeing. Even the term 'feeling' is in its origins a physical action before becoming, in the Lakoff and Johnson sense, psychologically metaphorised. Helping couples to look one another in the eye, to hold hands, mutually massage, to find oxytocin-releasing forms of body-to-body contact – not to mention sex! – are important parts of attachment-informed couple therapy.

10 Facing up to loss and destructiveness

If loss is the dark side of attachment, some couples come for help in order to separate and 'move on'. Helping them to progress from all-out war to 'civilised' separation, and the grief and bereavement that entails, is an important therapeutic skill. Therapists' capacity to 'contain' – i.e., acknowledge and survive – rage and hatred, and to maintain a safe space for this to happen, is essential. This may help the couple resolve the paradox that if an amicable separation were possible it might not have been necessary in the first place.

Attachment and the Family

In his role as Director of Children's Services at London's Tavistock Clinic in the 1940s, John Bowlby is credited with being a pioneer family therapist. Rather than slavishly sticking to the child psychoanalytic paradigm of individual therapy, he decided to work at times directly with parents and children (Bowlby, 1949; Byng-Hall, 1991). As well as his training in psychoanalysis and ethology, he was influenced by the nascent science of 'systems theory' and cybernetics. He deployed the ideas of feedback and control, in which care-seeker and care-provider mutually influence one another in order to maintain an appropriate balance between security and exploration.

'The family' is itself a systemic concept in that it is an abstract assemblage of constituent and contrasting elements or 'sub-units' – parents and children; males and females; the 'nuclear' family and the wider network of grandparents, uncles, aunts, cousins; humans and pets – as well as 'functions' – companionship, sexual pleasure, procreation, development, teaching, learning, cultural transmission, and nurturance.

The family's prime job provides the physical and psychological security necessary for children to grow and thrive. The basic attachment typology translates comfortably into family systems: some families are shaped by vertical forms of organised insecurity. When control is uni-directionally vested in the parents, children 'obey orders', do as they are told, avoid affective expression, while autonomy and rebelliousness tend to be suppressed. Safety is achieved by keeping the outside world at bay, often at the expense of creativity and fun. In the enmeshed pattern, an excess of democracy prevails – as antidote to the ever-present threat of loss, inattention, and insecurity. Family members 'live in one another's pockets', furiously text and tweet, and need reassurance that help is instantly at hand. Here the security imperative overrides childrens' need for independence and self-reliance. Chaotic and disorganised families especially increase children's risk of physical and psychological pathology.

Several attachment-influenced therapists have developed theory and practice which combine systems theory with attachment (see Byng-Hall, 1991; Crittenden, 2006; Dallos, 2014). Again, we will here point to a few salient therapeutic themes.

Intergenerational transmission

The finding that attachment patterns transmit across the generations remains one of the seminal discoveries of post-Bowlby attachment studies (Fonagy, Steele, & Steele, 1991; Main et al., 1985). The idea of 'ghosts in the nursery' (Fraiberg, 1980) and 'family scripts' (Byng-Hall, 1991) capture the way in which enduring stories and myths shape how families approach tasks, including the provision of security.

For example, the traumatic death of a child in one generation, through illness or accident, will influence the way that child's siblings approach parenthood when their turn comes. They may find themselves flooded with overwhelming anxiety when *their* children reach the age at which their sibling died. The other unbereaved parent, with a different 'script', may find this 'irrational'. Surviving children may react with compliance, thereby inhibiting healthy exploration, or defiantly take unnecessary risks, stimulating parental over-reaction, leading to bitter parental conflict about how this should be handled. Sometimes these traumatic scripts can impact 'unto the seventh generation', as the following example shows.

The Jones diaspora

Mr Jones sought help when he felt the need for 'truth and reconciliation' with his now grown-up children, whom he had left in their early years when his marriage broke down, and with whom he had maintained only intermittent contact since. He sensed that they carried a lot of unexpressed anger and disappointment that needed to be ventilated if their relationship was to get on to a better footing. The three children each lived in different continents, and on the rare occasions when they did meet, arguments often broke out. Gathered together in a family therapy session it emerged that Mr Jones' great-great-grandfather, some hundred years earlier, had been the perpetrator of a familicide at aged 60 (the age Mr Jones himself had just reached). In what appeared to be an episode of psychotic depression, he had killed his wife, then his grown-up daughter, and finally himself. This had been a dark family secret that Mr Jones had only learned about on his own father's deathbed. After the trauma, the surviving members of the family had dispersed to the then colonies, leaving Mr Jones' grandfather to deal with the aftermath.

The therapist attempted to summarise this horrible family script as 'safety in separation': proximity, physical, let alone emotional, was potentially lethal. Ironically, the 'Jones diaspora' could be understood as an attempt to *preserve* the family by stretching it to its geographic and psychological limits. For the present-day protagonists, understanding how their life-choices might have been unconsciously shaped by these historical forces was helpful, reducing guilt and blame, and fostering a wish to make reparation, and feel safe enough to hold more closely together.

Triangulation and distance-regulation

The psychoanalytic Oedipus model posits a child caught between love and hate: the wish to possess the mother and fear of paternal retribution. An attachment gloss on this draws on neo-Darwinist concepts of the divergent genetic imperatives for parent and child (Hrdy, 1999). The child's security depends directly on the mother, so the more she is his exclusive property the better; the role of the father and of siblings may conflict with this, although the father's (and in his absence, the grandparents') capacity to support the nursing mother will impact on the infant's survival. Meanwhile, the mother's genetic future depends only in part on the child: with the father she can make, or may have made, more children, even if one fails to survive. Although these considerations become less pressing where infant mortality rates are low, they remain part of the human archaic inheritance. A crucial part of the maturational process for the 'Oedipal' child is to accept that parents will pursue their own interests and pleasures, even at the expense of his or her own. The payoff for this acceptance is an inner sense perspective and the capacity to live and think independently (Britton, 2015).

Attachment-influenced systemic thinking turns this model on his head, in the sense that it is *parental* pathology that inhibits the child's healthy individuation, rather than the child's unresolved 'Oedipal' wishes. Byng-Hall (1991) describes how children can become 'distance regulators' between dysfunctional parents. Rather than being free to explore, backed up by security when needed, the 'triangulated' child acts as a buffer or link-person between parents whose affect co-regulation is problematic: estranged, or enmeshed, or alternating between the two. In extreme examples, all communication between the parents is directed 'through' the trapped child.

Drawing on Minuchin's pioneering work, Dallos (2014) argues that in eating disorders the role of the child's symptoms is to bring disconnected parents together in mutual concern about their offspring's weight. The converse is seen in cases of parental neglect, where 'the children of lovers are orphans', an aphorism that applies often to fractured families where a step-parent consumes all of one parent's interests at the expense of the children. Here the triangulated child's symptoms represent attempts to reunite a severed family.

Attachment-informed Family Therapy

Attachment-oriented family therapists conduct family sessions in ways that aim to consolidate security, enhance affect-regulation, and manage and resolve conflict. Here are four salient aspects.

1 Modelling the parameters of secure attachment

To repeat our mantra: therapists must be 'always in control, but never controlling'. This embodies the virtues of 'mid-rangeness', modelling and encouraging the parents to do likewise. Conversations that threaten to get out of hand are cooled. Members who dominate are restrained, while those who are silent are encouraged to speak up. Turn-taking, listening, and ownership of feelings are orchestrated and validated. Spontaneous expressions of feeling, whether verbal, or with younger members through drawing or movement, are encouraged and reflected upon. The aim of the work is always exploratory, in a safe-enough context guaranteed by the therapist. The therapist communicates the confidence that as an overall sense of security grows, the family will find ways for itself of solving its problems.

2 Engagement and 'difficultness'

By definition, families coming for help are in difficulty. The family as a whole may be problematic; there may be a particularly 'difficult' member; every therapy session will have its moments of difficulty. The skilfulness of therapists is most in evidence here. Attachment-informed therapists will be aware that non-engagement, whether by a family as a whole or an individual member, has its own logic, typifying the avoidant style of organised insecurity. While respecting the wariness that previous experiences of rejection or neglect evoke, they will be determined in their efforts not to be brushed off or rejected.

In-session avoidance, denigration, and distancing require 'joining' strategies such as sitting next to the 'difficult' member, and sometimes 'ganging up' with them – including against oneself – in a playful way ('*Your husband, impressive as he is, can be a bit overpowering at times; he seems to have all the answers*'; '*I can well understand your reluctance to come here today; maybe I'm just one of a long list of "experts" who have let you down*'). The guiding principle here is: 'The more you (the therapist) feel off-put, angry with, or blaming of a particular family member, the more that person needs attention and security as an urgent first step before the family as a whole can be helped.'[4]

3 Mentalising and 'circular questioning'

Therapists of all persuasions probably over-value their stock-in-trade of mentalising, self-questioning, and psychologising. Many successful families just 'get on with it' without too much introspection or navel-gazing. But the evidence shows that *implicit* mentalising characterises mothers of secure children (Meins et al., 2001; Shai & Belsky, 2017), seeing their offspring as separate beings with minds, feelings, and perspectives of their own. Problematic families, where such implicit strategies are deficient, need to be helped to instil the skills of explicit mentalising, and to use it to tackle problems.

The technique of 'circular questioning', devised by the 'Milan School' of family therapy (Palazolli-Selvini et al., 1980), is essentially a mentalising method. One member of the family is asked what he or she thinks another might be thinking. For example (to parents), '*What do you think might have been going through the children's minds when you two had that slanging match the other night?*', or (to sibling A), '*How do you think B [another sibling] feels when Dad always gives you the first pick of the roast dinner?*' The aim is to induce a family current of thinking and feeling in which members can begin to 'see themselves from the outside, and others from the inside'.

4 The 'Positive Connotation'

Bowlby saw 'adaptation' as crucial to the attachment dynamic. Insecure attachment represents a 'positive' strategy to stay safe within a given 'suboptimal' environment. Family therapists offer a 'positive connotation', 'prescribing the symptom' position *vis-à-vis* their families. Thus, for example, saying to a griping and complaining mother of two adolescent boys things like: '*I think it's really important you go on moaning and nagging them, otherwise they'd get* much *too fond of you, and never get round to leading their own lives and leaving home.*[5] The therapist here assumes a playful, ironic, court-jester, as-if role that models mentalising and healthy detachment, as well as validating families' attempts to stay safe despite developmental and sociological adversity.

Summary

- The principles of attachment-informed therapy can readily be transposed to working with couples and families.

- Insecure individuals tend to have less stable marriages than their secure counterparts.

- Marriage can be seen as a 'benign bind' embodying hopes for resolution of dysfunctional attachment patterns.

- Johnson's 'attachment injury' underlies many marital conflicts.

- There is a disruptive aspect to sexuality which means that it both challenges and potentially deepens attachment security.

- Symptomatic children may act as 'distance regulators' in marital conflict.

- Fostering the parameters of secure attachment – consistency, mentalising, turn-taking, and conflict resolution – are the hallmarks of couple and family therapy.

Notes

1. While mindful of patriarchal implications, we use the term 'marriage' to denote long-term conjugal relationships between adults of whatever gender, irrespective of their formal, legal, or religious status.
2. As it was once jocularly put to JH, 'You attachment guys never seem to get round to fucking'!
3. A phenomenon known as the 'Westermark effect' (Spain, 1987), probably mediated by olfactory cues.
4. Sebastian Kraemer (personal communication, JH, August 2016) points out that this valuation of every member's contribution, however irrelevant or irritating-seeming, derives from the 'work group' principles devised in part by Bowlby at the Tavistock Clinic in the 1940s as an outgrowth of the War Office Selection Boards (Kanter, 2007).
5. We are grateful, again, to Sebastian Kraemer (personal communication, JH, August 2016) for the outlines of this example.

15

Attachment and Society

We are nearing the end of our journey. In this final chapter we zoom yet further out to consider how attachment themes play out in wider society.

Let's first return to two of the general principles that have informed this book's approach. First are the parallels between the attachment and the immune systems.[1] The function of both is to keep the individual safe. The immune system is primed to recognise and attack disease-vectors; attachment's purpose is to protect the vulnerable from predators and mitigate the adverse consequences of unregulated emotion. The immune system is a social as well as an individual phenomenon. The feeding mother's antibodies protect her infant via colostrum. Her immune 'experience' is thus interpersonally transmitted. Similarly, intergenerational patterns of attachment mean that parental attachment styles shape those of their infants. Immunisation programmes strengthen children's immune defences. Society plays a vital role in strengthening its members' immune systems. Comparably, positive parenting preventative programmes, such as 'Minding the Baby®' (Sadler et al., 2013; Slade, Sadler et al., 2017), alter the attachment environment, aiming to counteract the socially disastrous consequences of poverty, stress, and disruption on children's psychological development.

A second leitmotiv throughout this book is the balance in the search for security between control and collaboration. The management of uncertainty, and the anxiety it arouses, can be plotted along these two dimensions.[2]

To the extent that one is 'in control of oneself', the less likely one is to be driven by the unpredictable forces of the unconscious – rage, envy, sexuality, terror. If one is in control of those in one's immediate environment – human and non-human – the inherent unpredictability of other people and nature itself is reduced. Control can be thought of as a 'vertical' uni-directional strategy for managing anxiety.

In collaborative, or 'horizontal', strategies, by contrast, uncertainty and unpredictability is shared *across* the group, with a degree of division of labour, as seen in social avian species where the vigilance of some enhances foraging in others (D. S. Wilson, 2015). Each pattern is adaptive to specific environments. The life-threatening vagaries of sailing, or warfare, mean that a vertical chain of command is essential; orders must be obeyed. In less hostile settings, democratic polyphony fosters cross-fertilisation, innovation, and creativity.

Difficulties arise when there is a discrepancy between strategy and prevailing environmental conditions. In the Second World War, the UK coalition government exercised a degree of control that would not have been acceptable in peacetime; 1945 saw a democratic revolution in which the revered war leader Winston Churchill was ousted in favour of the Social Democratic Clement Attlee. Meanwhile, under Stalin, the Soviet Union persisted with a centralised control system that eventually led to the demise of the Communist regime.

Transposing these principles to attachment, extreme control with minimal collaboration characterises avoidant caregiver–infant relationship patterns. In the insecure-anxious form, both control and collaboration are out of kilter: the caregiver is inconsistent and unpredictable and the infant feels unheard. In disorganised attachment, the 'frightened' caregiver (Lyons-Ruth & Jacobvitz, 2016) offers minimal control and 'excessive' collaboration, sowing the seeds of later role reversal. In the 'frightening' disorganised pattern, a combination of control and failure of mentalising leads the caregiver to underestimate the child's vulnerability, treating the unequal as equal.

An important take-home message of attachment for therapists is that secure attachment is typically 'mid-range' (Beebe et al., 2012). The caregiver is ultimately in control, in the sense that parents set the boundaries for bedtimes, meal-times, and environmental safety. At the same time, secure-making parents' mentalising capacities enable them to listen to their children, anticipate their wants and needs, be prepared to make age-appropriate concessions, and engage in collaborative, turn-taking conversations and play.

Similar typologies can be applied to attachment-informed client–therapist relationships. The boundaries of the setting are the responsibility of the therapist, although they are to some extent negotiable. Within the relational framework so established, the atmosphere needs to be control-free and democratic. Therapists are 'in control, but not controlling'. The client's and therapist's voices are of equal status and value, with the shared aim of moving towards mutual understanding or a 'fusion of horizons' (Stern, 2010). This is not to deny the desirable 'lopsidedness' of the relationship, or devalue the role of therapists' knowledge and expertise. Both depend on the therapist's skill in creating a secure context – a capacity which is, to an extent, synonymous with 'technique'.

We have described how Bayesian principles shape pychobiological responses to living in an inherently uncertain world, in which predictions are based on prior experience (aka 'transference' and/or IWMs), but, in health, are shaped and updated in the light of current perceptions. Implicit in this is the precept that the capacity to tolerate uncertainty is a feature of psychological well-being.[3] The 'horizontal' 'extended self' strategies found in secure attachment are in most circumstances more adaptive than control-dominated, top-down patterns of insecure attachments. Recent computational studies of behavioural strategies across the animal kingdom (Laland, 2017) confirm this, suggesting that informed learning based on 'epistemic trust' outperforms go-it-alone or slavish copying. Secure attachment with its inherent 'horizontal' learning processes – tops the bill, although in extreme circumstances, e.g. when the environment is highly unpredictable, changing rapidly, or when entering virgin territory, more insecure patterns come into their own, which is presumably why, from an evolutionary point of view, they remain part of the human repertoire.

The Sociology of Attachment

The sociologist Peter Marris (1996) has applied attachment ideas to the *management of uncertainty* in a society-wide context. He argues that two prototypical patterns are to be found – either collective sharing of the burden of uncertainty through mutual support, progressive taxation, and universal benefits; or top-down control and unequal distribution of security.

Marris suggests that the shift from the welfare-ism and relative equality of the 1970s to the neo-liberal societies of the present day have brought the latter pattern to the fore. Increasing economic, occupational, and social inequality mean that those with power and control use their position to 'export' insecurity to the vulnerable and weak, to both groups' great disadvantage. This happens in a variety of ways. Large corporations sub-contract work to a range of suppliers. This enhances corporate power and lowers multinationals' exposure to insecurity. Corporations are freed from worker representation, no longer have to provide benefits for their employees, can shift contracts at will depending on circumstances, and play one contractor off against another to minimise costs. International capital minimises their tax burden by moving to low-tax locations. Corporate security is inversely related to the lack of it by employees, who are often on 'zero hours contracts', uncertain as to their work pattern each week, de-skilled, and depressed by the massive differential between top executive pay and basic wages. Marris sees this 'vertical' imbalance as self-defeating, undermining the fabric of society, which depends on trust, reciprocity, and an economically and psychologically confident workforce.

Pickett and Wilkinson (2009) provide empirical evidence consistent with Marris's arguments. They plot the social impact of the wealth gap between rich and poor as measured in the advanced countries of the world, and between different states in the USA. There is a strong correlation in both samples between inequality and indices of social disruption. Above a certain level of income, irrespective of absolute wealth, the greater the gap between rich and poor, the greater the incidence of depression and schizophrenia, teenage pregnancy, homicide, drug and alcohol addiction, obesity, and child abuse. The authors attribute these effects to the impact of material and psychological insecurity, leading to worries about status, role, self-worth, and uncertainty about the future and the fate of one's children. All of this, they argue, fosters the pursuit of short-term goals, even if these are ultimately self-defeating. Income inequality impacts of quality of life for rich and poor alike, albeit in different – and unequal – ways.

What is the relevance for psychotherapists of this excursion into the sociology of attachment and inequality? Consider a specific psychiatric condition, commonly referred for psychotherapy, borderline personality disorder (BPD). As with other forms of social and relational disturbance, the country-by-country and US state-by-state incidence of BPD correlates with the gap between rich and poor: the bigger the gap, the greater the prevalence (Pickett & Wilkinson, 2015).

Why might this be so, and what might be done to redress the extent of this disabling condition? BPD can be thought of as a 'disease of civilisation', comparable to conditions such as hypertension, obesity, diabetes, and heart disease, which were virtually absent in pre-industrial societies, and arising out of the social and economic conditions of 'advanced' societies, so called. Income inequality and social stratification underpin the disorganisation, disorientation, and trauma which form the seedbed for BPD. A key point in Pickett and Wilkinson's (2009) work is that economic inequality diminishes wellbeing *across the social class spectrum*, not just amongst the poor.

This, we argue, pushes up the prevalence of BPD in all social groups. Material or status insecurity can mean that parents are in a constant state of arousal and cannot attend to or mentalise their children. Low self-esteem associated with a sense of 'failure', whether material or psychological, leads to collapse and lack of confidence in meeting the challenges of parenthood. Short-term escape into drugs, alcohol, abandonment, or abusive sex beckons. Social victimisation, exclusion, racism, bigotry, denigration, and scapegoating add to feelings of hopelessness. While under 'classical' manufacturing capitalism, economic insecurity enhances mutual solidarity, neoliberalism and the shift to service industries and the 'gig economy' disrupts wider family networks as dispersal and economic pressure intensifies.

For the privileged, Piketty (2013) argues, the global shift from manufacturing to financial investment means that markets have a built-in tendency to instability and 'crisis', as the value of capital and wages increasingly diverge, thereby reducing the purchasing power of the poor, and ultimately undermining the security of the rich as well. They too are living in a 'vertical' or 'top-down' universe in which security and collaboration are discouraged. All these various cultural circumstances potentiate 'borderline' adaptations and social structures.

Disorganised families are especially liable to trauma, which tends to go hand-in-hand[4] with BPD (van der Kolk, 2014). A shared sense of family goals and identity may be absent. The mutual economy of parents and children is distorted. Children are seen as 'takers', depriving the parent of sleep and resources; conversely, abusive parents use children for their own ends, as receptacles for unwanted feelings, or, in cases of abuse, as sexual objects. The atmosphere is 'vertical', in which victim/victimiser (the child or parent may occupy either pole) roles predominate. In the absence of mentalising skills, monitoring and learning from experience are weak or non-existent: dysfunctional patterns merely repeat themselves. Sanctions tend to be absent or extreme: from empty threats to disproportionate and violent responses. Children are not seen in a mentalising way as having their own thoughts, feelings, and legitimate desires, and tend either to be controlled or neglected. A wider family to which parent or parents can turn when their own attachment needs are activated is often missing or divided.

In secure families, by contrast, parents, sensitive to the age and abilities of their offspring, are able to handle sibling rivalry, and to ensure a 'fair' balance between their own needs, individually and as a couple – for solitude, sex, sharing – and those of the children, making sure that rewards are earned and persistent 'free-riding' is discouraged. A collaborative culture prevails, in which the children's voices are heard, and, with due allowance for age and maturity, permitted to influence decisions over bedtimes, pocket-money, holiday destinations, homework duration, chores, etc. Feedback is encouraged. Sanctions are in the hands of parents, and start at the mildest level before going up the scale. There are agreed ways of resolving disputes, in which parents have the final say, but, within those limits, children have a degree of autonomy – what foods they prefer, how messy their room is, how they choose to spend their allotted 'screen time', etc.

'Diseases of civilisation' are often characterised as 'lifestyle' problems. Remediation tends to target individual behaviours, e.g. anti-obesity, fitness-enhancing, and anti-smoking programmes. Laudable though these are, the social and political context in which they arise is ignored or approached with extreme caution by politicians. It took half a century between the discovery of the link between smoking and lung cancer and heart disease to establish a smoking-ban in public places. This now exemplary example of society-level prevention has yet to be emulated in the field of diet and activity, or – most relevant to our project – a society-wide commitment to child, parent, and family security and safety.

Change is inherent in biological and cultural evolution. In most species, including our own, the main drivers of change are either ecological – i.e. environmental circumstances – or, in the case of cultural evolution, unwitting, unconscious, or imposed via social structures. But the neo-Darwinist group of D. S. Wilson et al. (2014) argue that despite being at the mercy of circumstances, and dependent on natural selection to produce adaptation, humans are also endowed with the capacity for *intentional change*.

From Wilson's evolutionary perspective, collaboration, sharing, and altruism co-exist in the human psyche alongside egotism, narcissism, and competitiveness. Even from the perspective of 'enlightened self-interest', generosity and sharing enhances an individual's reputation and hence their social, sexual, and economic capital. The role of psychotherapy is to champion and promote 'intentional change' towards greater security for individuals, families, and small groups. Marris's arguments for greater attachment security in society at large are the political top-down counterpart of this bottom-upwards approach to inequality and disadvantage.

We end, therefore, with an implicit preventative message that flows from attachment-informed psychotherapy. We have moved from the intimacy of the mother–infant bond to couples, families, groups, and wider society. Although liberal in his views, Bowlby was ever the cautious scientist. His whole project was steered by the need to find solid evidence with which to buttress therapeutic speculation. But he was also a committed social reformer. We end with his passionate plea, no less relevant today than when it was written:

> Man and woman power devoted to the production of material goods counts a plus in all our economic indices. Man and woman power devoted to the production of happy, healthy, and self-reliant children in their own homes does not count at all. We have created a topsy turvy world. ... The society we live in is ... in evolutionary terms ... a very peculiar one. There is a great danger that we shall adopt mistaken norms. For, just as a society in which there is a chronic insufficiency of food may take a deplorably inadequate level of nutrition as its norm, so may a society in which parents of young children are left on their own with a chronic insufficiency of help, take this state of affairs as its norm. (Bowlby, 1988: 6)

Attachment, we suggest, offers a perspective that is both humanistic and optimistic. It is humanistic because it focuses on the totality of a life, people's inner landscape and actual relationships, and the developmental and current contexts from which they emerge. It is humanistic, too, because only by establishing and protecting connections with our fellow humans is it safe to go out into the world.

It is optimistic because our struggles, degrees of 'insanity', and capacity for hatred, violence, and destruction are seen not as evidence of an in-built drive to destroy, but as forms of relational communication. They represent the need to connect, re-work pain, or even defy the ultimate vulnerability and improbability of life, however seemingly self-defeating these efforts appear. It is optimistic, finally, because attachment theory sees the urge to connect as always dynamic, and thus mutable. Mobilising this mutability is the psychotherapist's task. We hope in these pages to have helped show some of the steps, large and small, by which this can come about.

Summary

- Like families, societies 'export' insecurity from stronger to weaker members.

- Borderline personality can, from this perspective, be seen as a 'disease of civilisation'.

- The social message of attachment is to help move societies on from knowing the 'price of everything and the value of nothing'.

- This entails fostering psychotherapy's capacity to enhance healthy developmental processes in children, adults, and families.

16

Epilogue

One of the pitfalls – and pleasures – of conversation is that one never quite knows what one is trying to say until one has said it. That applies as much to written as it does to spoken conversation, as well as to the therapeutic communications which form a major theme of this book. To misquote, in our end is our beginning: it has taken us a long time to get to this point. Below, now on our very last page, we distil the book's take-home message into ten brief points. The next couple of paragraphs present a prose version of them.

Based on science and clinical practice, and starting from the mother–infant relationship, we have aimed to show how attachment thinking illuminates and facilitates the processes of psychotherapy – neurophysiological, psychological, and interpersonal. We have described *'biobehavioural synchrony'* between therapist and client; how insecure attachments can compromise and limit this; and how therapy helps move from dissonant towards more harmonious timings. We show how clients return to a developmental *'sensitive period'* where, with the help of *affect co-regulation*, opportunities and challenges can be met collaboratively, in contrast to the helplessness, go-it-aloneness, or isolation of psychological disability. The *trust* associated with nascent secure attachment forms the basis for learning and exploration in the consulting room and the wider world.

In contrast to the freedoms associated with secure attachment lie the tug and pull of 'automatic mode' relational expectations and adaptations to the sub-optimal caregiving environments and *threats* to which clients have been exposed. A key attachment contribution is the concept of *mentalising* – the capacity to stand back and 'think about thinking', one's own and others. To use Green's (2014) camera analogy, mentalising can be seen as a move from 'automatic' to 'manual' modes of relating. Therapy is a 'school for mentalising' in which therapist and client jointly scrutinise the client's thoughts, feelings and actions as they arise in therapy – i.e. transference – and their extra-therapeutic life. When things go well, clients gradually incorporate mentalising into their repertoire of daily living skills.

Another benefit of the entrainment, synchrony, and sensitive period reawakening entailed in therapy is that *exploration, experiment, and surprise replace avoidance, inappropriate dependency, and chaos*. Hands held (meta-phorically mainly), terrors can be faced, not fled from. Conversation moves towards *mutual exchange* and 'fusion of horizons' rather than distancing, parallel lines, or narratives of victimhood and helplessness. Through the instantiation of secure attachment, *earned security*, therapy returns to its clients a sense of *agency and connection* which their insecure attachments have hitherto denied them.

These processes, we maintain, constitute an observational and science-based *meta-narrative of therapeutic engagement and change* applicable to a range of therapies. We hope there has been something useful and interesting here for everyone! Which is not to underestimate the originality and challenge of the attachment paradigm, specific features of which include, in addition to the themes highlighted above, *positive connotation*, *radical acceptance*, and acknowledgement of the *pain of loss and limitation*.

Here then are the book's main messages.

From insecure...	...via therapeutic...	....to secure attachment
Unregulated affect	Co-regulation sensitivity, mirroring, play	Self-regulation and mature co-regulation
Pre-mentalising modes: teleology, equivalence, fantasy	Devil is in the detail; transference mentalising with therapist	Mentalising skills
Passivity, lack of agency	Emphasis on client choice	Sense of autonomy and agency
Low self-esteem, victim mode	Benign, non-judgemental, non-conditional radical acceptance	Good self-esteem; good-enoughness in self and world-view
'Vertical' routes to security	Collaborative culture in therapy	'Horizontal' 'democratic' modes
Avoidance of unbound energy and uncertainty	Therapist reticence as 'enigmatic signifier'	Tolerance of surprise and capacity to learn from experience
'Looming' or disengagement	Balance and regulation – up when down, down when up	'Mid-range' playfulness
Hormonal disengagement	Oxytocin and dopaminergic entrainment	Biobehavioural synchrony
Self-sufficiency	Opening sensitive period of mutual influence	Epistemic trust and 'university of life'
Inhibition of exploration for sake of security	*In vivo* security/exploration balance shifted	Exploration, learning from others and from experience

Or, to put it another way, attachment-informed psychotherapy addresses heart (affect regulation), head (mentalising), and hand (agency and connection). We hope in the course of this book we have touched – moved even – our readers in all three zones.

Notes

1. If the recent interest in the relationship between inflammation and depression proves well-founded (e.g., Iwata, Ota, & Duman, 2013), this may prove to be more than an analogy.
2. The model developed here bears a close resemblance to both Bartholomew's matrix (1990) and Crittenden's 'circumplex model' (2006), which similarly see different attachment styles in terms of strategies for managing uncertainty.
3. This view is also widely held in psychoanalytic circles under the rubric of 'negative capability', Keats' valuation of 'being in uncertainties, mysteries, doubts, without any irritable reaching after fact and reason' (see Bion, 1970).
4. Or, typically, hand in search of absent helping hand.

Selected Attachment Bibliography

Allen, J. (2012a). *Mentalizing in the development and treatment of attachment trauma*. London: Karnac.

Allen, J. (2012b). *Restoring mentalising in attachment relationships: Treating trauma with plain old therapy*. New York: American Psychiatric Association.

Allen, J., & Fonagy, P. (2006). *Handbook of mentalization-based treatment*. New York: Wiley.

Allen, J., Fonagy, P., & Bateman, A. (2008). *Mentalising in clinical practice*. Washington, DC: American Psychiatric Publishing.

Bateman, A., & Fonagy, P. (2004). *Psychotherapy for borderline personality disorder: Mentalization-based treatment*. New York: Oxford University Press.

Bateman, A., & Fonagy, P. (2006). *Mentalization-based treatment for borderline personality disorder: A practical guide*. New York: Oxford University Press.

Brisch, K.-H. (2002). *Treating attachment disorders: From theory to therapy*. New York: Guilford Press.

Cassidy, J., & Shaver, P. (Eds.). (2016). *Handbook of attachment* (3rd ed.). New York: Guilford Press.

Daniel, S. (2014). *Adult attachment patterns in a treatment context: Relationship and narrative*. London: Routledge.

Diamond, D., Blatt, S., & Lichtenberg, J. (Eds.). (2007). *Attachment and sexuality*. New York: Analytic Press.

Eagle, M. (2013). *Attachment theory and psychoanalysis: Theory, research, and clinical implications*. New York: Guilford Press.

Exquero, A. (2017). *Encounters with John Bowlby*. Hove: Routledge.

Fonagy, P. (2001). *Attachment theory and psychoanalysis*. New York: Other Press.

Holmes, J. (1993/2013) *John Bowlby and attachment theory*. London: Routledge.

Johnson, S., & Whiffen, V. (2005). *Attachment processes in couple and family therapy*. New York: Guilford Press.

Maunder, R., & Hunter, J. (2015). *Love, fear, and health: How our attachments to others shape health and health care*. Toronto: University of Toronto Press.

Mikulincer, M., & Shaver, P. (2016). *Attachment in adulthood* (2nd ed.). New York: Guilford Press.

Obegi, J., & Berant, E. (Eds.). (2009). *Attachment theory and research in clinical work with adults*. New York: Guilford Press.

Oppenheim, D., & Goldsmith, D. (Eds.). (2007). *Attachment theory in clinical work with children: bridging the gap between research and practice*. New York: Guilford Press.

Owen, I. (2017). *On attachment: The view from developmental psychology*. London: Karnac.

Sable, P. (2000). *Attachment and adult psychotherapy*. New York: Jason Aronson.

Shiller, V. (2017). *The attachment bond: Affectional ties across the lifespan*. New York: Lexington Books.

Steele, H., & Steele, M. (Eds.). (2008). *Clinical applications of the adult attachment interview*. New York: Guilford Press.

Wallin, D. (2007). *Attachment in psychotherapy*. New York: Guilford Press.

References

Ackerman, S. J., Benjamin, L. S., Beutler, L. E., Gelso, C. J., Goldfried, M. R., Hill, C., & Rainer, J. (2001). Empirically supported therapy relationships: Conclusions and recommendations of the Division 29 Task Force. *Psychotherapy, 38,* 495–497.

Ainsworth, M. D. S. (1967). *Infancy in Uganda.* Baltimore, MD: Johns Hopkins University Press.

Ainsworth, M. D. S. (1983). Mary D. Salter Ainsworth. In A. N. O'Connell & N. F. Russo (Eds.), *Models of achievement: Reflections of prominent women in psychology* (pp. 200–219). New York: Columbia University Press.

Ainsworth, M. D. S., Blehar, M. C., Waters, E., & Wall, S. (1978). *Patterns of attachment: A psychological study of the strange situation.* Hillsdale, NJ: Erlbaum.

Ainsworth, M. D. S., & Wittig, B. A. (1965). Attachment and exploratory behavior of one-year-olds in a strange situation. In B. M. Foss (Ed.), *Determinants of infant behavior* (Vol. 4) (pp. 111–136). New York: Wiley.

Akhtar, S. (Ed.). (2009). *Good feelings: Psychoanalytic reflections on positive emotions and attitudes.* London: Karnac.

Alexander, F., & French, T. (1946). *Psychoanalytic therapy.* New York: Ronald Press.

Allen, J. (2012a). *Mentalizing in the development and treatment of attachment trauma.* London: Karnac.

Allen, J. (2012b). *Restoring mentalising in attachment relationships: Treating trauma with plain old therapy.* New York: American Psychiatric Association.

Allen, J., Fonagy, P., & Bateman, A. (2008). *Handbook of mentalizing in mental health practice.* Arlington, VA: American Psychiatric Association Publishing.

Austin, J. (1962). *How to do things with words.* Oxford: Oxford University Press.

Avdie, E. (2008). Analysing talk in the talking cure: Conversation, discourse, and narrative analysis of psychoanalytic psychotherapy. *European Psychotherapy, 8,* 69–87.

Avdie, E. (2012). Exploring the contribution of subject positioning to studying therapy as a dialogical enterprise. *International Journal for Dialogical Science, 6,* 61–79.

Bakermans-Kranenburg, M. J., Dobrova-Krol, N. A., & van IJzendoorn, M. H. (2011). Impact of institutional care on attachment disorganization and insecurity of Ukrainian preschoolers: Protective effect of the long variant of the serotonin transporter gene (5HTT). *International Journal of Behavioral Development, 36*, 11–18.

Bakermans-Kranenburg, M. J., & van IJzendoorn, M. H. (2009). The first 10,000 Adult Attachment Interviews: Distribution of adult attachment representations in non-clinical and clinical groups. *Attachment and Human Development, 11*, 223–263.

Bakermans-Kranenburg, M. J., & van IJzendoorn, M. H. (2016). Attachment, parenting, and genetics. In J. Cassidy & P. Shaver (Eds.), *Handbook of attachment* (3rd ed.) (pp. 155–179). New York: Guilford Press.

Balint, M. (1968). *The basic fault.* London: Tavistock.

Barel, E., van IJzendoorn, M. H., Sagi-Schwartz, A., & Bakermans-Kranenburg, M. J. (2010). Surviving the Holocaust: A meta-analysis of the long-term sequelae of a genocide. *Psychological Bulletin, 136*, 677–698.

Barratt, B. (2016). *Radical psychoanalysis.* Hove: Routledge.

Bartholomew, K. (1990). Avoidance of intimacy: An attachment perspective. *Journal of Social and Personality Relationships, 7*, 147–178.

Bartholomew, K., & Allison, C. (2006). An attachment perspective on abusive dynamics in intimate relationships. In M. Mikulincer & G. Goodman (Eds.), *Dynamics of romantic love* (pp. 201–227). New York: Guilford Press.

Bateman, A., & Fonagy, P. (2004). *Psychotherapy for borderline personality disorder: Mentalization-based treatment.* New York: Oxford University Press.

Bateman, A., & Fonagy, P. (2009). Randomized controlled trial of outpatient mentalization-based treatment versus structured clinical management for borderline personality disorder. *American Journal of Psychiatry, 166*, 1355–1364.

Bateman, A., & Holmes, J. (1995). *Introduction to psychoanalysis.* London: Routledge.

Bateson, G., Jackson, D., Haley, J., & Weakland, J. (1956). Toward a theory of schizophrenia. *Behavioral Science, 1*(4), 251–254.

Beebe, B., & Lachmann, F. (2013). *The origins of attachment: Infant research and adult treatment.* New York: Routledge.

Beebe, B., Lachmann, F., Markese, S., & Bahrick, L. (2012). On the origins of disorganized attachment and internal working models. *Psychoanalytic Dialogues, 22*, 352–374.

Belloc, H. (2007). *Cautionary tales.* London: Blackwood.

Belsky, J. (1997). Attachment, mating, and parenting: An evolutionary interpretation. *Human Nature, 8*(4), 361–381.

Belsky, J., Bakermans-Kranenburg, M. J., & van IJzendoorn, M. H. (2007). For better and for worse: Differential susceptibility to environmental influences. *Current Directions in Psychological Science, 16*(6), 300–304.

Belsky, J., Houts, R., & Fearon, P. (2010). Infant attachment security and the timing of puberty: Testing an evolutionary hypothesis. *Psychological Science, 21*(9), 1195–1201.

Benedek, T. (1959). Parenthood as a developmental phase. *Journal of the American Psychoanalytical Association, 7*, 389–417.

Berger, P. (1970). *The social construction of reality: A treatise in the sociology of knowledge*. London: Penguin.

Berman, M. (1983). *All that is solid melts into air*. London: Verso.

Bifulco, A. (2009). Risk and resilience in young Londoners. In D. Brom, R. Pat-Horenczyk, & J. Ford (Eds.), *Treating traumatised children: Risk, resilience and recovery* (pp. 56–92). London: Routledge.

Bion, W. R. (1962). A theory of thinking. *International Journal of Psycho-Analysis, 43*. Reprinted in *Second thoughts* (1967).

Bion, W. (1970). *Attention and interpretation*. London: Tavistock.

Bollas, C. (1989). *The shadow of the object: Psychoanalysis of the unthought known*. New York: Columbia University Press.

Bonanno, G. A., & Burton, C. L. (2013). Regulatory flexibility: An individual differences perspective on coping and emotion regulation. *Perspectives on Psychological Science, 8*(6), 591–612.

Bowlby, J. (1940). The influence of the early environment in the development of neurosis and neurotic character. *International Journal of Psychoanalysis, 21*, 154–178.

Bowlby, J. (1944). Forty-four juvenile thieves: Their characters and home-life. *International Journal of Psychoanalysis, 25*, 19–52.

Bowlby, J. (1949). The study and reduction of group tensions in the family. *Human Relations, 2*, 123–128.

Bowlby, J. (1958). The nature of the child's tie to his mother. *International Journal of Psychoanalysis, 39*, 350–373.

Bowlby, J. (1960). Separation anxiety. *International Journal of Psychoanalysis, 41*, 89–113.

Bowlby, J. (1961). Processes of mourning. *International Journal of Psychoanalysis, 42*, 317–340.

Bowlby, J. (1969). *Attachment and loss: Volume I: Attachment*. International Psychoanalytical Library, 79: 1–401. London: Hogarth Press and the Institute of Psychoanalysis.

Bowlby, J. (1973). *Attachment and loss: Volume II: Separation, anxiety, and anger*. International Psychoanalytical Library, 95: 1–429. London: Hogarth Press and the Institute of Psychoanalysis.

Bowlby, J. (1979). On knowing what you are not supposed to know and feeling what you are not supposed to feel. *Canadian Journal of Psychiatry, 24*(5), 403–408.

Bowlby, J. (1980). *Attachment and loss: Volume III: Loss, sadness and depression*. International Psychoanalytical Library, 109: 1–462. London: Hogarth Press and the Institute of Psychoanalysis.

Bowlby, J. (1984). Violence in the family as a disorder of the attachment and caregiving systems. *American Journal of Psychoanalysis, 44*, 9–27.

Bowlby, J. (1988). *A secure base: Clinical implications of attachment theory*. London: Routledge.

Bowlby, J. (1991). *Charles Darwin*. London: Hutchinson.

Bowlby, J., & Robertson, J. (1952). A two-year-old goes to hospital. *Proceedings of the Royal Society of Medicine, 46*, 425–427.

Brassard, A., & Johnson, S. (2016). Couple and family therapy: An attachment perspective. In J. Cassidy & P. Shaver (Eds.), *Handbook of attachment* (3rd ed.) (pp. 805–823). New York: Guilford Press.

Bretherton, I. (1992). The origins of attachment theory: John Bowlby and Mary Ainsworth. *Developmental Psychology, 28*(5), 759–775.

Britton, R. (2015). *Between mind and brain*. London: Karnac.

Browning, R. (1855/2000). Andrea del Sarto. In *Selected poems* (D. Karlin, Ed.). London: Penguin.

Burkhardt, R. (2005). *The science of behaviour: Konrad Lorenz, Niko Tinbergen and the founding of ethology*. Chicago, IL: University of Chicago Press.

Byng-Hall, J. (1991). An appreciation of John Bowlby: His significance for family therapy. *Journal of Family Therapy, 13*, 5–16.

Callaghan, B., & Tottenham, N. (2016). The neuro-environmental look of plasticity: A cross-species analysis of parental effects on emotion circuitry development following typical and adverse caregiving. *Neuropsychopharmacology Reviews, 41*, 163–176.

Carlson, E. (1998). A prospective longitudinal study of attachment disorganisation/disorientation. *Child Development, 69*, 1107–1128.

Carvalho, A., Rea, I. M., Parimon, T., & Cusack, B. J. (2014). Physical activity and cognitive function in individuals over 60 years of age: A systematic review. *Journal of Clinical Interventions in Aging, 9*, 661–682.

Casement, P. (1982). *On learning from the patient*. London: Tavistock.

Caspi, A., Hariri, A. R., Holmes, A., Uher, R., & Moffitt, T. E. (2010). Genetic sensitivity to the environment: The case of the serotonin transporter gene and its implications for studying complex diseases and traits. *American Journal of Psychiatry, 167*(5), 509–527.

Caspi, A., Sugden, K., Moffitt, T. E., Taylor, A., Craig, I. W., Harrington, H., Poulton, R. (2003). Influence of life stress on depression: Moderation by polymorphism in the 5-HTT Gene. *Science, 18*, 386–389.

Cassidy, J. (1994). Emotion regulation: Influences of attachment relationships. *Monographs of the Society for Research in Child Development, 59*(2–3), 228–249.

Cassidy, J. (2016). The nature of the child's ties. In J. Cassidy & P. Shaver (Eds.), *Handbook of attachment: Theory, research, and clinical applications* (3rd ed.) (pp. 3–24). New York: Guilford Press.

Castonguay, L., & Hill, C. (Eds.). (2012). *Transformation in psychotherapy*. Washington, DC: American Psychological Association.

Centers for Disease Control and Prevention (2009). Parent Training Programs: Insight for Practitioners. Atlanta (GA): Centers for Disease Control (www.cdc.gov/violenceprevention/pdf/parent_training_brief-a.pdf).

Champagne, F. A. (2008). Epigenetic mechanisms and the transgenerational effects of maternal care. *Frontiers in Neuroendocrinology, 29*, 386–397.

Choi-Kain, L. W., & Gunderson, J. G. (2008). Mentalization: Ontogeny, assessment, and application in the treatment of borderline personality disorder. *American Journal of Psychiatry, 165*(9), 1127–1135.

Clark, A. (2016). *Surfing uncertainty*. Oxford: Oxford University Press.

Coan, J. (2016). Attachment and neuroscience. In J. Cassidy & P. Shaver (Eds.), *Handbook of attachment* (3rd ed.) (pp. 242–269). New York: Guilford Press.

Coan, J. A., Schaefer, H. S., & Davidson, R. J. (2006). Lending a hand: Social regulation of the neural response to threat. *Psychological Science, 17*(12), 1032–1039.

Cooper, P. J., De Pascalis, L., Woolar, M., Romaniuk, H., & Murray, L. (2015). Attempting to prevent postnatal depression by targeting the mother–infant relationship: A randomized controlled trial. *Primary Health Care Research & Development, 16*(4), 383–397.

Craik, K. (1943). *The nature of explanation*. Cambridge: Cambridge University Press.

Crittenden, P. M. (1990). Internal representational models of attachment relationships. *Infant Mental Health Journal, 11*(3), 259–277.

Crittenden, P. M. (2006). A dynamic-maturational model of attachment. *Australian & New Zealand Journal of Family Therapy, 27*(2), 105–115.

Crowell, J., Fraley, C., & Roisman, G. (2016). Measurement of individual differences in adult attachment. In J. Cassidy & P. Shaver (Eds.), *Handbook of Attachment* (3rd ed.) (pp. 598–638). New York: Guilford Press.

Cyr, C., Euser, E., Bakermans-Kranenburg, M., van IJzendoorn, M. (2010). Attachment security and disorganization in maltreating and high risk families: A series of meta-analyses. *Development and Psychopathology, 22*, 87–108.

Dallos, R. (2014). Starving for affection: Attachment narrative therapy for eating disorders. In A. Danquah & K. Berry (Eds.), *Attachment theory in mental health* (pp. 129–154). London: Routledge.

Daly, K., & Mallinckrodt, B. (2009). A grounded-theory model of experts' approach to psychotherapy for clients with attachment avoidance or attachment anxiety. *Journal of Counseling Psychology, 56*, 549–563.

Damasio, A. (1999). *The feeling of what happens: Body and emotion in the making of consciousness*. New York: Harcourt.

Daniel, S. (2014). *Adult attachment patterns in a treatment context: Relationship and narrative*. London: Routledge.

Davidson, R., & McEwen, B. (2012). Social influences on neuroplasticity: Stress and interventions to promote well-being. *Nature Neuroscience, 15*(5), 689–695.

Davies, B., & Harré, R. (1990). Positioning: The discursive production of selves. *Journal for the Theory of Social Behaviour, 20*, 43–63.

Davies, W. H. (1908/2011). *Autobiography of a supertramp*. London: Melville.

Dawkins, R. (1978). *The selfish gene*. Oxford: Oxford University Press.

Dennett, D. (1987). *The intentional stance*. Cambridge, MA: MIT Press.

Dennett, D. (2006). *Breaking the spell: Religion as a natural phenomenon*. New York: Viking.

Dozier, M., Cue, K., & Barnett, L. (1994). Clinicians as caregivers: Role of attachment organization in treatment. *Journal of Consulting and Clinical Psychology, 62*, 793–800.

Dozier, M., Peloso, E., Lewis, E., Laurenceau, J., & Levine, S. (2008). Effects of an attachment-based intervention on the cortisol production of infants and toddlers in foster care. *Development and Psychopathology, 20*(3), 845–859.

Dumontheil, I., Apperly, I. A., & Blakemore, S. J. (2010). Online usage of theory of mind continues to develop in late adolescence. *Developmental Science, 13*(2), 331–338.

Eagle, M. (2007). Attachment and sexuality. In D. Diamond, S. Blatt, & J. Lichtenberg (Eds.), *Attachment and sexuality* (pp. 27–50). New York: Analytic Press.

Eagle, M. (2011). *From classical to contemporary psychoanalysis*. London: Routledge.

Egeland, B., Jacobvitz, D., & Sroufe, L. A. (1988). Breaking the cycle of abuse. *Child Development, 59*, 1080–1088.

Eliot, T. S. (1963). The wasteland. In *Collected poems*. London: Faber.

Erikson, E. H. (1950). *Childhood and society*. New York: W. W. Norton.

Fairbairn, R. (1952). *Psychoanalytic studies of personality*. London: Hogarth.

Fear, R. (2016). *Attachment theory: Working towards learned security*. London: Karnac.

Fearon, P., Tomlinson, M., Kumsta, R., Skeen, S., Murray, L., Cooper, P., and Morgan, B. (2016). Poverty, early care and stress reactivity in adolescence: Findings from a prospective, longitudinal study in South Africa. *Development and Psychopathology*. ISSN 1469-2198.

Fearon, R. P., Target, M., Sargent, J., Williams, L. L., McGregor, J., Bleiberg, E., & Fonagy, P. (2006). Short-term mentalization and relational therapy (SMART): An integrative family therapy for children and adolescents. In J. G. Allen & P. Fonagy (Eds.), *Handbook of mentalization-based treatment* (pp. 201–222). Chichester, England: Wiley.

Feldman, R. (2015a). Sensitive periods in human social development: New insights from research on oxytocin, synchrony, and high-risk parenting. *Development and Psychopathology, 27*, 369–395.

Feldman, R. (2015b). The adaptive human parental brain: Implications for children's social development. *Trends in Neuroscience, 38*, 387–399.

Felitti, V., Anda, R., Nordenberg, D., Williamson, D. F., Spitz, A. M., Edwards, B., & Marks, J. S. (1998). Relationships of childhood abuse and household dysfunction to many of the leading causes of death in adults: The Adverse Childhood Experiences Study. *American Journal of Preventive Medicine, 14*, 245–258.

Fonagy, P. (1991). Thinking about thinking: Some clinical and theoretical considerations in the treatment of a borderline patient. *International Journal of Psychoanalysis, 72*, 639–656.

Fonagy, P. (2003). Psychoanalysis today. *World Psychiatry, 2*(2), 73–80.

Fonagy, P., & Allison, E. (2014). The role of mentalizing and epistemic trust in the therapeutic relationship. *Psychotherapy, 51*(3), 372–380.

Fonagy, P., & Bateman, A. W. (2006). Mechanisms of change in mentalization-based treatment of BPD. *Journal of Clinical Psychology, 62*(4), 411–430.

Fonagy, P., Gergely, G., Jurist, E., & Target, M. (2002). *Affect regulation, mentalization, and the development of the self.* New York: Other Press.

Fonagy, P., Gergely, G., & Target, M. (2007). The parent–infant dyad and the construction of the subjective self. *Journal of Child Psychology and Psychiatry, 48,* 288–328.

Fonagy, P., Rost, F., Carlyle, J. A., McPherson, S., Thomas, R., Fearon, P., & Taylor, D. (2015). Pragmatic randomized controlled trial of long-term psychoanalytic psychotherapy for treatment resistant depression: The Tavistock Adult Depression Study (TADS). *World Psychiatry, 14*(3), 312–321.

Fonagy, P., Steele, H., & Steele, M. (1991). Maternal representations of attachment during pregnancy predict organization of infant–mother attachment at one year of age. *Child Development, 62,* 891–905.

Fonagy, P., Steele, M., Steele, H., Higgitt, A., & Target, M. (1994). The Emanuel Miller Memorial Lecture 1992: The theory and practice of resilience. *Journal of Child Psychology and Psychiatry, 35*(2), 231–257.

Fonagy, P., Steele, M., Steele, H., Leigh, T., Kennedy, R., Mattoon, G., & Target, M. (1995). Attachment, the reflective self, and borderline states: The predictive specificity of the Adult Attachment Interview and pathological emotional development. In S. Goldberg, R. Muir, & J. Kerr (Eds.), *Attachment theory: Social, developmental and clinical perspectives* (pp. 233–278). New York: Analytic Press.

Fonagy, P., & Target, M. (1996). Playing with reality: Theory of mind and the normal development of psychic reality. *International Journal of Psychoanalysis, 77,* 217–233.

Fonagy, P., & Target, M. (1997). Attachment and reflective function: Their role in self-organization. *Development and Psychopathology, 9,* 679–700.

Fonagy, P., & Target, M. (1999). Toward understanding violence: The use of the body and the role of the father. In R. Perelberg (Ed.), *Psychoanalytic understanding of violence and suicide* (pp. 14–36). London: Routledge.

Fonagy, P., & Target, M. (2007). The rooting of the mind in the body: New links between attachment theory and psychoanalytic thought. *Journal of the American Psychoanalytic Association, 55,* 411.

Fonagy, P., Target, M., Steele, H., & Steele, M. (1998). Reflective-functioning manual, Version 5.0, for application to Adult Attachment Interviews. Unpublished research manual, University College, London.

Fraiberg, S. (1980). *Clinical studies in infant mental health.* New York: Harcourt Brace.

Francis, D. D., Caldji, C., Champagne, F., Plotsky, P., & Meaney, M. J. (1999). The role of corticotropin-releasing factor – norepinephrine systems in mediating the effects of early experience on the development of behavioral and endocrine responses to stress. *Biological Psychiatry, 46,* 1153–1166.

Frankl, V. (1946/2006). *Man's search for meaning.* Boston, MA: Beacon Press.

Freud, A. (1936). *The ego and the mechanisms of defence.* London: Hogarth.

Freud, S. (1900). The interpretation of dreams. *The standard edition of the complete psychological works of Sigmund Freud* (Vol. 3). London: Hogarth.

Freud, S. (1913). On the beginning of treatment. *The standard edition of the complete psychological works of Sigmund Freud* (Vol. 12). London: Hogarth.

Freud, S. (1916). Introductory lectures on psycho-analysis. *The standard edition of the complete psychological works of Sigmund Freud* (Vol. 15). London: Hogarth.

Freud, S. (1923). The ego and the Id. *The standard edition of the complete psychological works of Sigmund Freud* (Vol. 19). London: Hogarth.

Freud, S. (1937). Analysis terminable and interminable. *The standard edition of the complete psychological works of Sigmund Freud* (Vol. 23). London: Hogarth.

Freud, S., & Breuer, J. (1895). Studies in hysteria. *The standard edition of the complete psychological works of Sigmund Freud* (Vol. 2). London: Hogarth.

Friston, K. (2010). The free energy principle: A unified brain theory? *Nature Reviews Neuroscience, 11*, 127–138.

Gabbard, G. (2016). *Boundaries and boundary violations in psychoanalysis* (2nd ed.). Arlington, VA: American Psychiatric Association Publishing.

Gabbard, G., & Horowitz, M. (2009). Insight, transference interpretations and therapeutic change in the dynamic psychotherapy of Borderline Personality Disorder. *American Journal of Psychiatry, 166*, 518–521.

George, C., Kaplan, N., & Main, M. (1996). Adult Attachment Interview protocol (3rd ed.). Unpublished manuscript, University of California, Berkeley.

Gergely, G., & Watson, J. (1996). The social biofeedback model of parent–infant mirroring. *International Journal of Psychoanalysis, 77*, 1181–1197.

Goodyear, I. M., Reynolds, S., Barrett, B., Byford, S., Dubicka, B., Hill, J., & Fonagy, P. (2017). Cognitive behavioural therapy and short-term psycho-analytical psychotherapy versus a brief psychosocial intervention in adolescents with unipolar major depressive disorder (IMPACT): A multi-centre, pragmatic, observer-blind, randomised controlled superiority trial. *Lancet Psychiatry, 4*(2), 109–119.

Goransson, K. (2009). *The binding tie: Chinese intergenerational relations in modern Singapore*. Honolulu, HI: University of Hawaii Press.

Gramsci, A. (1999). *Prison notebooks*. (Q. Hoare & G. N. Smith, Trans.). London: Elecbook.

Green, J. (2014). *Moral tribes*. London: Atlantic Books.

Grice, H. (1975). Logic and conversation. In P. Cole & J. Morgan (Eds.), *Speech acts* (pp. 41–58). New York: Academic Press.

Grienenberger, J., Kelly, K., & Slade, A. (2005). Maternal reflective functioning, mother–infant affective communication and infant attachment: Exploring the link between mental states and observed caregiving. *Attachment and Human Development, 7*, 299–311.

Grossman, K. E., Grossmann, K., & Waters, E. (Eds.). (2005). *Attachment from infancy to adulthood: The major longitudinal studies*. New York: Guilford Press.

Harlow, H. F. (1958). The nature of love. *The American Psychologist, 13*, 673–685.

Hauser, S., Allen, J., & Golden, E. (2006). *Out of the woods: Tales of resilient teens*. Cambridge, MA: Harvard University Press.

Hennenlotter, A., Dresel, C., Castrop, F., Ceballos-Baumann, A. O., Wohlschlager, A. M., & Haslinger, B. (2008). The link between facial feedback and neural activity within central circuitries of emotion: New insights from botulinum toxin-induced denervation of frown muscles. *Cerebral Cortex*, *19*(3), 537–542.

Heraclitus. (2008). *Fragments*. (J. Hillman, Trans.). London: Penguin. (Original work published 1846.)

Hesse, E. (2016). The Adult Attachment Interview: Protocol, method of analysis, and empirical studies: 1985–2015. In J. Cassidy & P. Shaver (Eds.), *Handbook of attachment* (3rd ed.) (pp. 553–597). New York: Guilford Press.

Hesse, E., & Main, M. (2000). Disorganized infant, child and adult attachment: Collapse in behavioral and attentional strategies. *Journal of the American Psychoanalytic Association*, *48*, 1097–1127.

Hicks, S. (2016). 'Forget your perfect offering': Improbable relationships and the muddy ground of formation, reformation, and transformation. *Australasian Journal of Psychotherapy*, *32*, 45–67.

Hinde, R. A. (1991). When is an evolutionary approach useful? *Child Development*, *62*, 671–675.

Hinshelwood, R. (2013). *Research on the couch*. Hove: Routledge.

Hobson, P. (2013). *Consultations in psychoanalytic psychotherapy*. London: Karnac.

Hobson, R. (1985). *The heart of psychotherapy*. London: Routledge.

Hofer, M. (1995). Hidden regulators in attachment and loss. In S. Goldberg, R. Muir, & J. Kerr (Eds.), *Attachment theory: Social, developmental, and clinical considerations* (pp. 357–376). Hillsdale, NJ: Analytic Press.

Holmes, J. (1996). *Attachment, intimacy, and autonomy: Using attachment theory in adult psychotherapy*. New York: Jason Aronson.

Holmes, J. (2001). *The search for the secure base: Attachment theory and psychotherapy*. London: Routledge.

Holmes, J. (2007). Sense and sensuality: Hedonic intersubjectivity and the erotic imagination. In D. Diamond, S. Blatt, & J. Lichtenberg (Eds.), *Attachment and sexuality*. Hillsdale, NJ: Analytic Press.

Holmes, J. (2010). *Exploring in security: Towards an attachment-informed psychoanalytic psychotherapy*. London: Routledge.

Holmes, J. (2014a). *John Bowlby and attachment theory* (2nd ed.). London: Routledge. (1st edition published 1993.)

Holmes, J. (2014b). *Attachments: Psychotherapy, psychiatry, psychoanalysis*. London: Routledge.

Holmes, J. (2015). Attachment theory in clinical practice: Personal account. *British Journal of Psychotherapy*, *31*, 208–238.

Holmes, J. (2016). Meaning without 'believing': attachment theory, mentalisation and the spiritual dimension of analytic psychotherapy. In C. Cook, A. Powell, & A. Sims (Eds.), *Spirituality in clinical practice* (pp. 145–159). London: Royal College of Psychiatrists Publications.

Holmes, J., & Bateman, A. (Eds.). (2002). *Integration in psychotherapy*. London: Routledge.

Holmes, J., & Lindley, R. (1997). *The values of psychotherapy*. London: Karnac.

Holmes, J. T. (2014). Countertransference before Heimann: An historical exploration. *Journal of the American Psychoanalytic Association*, 62(4), 603–629.

Hopkins, G. (1918/2008). *Collected poems and prose*. London: Penguin.

Hrdy, S. (1999). *Mother nature*. New York: Pantheon.

Hurry, A. (1998). *Psychoanalysis and developmental therapy*. London: Karnac.

Insel, T. R. (2000). Toward a neurobiology of attachment. *Review of General Psychology*, 4, 176–185.

Iwata, M., Ota, K., & Duman, R. (2013). The inflammasome: Linking psychological stress, depression, and systemic illnesses. *Brain, Behavior, and Immunity*, 31, 105–111.

Johnson, S., Makinen, J., & Millikin, J. (2001). Attachment injuries in couple relationships: A new perspective on impasses in couple therapy. *Journal of Marital and Family Therapy*, 27, 145–155.

Johnson, S., & Whiffen, V. (2005). *Attachment processes in couple and family therapy*. New York: Guilford Press.

Kahl, K. G., Winter, L., & Schweiger, U. (2012). The third wave of cognitive behavioural therapies: what is new and what is effective? *Current Opinion in Psychiatry*, 25, 522–528.

Kahneman, J. (2011). *Thinking: Fast and slow*. London: Allen Lane.

Kanter, J. (2007). John Bowlby, Interview with Dr Milton Senn. *Beyond the Couch: The Online Journal of the American Association for Psychoanalysis in Clinical Social Work*, Issue 2. Retrieved from: www.beyondthecouch. org/1207/bowlby_int.htm.

Keats, J. (1919/2007) Ode to a nightingale, in *Selected poems* (ed. J. Barnard). London: Penguin.

Kipling, R. (2014). *Captains courageous*. London: Signet Classics. (Original work published 1897.)

Klopfer, B., Ainsworth, M. D., Klopfer, W. F., & Holt, R. R. (1954). *Developments in the Rorschach technique* (Vol. 1). Yonkers-on-Hudson, NY: World Book Co.

Knox, J. (2010). *Self-agency in psychotherapy*. New York: W. W. Norton.

Kobak, R. R., & Sceery, A. (1988). Attachment in late adolescence: Working models, affect regulation, and representations of self and others. *Child Development*, 59(1), 135–146.

Kris, E. (1952). *Psychoanalytic explorations in art*. New York: International Universities Press.

Kuhn, T. (1977). *The essential tension: Selected studies in scientific tradition and change*. Chicago, IL: Chicago University Press.

Kundakovic, J., Gudsnuk, K., Herbstman, J. B., Tang, D., Perera, F., & Champagne, F. (2015). DNA methylation of BDNF as a biomarker of early-life adversity. *Proceedings of the National Academy of Sciences of the United States of America*, 112, 6807–6813.

Lacan, J. (1977). *Écrits*. London: Hogarth.

Lakoff, S., & Johnson, M. (2003). *The metaphors we live by* (2nd ed.). Chicago, IL: University of Chicago Press.

Laland, K. (2017). *Darwin's Unfinished Symphony: How culture made the human mind*. Princeton, NJ: Princeton University Press.

Lambert, M. (Ed.). (2015). *Bergin and Garfield's handbook of psychotherapy and behavior change* (6th ed.). Hoboken, NJ: Wiley.

Langer, S. (1951). *Philosophy in a new key*. New York: Academic Press.

Laplanche, J. (1999). *Essays on otherness*. New York: Routledge.

Lear, J. (2011). *A case for irony*. Cambridge, MA: Harvard University Press.

Lebel, C., Walton, M., Letourneau, N., Giesbrecht, G. F., Kaplan, B. J., & Dewey, D. (2016). Prepartum and postpartum maternal depressive symptoms are related to children's brain structure in preschool. *Biological Psychiatry, 80*, 859–868.

Lecours, S., & Bouchard, M. A. (1997). Dimensions of mentalization: Outlining levels of psychic transformation. *International Journal of Psycho-Analysis, 75*, 855–875.

LeDoux, J. (1996). *The emotional brain: The mysterious underpinnings of emotional life*. New York: Simon & Schuster.

Lemma, A., Roth, A., & Pilling, S. (2014). *The competencies required to deliver effective psychoanalytic/psychodynamic therapy*. Retrieved from www.ucl.ac.uk/CORE.

Levinas, E. (1961). *Totality and infinity*. (A. Lingis Trans,). London: Kluwer Academic Press.

Levine, S. (1957). Infantile experience and resistance to physiological stress. *Science, 126*, 405–411.

Lieberman, A. F., Ghosh Ippen, C., & Van Horn, P. (2015). *Don't hit my mommy: A manual for child–parent psychotherapy with young witnesses of family violence* (2nd ed.). Washington, DC: Zero to Three.

Lieberman, A. F., Padron, E., Van Horn, P., & Harris, W. (2005). Angels in the nursery: The intergenerational transmission of benevolent parental influences. *Infant Mental Health Journal, 26*, 504–520.

Lieberman, A. F., & Van Horn, P. (2008). *Psychotherapy with infants and young children: Repairing the effects of stress and trauma on early attachment*. New York: Guilford Press.

Lilienfeld, S., & Arkowitz, H. (2012). Are all psychotherapies created equal? *Scientific American Mind*. Retrieved from www.scientificamerican.com/article/are-all-psychotherapies-created-equal/.

Linehan, M. (1993). *Cognitive behavioral treatment of borderline personality disorder*. New York: Guilford Press.

Liotti, G. (2004). Trauma, dissociation, and disorganized attachment: Three strands of a single braid. *Psychotherapy: Theory, Research, Practice, Training, 41*(4), 472–486.

Litowitz, B. (2014). From switch-words to stitch-words. *International Journal of Psychoanalysis, 95*, 3–14.

Lorenz, K. (1961). *King Solomon's ring* (M. Wilson, Trans.). London: Methuen.

Luborsky, L., Rosenthal, R., Diguer, L., Andrusyna, T. P., Berman, J. S., Levitt, J. T., & Krause, E. D. (2002). The dodo-bird verdict is alive and well – mostly. *Clinical Psychology*, *9*, 2–12.

Luquet, P. (1981). *Le changement dans la mentalization. Revue Française de Psychanalyse*, *45*, 1023–1028.

Lyons-Ruth, K., Bronfman, E., & Parsons, E. (1999). Maternal frightened, frightening, or atypical maternal behavior and disorganized infant attachment patterns. In J. Vondra & D. Barnett (Eds.), Atypical attachment in infancy and early childhood among children at developmental risk. *Monographs of the Society for Research in Child Development*, *64*(3), 67–96.

Lyons-Ruth, K., & Jacobvitz, D. (2016). Attachment disorganization: Genetic factors, parenting contexts, and developmental transformation from infancy to adulthood. In J. Cassidy & P. Shaver (Eds.), *Handbook of attachment* (3rd ed.) (pp. 667–696). New York: Guilford Press.

Lyons-Ruth, K., Yellin, C., Melnick, S., & Atwood, G. (2005). Expanding the concept of unresolved mental states: Hostile/helpless states of mind on the Adult Attachment Interview are associated with disrupted mother–infant communication and infant disorganization. *Development and Psychopathology*, *17*(1), 1–23.

Madigan, S., Bakermans-Kranenburg, M., van IJzendoorn, M. H., Moran, G., Pederson, D. R., & Benoit, D. (2006). Unresolved states of mind, anomalous parental behavior, and disorganized attachment: A review of the transmission gap. *Attachment and Human Development*, *8*, 89–111.

Main, M. (1991). Metacognitive knowledge, metacognitive monitoring, and singular (coherent) vs. multiple (incoherent) models of attachment: Findings and directions for future research. In C. M. Parkes, J. Stevenson, & P. Marris (Eds.), *Attachment across the life cycle* (pp. 127–159). New York: Routledge.

Main, M. (1995). Recent studies in attachment: Overview, with selected implications for clinical work. In S. Goldberg, R. Muir, & J. Kerr (Eds.), *Attachment theory: Social, developmental, and clinical perspectives* (pp. 19–43). Hillsdale, NJ: Analytic Press.

Main, M. (2000). The organized categories of infant, child and adult attachment: Flexible vs. inflexible attention under attachment-related stress. *Journal of the American Psychoanalytic Association*, *48*, 1055–1095.

Main, M., & Cassidy, J. (1988). Categories of response to reunion with the parent at age 6: Predictable from infant attachment classifications and stable over a 1-month period. *Developmental Psychology*, *24*, 415–426.

Main, M. & Goldwyn, R. (1989) *Adult attachment rating and classification system*. Unpublished manuscript, University of California, Berkeley, Berkeley, CA.

Main, M., & Hesse, E. (1990). Parents' unresolved traumatic experiences are related to infant disorganized attachment status: Is frightened and/or frightening parental behavior the linking mechanism? In M. T. Greenberg,

D. Cicchetti, & E. M. Cummings (Eds.), *Attachment in the preschool years: Theory, research and intervention* (pp. 161–184). Chicago, IL: University of Chicago Press.

Main, M., Kaplan, N., & Cassidy, J. (1985). Security in infancy, childhood and adulthood: A move to the level of representation. *Monographs of the Society for Research in Child Development, 50*(1/2), 66–104.

Main, M., & Solomon, J. (1990). Procedures for identifying infants as disorganized/disoriented during the Ainsworth Strange Situation. In M. T. Greenberg, D. Cicchetti, & E. M. Cummings (Eds.), *Attachment in the preschool years: Theory, research and intervention* (pp. 121–160). Chicago, IL: University of Chicago Press.

Malan, D. (1979). *Individual Psychotherapy and the science of psychodynamics*. London: Routledge.

Marris, P. (1996). *The politics of uncertainty: Attachment in private and public life*. London: Routledge.

Marty, P. (1991). *La psychosomatique de l'adulte*. Paris: Laboratoire Delagrange.

Marx, K. (1888/1998). *The German ideology*. New York: Prometheus.

Matas, A., Arend, R., & Sroufe, L. A. (1978). Continuity of adaptation in the second year: The relationship between quality of attachment and later competence. *Child Development, 49*, 547–556.

Maunder, R., & Hunter, J. (2012). A prototype-based model of adult attachment for clinicians. *Psychodynamic Psychiatry, 40*, 549–573.

Maunder, R., & Hunter, J. (2015). *Love, fear, and health: How our attachments to others shape health and health care*. Toronto: University of Toronto Press.

McGilchrist, I. (2009). *The master and his emissary*. New Haven, CT: Yale University Press.

McGrayne, S. (2011). *The theory that would not die*. New Haven, CT: Yale University Press.

Meaney, M. (2001). Maternal care, gene expression, and the transmission of individual differences in stress reactivity across generations. *Annual Review of Neuroscience, 24*, 1161–1192.

Mears, R. (2005). *The metaphor of play*. London: Routledge.

Meins, E. (1999). Sensitivity, security, and internal working models: Bridging the transmission gap. *Attachment and Human Development, 3*, 325–342.

Meins, E., Fernyhough, C., Fradley, E., & Tuckey, M. (2001). Rethinking maternal sensitivity: Mothers' comments on infants' mental processes predict security of attachment at 12 months. *Journal of Child Psychology and Psychiatry, 42*(5), 637–648.

Meltzoff, A. N., & Moore, M. K. (1997). Explaining facial imitation: A theoretical model. *Early Development and Parenting, 6*(34), 179–192.

Mikulincer, M., & Shaver, P. (2005). Attachment security, compassion and altruism. *Current Directions in Psychological Science, 14*, 34–38.

Mikulincer, M., & Shaver, P. (2016). *Attachment in adulthood* (2nd ed.). New York: Guilford Press.

Miller, S. D., Hubble, M. A., & Duncan, B. L. (2007). *Supershrinks*. Retrieved from www.psychotherapynetworker.org.

Miller, S. D., Hubble, M. A., Chow, D., & Seidel, J. (2013). The outcome of psychotherapy: Yesterday, today and tomorrow. *Psychotherapy, 50,* 88–97.

Mizen, S. (2014). Towards a relational-affective model of personality disorder. *Psychoanalytic Psychotherapy, 28*(4), 357–378.

Monk, C., Feng, T., Lee, S., Krupska, I., Champagne, F., & Tycko, B. (2016). Distress during pregnancy: Epigenetic regulation of placenta glucocorticoid-related genes and fetal neurobehavior. *American Journal of Psychiatry, 173*(7), 705–713.

Morgan, H., & Shaver, P. (1999). Attachment processes and commitment to romantic relationships. In J. Adams & W. Jones (Eds.), *Handbook of interpersonal commitment and relationship stability* (pp. 109–124). New York: Plenum.

Nietzsche, F. (1988). *Twilight of the idols* (R. Hollingdale, Trans.). London: Penguin. (Original work published 1900.)

Noller, P., & Feeney, J. (2002). *Understanding marriage: Developments in the study of couple interactions.* Cambridge: Cambridge University Press.

Novick, K. K., & Novick, J. (2005). *Working with parents makes therapy work.* New York: Jason Aronson.

Oberman, L. M., Winkielman, P., & Ramachandran, V. S. (2007). Face to face: Blocking facial mimicry can selectively impair recognition of emotional expressions. *Social Neuroscience, 2,* 167–178.

Ogden, T. (1994). The analytic third: Working with intersubjective clinical facts. *International Journal of Psychoanalysis, 75,* 3–20.

Olds, D., Sadler, L., & Kitzman, H. (2007). Programs for parents of infants and toddlers: Recent evidence from randomized trials. *Journal of Child Psychology and Psychiatry, 48,* 355–391.

Oppenheim, D., & Koren-Karie, N. (2013). The insightfulness assessment: Measuring the internal processes underlying maternal sensitivity. *Attachment and Human Development, 15,* 545–561.

Palazolli-Selvini, M., Boscolo, M., Ceccin, G., & Prata G. (1980). Hypothesising – circularity neutrality. *Family Process, 19*(1), 3–12.

Panksepp, J. (2010). *The archeology of mind: Neural origins of human emotion.* New York: W. W. Norton.

Parens, H. (2009). Resilience. In S. Akhtar (Ed.), *Good feelings* (pp. 329–362). London: Karnac.

Pearson, J. L., Cohn, D. A., Cowan, P. A., & Cowan, C. P. (1994). Earned and continuous security in adult attachment: Relation to depressive symptomatology and parenting style. *Development and Psychopathology, 6,* 359–373.

Pedder, J. (2010). Termination reconsidered in G. Winship (Ed.), *Attachment and new beginnings: Reflections of psychoanalytic therapy* (pp. 76–84). London: Karnac.

Pickett, K., & Wilkinson, R. (2009). *The spirit level: Why more equal societies almost always do better.* London: Penguin.

Pickett, K., & Wilkinson, R. (2015). Income inequality and health: A causal review. *Social Science & Medicine, 128,* 316–326.

Piketty, T. (2013). *Capital in the 21st century* (A. Goldhammer, Trans.). Cambridge, MA: Harvard University Press.

Porges, S. P. (2011). *The polyvagal theory: Neurophysiological foundations of emotions, attachment, communication, and self-regulation.* New York: W. W. Norton.

Powell, B., Cooper, G., Hoffman, K., & Marvin, B. (2013). *The Circle of Security Intervention: Enhancing attachment in early parent–child relationships.* New York: Guilford Press.

Prigogine, I. (1980). *From being to becoming: Time and complexity in the physical sciences.* New York: Freeman.

Putnam, K., Harris, W., & Putnam, F. (2013). Synergistic childhood adversities and complex adult psychopathology. *Journal of Traumatic Stress, 26,* 435–442.

Reik, T. (1948). *Listening with the third ear: The inner experience of a psychoanalyst.* New York: Grove Press.

Rizzolati, G., & Sinigaglia, C. (2010). The functional role of the parieto-frontal mirror circuit: Interpretations and misinterpretations. *Nature Reviews Neuroscience, 11,* 264–274.

Robertson, J., & Robertson, J. (1952). *A Two–Year–Old Goes to Hospital* [Motion picture]. United Kingdom: Robertson Films.

Rogers, C. (1985). The necessary and sufficient features of therapeutic personality change. *Journal of Consulting and Clinical Psychology, 25,* 91–103.

Rogers, C. H., Floyd, F. J., Seltzer, M. M., Greenberg, J., & Hong, J. (2008). Long-term effects of the death of a child on parents' adjustment in mid-life. *Journal of Family Psychology, 22*(2), 203–211.

Rose, J., & Shulman, G. (Eds.). (2016). *The non-linear mind: Psychoanalysis of complexity in psychic life.* London: Karnac.

Rutherford, B., & Roose, S. (2014). A model of placebo response in antidepressant clinical trials. *American Journal of Psychiatry, 170,* 723–733.

Rutter, M. (2012). Resilience as a dynamic concept. *Development and Psychopathology, 24,* 335–344.

Rutter M., Kreppner, J., & Sonuga-Barke, E. (2009). Attachment insecurity, disinhibited attachment, and attachment disorders: where do research findings leave the concepts? *Journal of Child Psychology and Psychiatry, 50,* 529–543.

Ryle, A. (1990). *Cognitive analytic therapy.* London: Butterworth.

Sadler, L. S., Slade, A., Close, N., Webb, D. L., Simpson, T., Fennie, K., & Mayes, L. C. (2013). Minding the Baby®: Improving early health and relationship outcomes in vulnerable young families in an interdisciplinary reflective parenting home visiting program. *Infant Mental Health Journal, 34,* 391–405.

Safran, J. D., Muran, J. C., & Proskurov, B. (2009). Alliance, negotiation, and rupture resolution. In R. Levy & S. J. Ablon (Eds.), *Handbook of evidence based psychodynamic psychotherapy* (pp. 201–225). New York: Humana Press.

Sander, L. (1977). The regulation of exchange in the infant–caregiver system. In M. Lewis & L. Rosenblum (Eds.), *Interaction, conversation and the development of language* (pp. 133–156). New York: John Wiley & Sons.

Saunders, R., Jacobvitz, D., Zaccagnino, M., Beverung, L., & Hazen, N. (2011). Pathways to earned security: The role of alternative support figures. *Attachment and Human Development, 13,* 403–420.

Saxbe, D. E., & Repetti, R. L. (2010). No place like home: Home tours correlate with daily patterns of mood and cortisol. *Personality and Social Psychology Bulletin, 36*(1), 71–81.

Schore, J. R., & Schore, A. N. (2008). Modern attachment theory: The central role of affect regulation in development and treatment. *Clinical Social Work Journal, 36,* 9–20.

Schuengel, C., Bakermans-Kranenburg, M. J., & van IJzendoorn, M. H. (1999). Frightening maternal behavior linking unresolved loss and disorganized infant attachment. *Journal of Consulting and Clinical Psychology, 67*(1), 54–63.

Sen, A. (1982). *Poverty and famines: An essay on entitlement and deprivation.* New York: Oxford University Press.

Shai, D., & Belsky, J. (2017). Parental embodied mentalizing: How the nonverbal dance between parents and infants predicts children's socio-emotional functioning. *Attachment and Human Development, 19,* 191–219.

Shedler, J. (2010). The efficacy of psychodynamic psychotherapy. *American Psychologist, 65,* 98–109.

Shonkoff, J. P. (2012). Leveraging the biology of adversity to address the roots of disparities in health and development. *Proceedings of the National Academy of Sciences in the United States of America, 109* (Suppl. 2), 17302–17307.

Siskind, D. (1997). *Working with parents: Establishing the essential alliance in child psychotherapy and consultation.* New York: Jason Aronson.

Slade, A. (1988). The quality of attachment and early symbolic play. *Developmental Psychology, 23*(1), 78–85.

Slade, A. (1994). Making meaning and making believe: Their role in the clinical process. In A. Slade & D. Wolf (Eds.), *Children at play* (pp. 81–110). New York: Oxford University Press.

Slade, A. (1999). Representation, symbolization and affect regulation in concomitant treatment of a mother and child: Attachment theory and child psychotherapy. *Psychoanalytic Inquiry, 19,* 797–830.

Slade, A. (2000). The development and organization of attachment: Implications for psychoanalysis. *Journal of the American Psychoanalytic Association, 48,* 1147–1174.

Slade, A. (2004). The move from categories to process: Attachment phenomena and clinical evaluation. *Infant Mental Health Journal, 25,* 269–283.

Slade, A. (2005). Parental reflective functioning: An introduction. *Attachment & Human Development, 7*(3), 269–281.

Slade, A. (2006). Reflective parenting programs: Theory and development. *Psychoanalytic Inquiry, 26,* 640–657.

Slade, A. (2008a). The implications of attachment theory and research for adult psychotherapy: Research and clinical perspectives. In J. Cassidy & P. Shaver (Eds.), *Handbook of attachment* (2nd ed.) (pp. 762–782). New York: Guilford Press.

Slade, A. (2008b). Mentalization as a frame for parent work in child psychotherapy. In E. Jurist, A. Slade & S. Bergner (Eds.), *Mind to mind: Infant research, neuroscience and psychoanalysis* (pp. 307–334). New York: Other Press.

Slade, A. (2009). Mentalizing the unmentalizable: Parenting children on the spectrum. *Journal of Child, Infant, and Adolescent Psychotherapy, 8,* 7–21.

Slade, A. (2014). Imagining fear: Attachment, threat, and the dynamics of psychic experience. *Psychoanalytic Dialogues, 24,* 254–266.

Slade, A. (2016). Attachment and adult psychotherapy: Theory, research and practice. In J. Cassidy & P. Shaver (Eds.), *Handbook of attachment* (3rd ed.) (pp. 759–779). New York: Guilford Press.

Slade, A., Aber, L. A., Berger, B., Bresgi, I., & Kaplan, M. (2003). The Parent Development Interview – Revised. Unpublished manuscript, City University of New York.

Slade, A., Bernbach, E., Grienenberger, J., Levy, D., & Locker, A. (2015). Parental reflective functioning coding manual: For use with the Parent Development Interview. Unpublished manuscript, City University of New York.

Slade, A., Grienenberger, J., Bernbach, E., Levy, D., & Locker, A. (2005). Maternal reflective functioning and attachment: Considering the transmission gap. *Attachment and Human Development, 7,* 283–292.

Slade, A., & Holmes, J. (Eds.). (2014). *Attachment theory* (Vols. 1–6). London: Sage.

Slade, A., Sadler, L., Close, N., Fitzpatrick, S., Simpson, T., & Webb, D. (2017). Minding the Baby®: The impact of threat on the mother–baby and mother–clinician relationship. In S. Gojman de Millan, C. Herreman, & L. A. Sroufe (Eds.), *Attachment across cultural and clinical contexts* (pp. 182–205). London: Routledge.

Smith, Z. (2016) *Swing time*. London: Penguin Books.

Solomon, J., & George, C. (1996). Defining the caregiving system: Toward a theory of caregiving. *Infant Mental Health Journal, 17*(3), 183–197.

Southwick, S., Bonnano, G., Masten, S. A., Panter-Brick, C., & Yehuda, R. (2014). Resilience definitions, theory, and challenges: Interdisciplinary perspectives. *European Journal of Traumatology, 5,* doi: 10.3402/ejpt.v5.25338.

Spain, D. (1987). The Westermarck–Freud incest-theory debate: An evaluation and reformation. *Current Anthropology, 5*(28), 623–645.

Sroufe, L. A. (1979). The coherence of individual development: Early care, attachment, and subsequent developmental issues. *American Psychologist, 34*(10), 834–841.

Sroufe, L. A. (2005). Attachment and development: A prospective, longitudinal study from birth to adulthood. *Attachment & Human Development, 7*(4), 349–367.

Sroufe, L. A., Egeland, B., Carlson, E. A., & Collins, A. (2005). *The development of the person: The Minnesota study of risk and adaptation from birth to adulthood.* New York: Guilford Press.

Sroufe, L. A., & Fleeson, J. (1986). Attachment and the construction of relationships. In W. Hartup & Z. Rubin (Eds.), *Relationships and development* (pp. 51–71). Hillsdale, NJ: Erlbaum.

Sroufe, L. A., & Waters, E. (1977). Attachment as organizational construct. *Child Development, 48,* 1184–1199.

Steele, H., & Steele, M. (Eds.). (2008). *Clinical applications of the adult attachment Interview.* New York: Guilford Press.

Stern, D. (2010). *Partners in thought: Working with unformulated experience, dissociation, and enactment.* London: Routledge.

Stern, D. N. (1985). *The interpersonal world of the infant.* New York: Basic Books.

Stern, D. N. (1995). *The motherhood constellation: A unified view of parent–infant psychotherapy.* London: Karnac.

Stiles, W., Elliott, R., Llewelyn, S., Firth-Cozens, J., Margison, F., Shapiro, D., & Hardy, G. (1990). Assimilation of problematic experiences by clients in psychotherapy. *Psychotherapy: Theory, Research, Practice, Training, 27*(3), 411–420.

Stiles, W., & Shapiro, D. (1989). Use and abuse of the drug metaphor in psychotherapy process outcome research. *Clinical Psychology Review, 9,* 521–543.

Stovall-McClough, K. C., & Dozier, M. (2016). Attachment states of mind and psychopathology in adulthood. In J. Cassidy & P. Shaver (Eds.), *Handbook of attachment* (3rd ed.) (pp. 715–738). New York: Guilford Press.

Strachey, J. (1934). The nature of the therapeutic action in psychoanalysis. *International Journal of Psycho-analysis, 15,* 126–159.

Strathearn, L., Fonagy, P., Amico, J., & Montague, P. R. (2009). Adult attachment predicts maternal brain and oxytocin response to infant cues. *Neuropsychopharmacology, 34,* 2655–2666.

Strathearn, L., Li, J., Fonagy, P., & Montague, P. (2008). What's in a smile? Maternal responses to infant facial cues. *Paediatrics, 122,* 40–51.

Stupica, B. (2016). Rounding the bases with a secure base. *Attachment and Human Development, 18,* 373–390.

Sung, S., Simpson, J., Griskeviscius, V., Kuo, S., Schlomer, G., & Belsky, J. (2016). Secure mother–infant attachment buffers the effects of early life stress on the age of menarche. *Psychological Science, 27,* 667–674.

Suomi, S. (2016). Attachment in rhesus monkeys. In J. Cassidy & P. Shaver (Eds.), *Handbook of attachment* (3rd ed.) (pp. 133–154). New York: Guilford Press.

Talia, A., Daniel, S. I., Miller-Bottome, M., Brambilla, D., Miccoli, D., Safran, J. D., & Lingiardi, V. (2014). AAI predicts patients' in-session interpersonal behavior and discourse: A 'move to the level of the relation' for attachment-informed psychotherapy research. *Attachment & Human Development, 16*(2), 192–209.

Target, M. (2007). Is our sexuality our own? An attachment model of sexuality based on early affect mirroring. *British Journal of Psychotherapy, 23,* 517–530.

Taylor, B. (2014). *The Last asylum.* London: Penguin.

Tottenham, N. (2014). The importance of early experiences for neuro-affective development. In S. Anderson & D. Pine (Eds.), *The neurobiology of childhood* (Vol. 16) (pp. 109–129). Berlin: Springer.

Tronick, E. (2007). *The neurobehavioral and social-emotional development of infants and children.* New York: W. W. Norton.

Tuber, S., & Calflisch, J. (2011). *Starting treatment with children and adolescents.* London: Routledge.

Tudor-Hart, J. (1971). The inverse care law. *Lancet, 297,* 405–412.

Van der Horst, F. C. P., Van der Veer, R., & van IJzendoorn, M. H. (2007). John Bowlby and ethology: An annotated interview with Robert Hinde. *Attachment & Human Development, 9*(4), 321–335.

van der Kolk, B. (2014). *The body keeps the score: Brain, mind, and body in the healing of trauma.* New York: Penguin.

van Dikjen, S., van der Veer, R., van IJzendoorn, M. H., & Kuipers, H. J. (1998). Bowlby before Bowlby: The sources of an intellectual departure in psychoanalysis and psychology. *Journal of the History of the Behavioural Sciences, 34*(3), 247–269.

van IJzendoorn, M. (1995). Adult attachment representations, parental responsiveness, and infant attachment: a meta-analysis on the predictive validity of the Adult Attachment Interview. *Psychological Bulletin, 117,* 387–403.

van IJzendoorn, M. H., & Bakermans-Kranenburg, M. J. (2006). DRD4 7-repeat allele moderates the association between parental unresolved loss or trauma and infant disorganization. *Attachment and Human Development, 8,* 291–307.

van IJzendoorn, M. H., & Bakermans-Kranenburg, M. J. (2009). Attachment security and disorganisation in maltreating families and orphanages. In M. van IJzendoorn (Ed.), *Encyclopedia on early childhood development: Attachment* (pp. 30–34). Retrieved from www.child-encyclopedia.com/sites/default/files/dossiers-complets/en/attachment.pdf#page=30.

van IJzendoorn, M. H., & Bakermans-Kranenburg, M. J. (2012). A sniff of trust: Meta-analysis of the effects of intranasal oxytocin administration on face recognition, trust to in-group, and trust to out-group. *Psychoneuroendocrinology, 37,* 438–443.

Vaughn, B., Egeland, B., Sroufe, L. A., & Waters, E. (1979). Individual differences in infant–mother attachment at twelve and eighteen months: Stability and change in families under stress. *Child Development, 50,* 971–975.

Veale, D. (2007). Cognitive-behavioural therapy for obsessive-compulsive disorder. *Advances in Psychiatric Treatment, 13,* 438–446.

Vygotsky, L. (1978). *Mind in society: The development of higher psychological processes* (Rev. ed.). Cambridge, MA: Harvard University Press.

Wallin, D. (2007). *Attachment in psychotherapy*. New York: Guilford Press.

Wampold, B. (2015). *The great psychotherapy debate: Models, methods and findings* (2nd ed.). Hillsdale, NJ: Jason Aronson.

Wang, H., Duclot, F., Liu, Y. et al. (2013). Gene switches make prairie voles fall in love. *Nature Neuroscience*, http://dx.doi.org/10.1038/nn.3420.

Waters, E. (1978). The reliability and stability of individual differences in infant–mother attachment. *Child Development*, 49(2), 483–494.

Waters, E., Wippman, J., & Sroufe, L. A. (1978). Attachment, positive affect, and competence in the peer group: Two studies in construct validation. *Child Development*, 50, 821–829.

Weiss, J., & Sampson, H. (1986). *The psychoanalytic process: Theory, clinical observations, and empirical research*. New York: Guilford Press.

Weiste, E., & Peräkylä, A. (2014). Prosody and empathic communication in psychotherapy interaction. *Psychotherapy Research*, 24(6), 687–701. Retrieved from www.tandfonline.com/doi/full/10.1080/10503307.2013.87 9619.

Werner, H., & Kaplan, B. (1963). *Symbol formation*. New York: Wiley.

Whitehead, A. (1916). The organization of thought. *Science*, 22, 409–419.

Widlocher, D. (2002). *Infantile sexuality and attachment*. New York: Other Press.

Wilson, D. S. (2015). *Does altruism exist?* New Haven, CT: Yale University Press.

Wilson, D. S., Hayes, S., Biglan, A., & Embry, D. (2014). Evolving the future: Towards a science of intentional change. *Behavioural and Brain Sciences*, 37, 395–460.

Wilson, E. O. (2012). *The social conquest of earth*. New York: W. W. Norton.

Wimmer, H., & Perner, J. (1983). Beliefs about beliefs: Representation and constraining function of wrong beliefs in young children's understanding of deception. *Cognition*, 13, 103–128.

Winnicott, D. W. (1965). *Maturational processes and the facilitating environment*. London: Karnac.

Winnicott, D. (1971). *Playing and reality*. London: Penguin.

Wittgenstein, L. (1967). *The blue and brown books*. Oxford: Blackwell.

Wolpert, D. M., & Ghahramani, Z. (2000). Computational principles of movement neuroscience. *Nature Neuroscience*, 3, 1212–1217.

Wordsworth, W. (1802/1984) *Collected poems*. London: Penguin.

Zeanah, C. H., & Smyke, A. (2009). Attachment disorders. In C. H. Zeanah (Ed.), *Handbook of infant mental health* (3rd ed.) (pp. 421–435). New York: Guilford Press.

Index